ECONOMIC GROWTH
IN A FREE MARKET

ECONOMIC GROWTH IN A FREE MARKET

George H. Borts and
Jerome L. Stein

COLUMBIA UNIVERSITY PRESS
New York and London 1964

George H. Borts and Jerome L. Stein are Professors of
Economics at Brown University.

TO OUR PARENTS

PREFACE

This book presents the results of research that has been undertaken by the two authors at the Economics Department of Brown University with the aid of several foundation grants.

In 1952 the department established a College-Community Research Program which was financed in part by grants-in-aid from the Committee for Economic Development and from the Fund for Adult Education. The initial research topic chosen was the competitive position of the Rhode Island economy. Several monographs on the various aspects of the Rhode Island economy were written by us and by other members of the Department.

The problems uncovered in these monographs suggested that we extend the scope of our interests to the economies of the component states of the United States. In 1957 the Economics Department received a three-year grant from the Ford Foundation to study regional economic maturity in the United States. During this period, we published articles on economic growth and maturity which contained the rudiments of the analytical framework used in this book.

In 1960 the department received a five-year grant from the Ford Foundation to develop a graduate training program in regional economic development in the United States. We have benefited from the advice and criticism of our colleagues, Merton P. Stoltz, Philip Taft, Michael Brennan, and Martin Beckmann. In addition, we are indebted to comments and suggestions by Daniel Creamer, Richard Muth, and Harvey S. Perloff. Moreover, the doctoral dissertations written by our graduate students in the regional economic development program have extended our knowledge of the process of economic growth.

GEORGE H. BORTS

JEROME L. STEIN

Providence, Rhode Island
January, 1964

CONTENTS

PREFACE   vii

1. THE FRAMEWORK FOR AN ANALYSIS OF ECONOMIC GROWTH AMONG OPEN ECONOMIES   3

2. EMPIRICAL REGULARITIES IN THE PROCESS OF GROWTH AND DECLINE   19

3. A CRITIQUE OF A SIMPLE AGGREGATIVE THEORY OF GROWTH   48

4. INTERSTATE DIFFERENCES IN RATES OF GROWTH OF MANUFACTURING EMPLOYMENT   65

5. INTERINDUSTRY REPERCUSSIONS OF GROWTH AND DECLINE   87

6. MODELS OF GROWTH AND ALLOCATION   101

7. ECONOMIC GROWTH, DISTRIBUTION OF INCOME, AND MOVEMENT OF CAPITAL   124

8. INTERTEMPORAL EFFICIENCY AND ACTUAL GROWTH PATTERNS   162

9. GOVERNMENT POLICIES TOWARD GROWING AND DECLINING REGIONS   188

10. SUMMARY   206

NOTES   217

INDEX   233

ECONOMIC GROWTH
IN A FREE MARKET

I. THE FRAMEWORK FOR AN ANALYSIS OF ECONOMIC GROWTH AMONG OPEN ECONOMIES

Why do regions and countries experience different rates of economic growth? As the countries of the world liberalize trade and remove restrictions on the flow of long-term capital, what will happen to their rates of economic growth? These questions were raised by Adam Smith in 1776 and still engage the attention of modern economists. If there were full employment of resources in each country at all times, would growth rates tend to converge or diverge? Many different opinions exist on this subject.

Gunnar Myrdal, for example, asserts that there is a tendency inherent in the free play of market forces to perpetuate regional inequalities. His thesis is that

There are a small group of countries which are quite well off and a much larger group of extremely poor countries; . . . the countries in the former group are on the whole firmly settled in a pattern of continuing economic development, while in the latter group average progress is slower; . . . in recent decades the economic inequalities between developed and underdeveloped countries have been increasing.[1]

"If the forces in the capital market were given unhampered play, capitalists in underdeveloped countries would be exporting their capital."[2] These capital movements will aggravate the inequalities:

In the centres of expansion increased demand will spur investment, which in its turn will increase incomes and demand and cause a second round of investment, and so on. Savings will increase as a result of higher incomes but will tend to lag behind investment . . . . Studies in many countries have shown how the banking system, if not regulated to act differently, tends to become an instrument for siphoning off the savings from the poorer regions to the richer and more progressive ones where returns on capital are high and secure.[3]

A different point of view has been suggested by Simon Kuznets.[4] Retardation in the rate of growth of product per capita seems to occur in the majority of countries he examined. Two subperiods were distinguished for those countries with relatively long records. With few exceptions the rates of growth of population and of per capita product were lower in the second period than in the first period.

The general implication of such a pattern can be clearly perceived if we assume that countries do not enter upon modern economic growth simultaneously . . . . On this assumption, differences in timing of entry of the various countries upon modern economic growth mean correlative differences in the rates of growth of population, per capita, and total product. Countries that start later than others soon shift from a position lagging behind the early entrants into a position where their rates of growth are distinctly higher than those of the early entrants which meanwhile may have entered the retardation phase.[5]

Our object in this book is to explain the process of growth that occurs in a free-market area characterized by free trade and free movements of productive services under conditions of full employment. Myrdal bases his conclusions concerning the effects of free capital movements upon the experiences of the developed and the underdeveloped countries. We believe that the experiences of the component states of the United States of America are more relevant for a test of a theory of growth in a free-market area than are the experiences of countries with varying degrees of political instability and different restrictions upon private enterprise. By studying the U.S. experience, we are holding the political factors relatively constant and we can focus our attention upon the market forces.

Myrdal's views are logical; i.e., they contain no internal contradictions. The more rapidly growing regions are likely to import capital from the more slowly growing regions. Nevertheless, we adduce evidence to support the view that the rapidly growing regions have been the regions of low rather than of high per capita income. There has been a strong tendency for the convergence of per capita incomes among states within the United States. The evidence, therefore, is not compatible with Myrdal's theory of interregional differences in growth rates among open economies.

There is an important distinction between the actual and the ideal patterns of growth. Most of this book is devoted to positive economics: What has been the process of growth? Our conclusions concerning the nature of the growth process differ from Myrdal's. A completely different question is whether the observed or inferred growth process is optimal. Chapters 8 and 9 involve normative economics and evaluate the optimality of the observed growth process.

A GENERAL ANALYSIS OF THE SOURCES OF GROWTH

We may consider a simple economy which produces one output (Y) with the aid of labor services (N) and the services of the total stock of unconsumed previous outputs (K), i.e., capital. Technological change is assumed to increase output by g percent per year, given the inputs of labor and capital. Full employment is assumed to prevail, so that demand always equals supply. Let lower-case letters refer to percentage rates of growth. Then, the rate of growth of output is given by[6]

$$y = ak + bn + g \tag{1}$$

The letters a and b refer to the ratio of the marginal to the average product of capital and labor, respectively. There is no need to assume that they are constants, but it is useful and realistic to consider that their values change slowly over time. Since there are assumed to be constant returns to scale, we have $a + b = 1$.

Postulate that the rate of growth of capital in any state is such that the marginal product of capital is equal to the world interest rate r:

$$M = a \frac{Y}{K} = r \tag{2}$$

where M is the marginal product of capital and a is the ratio of the the marginal to the average product.[7] In so far as the interest rate is given, Y and K must grow at the same rate.

Solving Equation (1), with the condition that $y = k$, we obtain the equilibrium rate of growth of output and capital as

$$y = k = \frac{g}{1 - a} + n \tag{3}$$

The rate of growth is a linear combination of the rate of growth of the labor supply (n) and the rate of technological change (g).

If population grows at the same rate as the labor force, then per capita produced income grows at a rate $y - n$, or

$$y - n = \frac{g}{1 - a} \tag{4}$$

The rate of growth of per capita output is determined by g.

Capital imports into the region are defined as imports minus exports or, to say the same thing, absorption minus production. By definition, imports minus exports is equal to investment minus savings.[8] The magnitude of capital imports can be determined by comparing the rate of investment (I) with the rate of savings (S).

Assume that savings are proportional to output:

$$S = sY \tag{5}$$

Investment I is kK, by definition. Capital imports occur if kK exceeds sY. Since the rate of growth of capital is equal to y, the rate of growth of output, and since $M = a(Y/K) = r$, capital imports occur if and only if the rate of growth of output exceeds the ratio of domestic savings to capital:

$$y > s\frac{r}{a} \qquad (6)$$

The greater the rate of growth, the more likely it is that a state will import capital. If all states have similar savings-income ratios and similar shares of output received by capital, then the rapidly growing states will be importing capital from the slowly growing states.

A numerical example is interesting. If the world interest rate is 6 percent, the savings-income ratio is 20 percent, and capital receives one-third of the output in all countries, then countries that are growing faster than 3.64 percent per annum will import capital from those which are growing at slower rates.

The equilibrium world rate of interest will be such as to equate world investment with world savings:

$$\Sigma I_i = \Sigma r\left(\frac{s}{a}\right)_i K_i \qquad (7)$$

where the i subscript refers to country i. Solving for r, we obtain the expression

$$r = \frac{\Sigma I_i}{\Sigma (s/a)_i K_i} \qquad (8.1)$$

If s/a is the same in all countries, then the world interest rate is proportional to the world growth of capital, k:

$$r = \frac{a}{s} k \qquad (8.2)$$

If world capital is growing at 3 percent and a/s is $\frac{5}{3}$, then the world interest rate will be 5 percent.[9] When the world capital stock is growing, then the world interest rate is strictly positive.

To summarize, we have presented a general model of growth which is the framework of our subsequent analysis. This model is internally consistent in the sense that it determines the equilibrium regional growth rates, capital movements, and the world interest rate.

With the aid of the elementary model we can examine the logical foundations of Myrdal's conclusions. First, he claims that there will be permanent differences in the rates of growth of per capita output. The rate of growth of per capita output is given by Equation (4): it is the rate of technological change (*g*) divided by labor's share of output (1 − *a*). In so far as there are permanent differences among regions or countries in the rates of technological change, there will be permanent differences in the rate of growth of per capita output. As a result, there will be, eventually, a divergence among regions in output per capita. Second, he claims that the poor countries will be exporting capital to the rich countries. If the rate of growth in the poor countries is less than that prevailing in the rich countries and if *s/a* is not very different among countries, then his conclusion follows logically from our model.

The crucial question is one of fact. Is the rate of growth greater in the regions with initially high per capita incomes or greater in the poorer regions? Is there a tendency for per capita incomes among regions to diverge or converge? These empirical questions are answered in the subsequent chapters of this book. Myrdal's argument is not general. It does not accord with the U.S. experience. There has been a tendency among U.S. regions for per capita incomes to converge. The states with the initially low per capita outputs tended to have higher rates of growth of per capita output than did the initially richer states.

GROWTH AND TECHNOLOGICAL CHANGE IN A MULTISECTOR ECONOMY

The model developed above was a simplification of reality. It assumed that the region produced one good that could be consumed or invested. In reality regions produce a multiplicity of goods. When a variety of goods are produced, what is the meaning of an aggregative production function? What role in the growth process is played by changes in the terms of trade? The crucial variable in the above model is the rate of technological change, but what is the economic meaning of that term? The key to the understanding of the growth process lies in the answers to these questions.

Interregional Differences in the Rate of Technological Change. Why should there be interregional differences in the rates of technological change? In a market economy technological changes are likely to be widely diffused. The extent of this diffusion depends upon the type of economic activity being carried on and on the nature of the change itself. We might consider the extremes of extractive industries, on the one hand, and manufacturing, construction, services, and transport on the other. In extractive industries technological change in the forms of discovery of new resources or new techniques will have a differential regional impact because of the unequal distribution of this activity among regions and the unequal distribution of the new discovery or technique among the existing activities.

In the second group of industries, technological change in the form of new techniques of production or management will have a differential regional impact only if there is differential response to the new knowledge which is made available. A new manufacturing process or a new machine is, under competition, available to all. While it may be introduced more rapidly in one place than another, this difference is a result of the alertness of entrepreneurship in different places and the possibilities for expansion generated by the other economic determinants of growth. Technological change may appear to have a differential regional impact because its introduction depends upon the rate of current gross investment. If gross investment is more important in one region than another, it may appear that technological change is occurring more rapidly there as well.

Technological change in the form of improved efficiency of the labor force is likely to have a differential regional impact because of the demographic characteristics of the population. Rural inhabitants are likely to have less schooling than urban. They are also likely to be strangers to factory technology and urban business methods. Starting from these initial conditions of inequality which result from the differential regional distribution of rural populations, the improvement in skills due to education and to acquaintance with urban society may be considerable.

As a practical matter, it is extremely difficult to observe and quantify technological changes of the sort described.[10] This problem is accentuated when we measure the economic performance of different regions. We can measure their output and its growth and their labor force and its growth, and we can approximate their growth of capital. It may not be possible in practice to measure the differential regional impact of technological change, although it undoubtedly exists and plays a role in regional growth phenomena. We would suggest, however, that technological change plays a reinforcing role which accentuates the effects of investment and labor force growth. We do not believe that it acts counter to the other major influences which we can observe and quantify.

In addition to these three forces, a fourth factor making for economic growth and included under the heading of technological change is the improved efficiency of the economic system. Any economy, whether or not it is organized by means of markets, displays a set of production goals for its resources. The efficiency of the system is a concept that describes the success with which these goals are met. In the market economy, these goals are represented by the relative prices of various outputs, and the efficiency of the system may under certain circumstances be measured by the value of output that its resources produce. Any redistribution of productive resources that yields a higher value of output may be said to provide an increase in efficiency, for the same resources are then yielding a higher total return. Provided that the prices used to weight the various outputs reflect the free choices of consumers and producers, and assuming perfect competition with no external effects, we may consider an increase in income through greater efficiency a type of economic growth. It might seem that improved efficiency could yield only small increments of output and therefore is less important than the other forces included under technical change. In fact, however, Massell, in a valuable study of technical change, concluded that approximately one-third of the measured technical change resulted from a more efficient interindustry allocation of resources.[11]

A formal analysis of these points will give us a deeper insight into the role of technological change in a study of economic growth. Suppose there are h industries in a region, each with a production function subject to constant returns to scale. If we use subscripts to denote industries, the value of output in constant prices is Y_i, the value of the capital input is K_i, and the labor input is L_i. Since there are constant returns to scale, we have

$$Y_i = m_i K_i + w_i L_i \qquad (i = 1, 2, \ldots, h) \qquad (9)$$

where m_i is the marginal rate of return on capital and w_i is the marginal value product of labor. If competition equalized the marginal rates of return on capital and the marginal value product of labor among industries such that $m_i = m$ and $w_i = w$, then

$$Y = mK + wL \qquad (10)$$

Given K and L, we have the value of output in constant prices Y a maximum when $m_i = m$ and $w_i = w$ for all industries. In reality there may be disequilibrium such that the average m_i, denoted by m', and the average w_i, denoted by w', are not equal to m and w, respectively (where the latter are the equilibrium values). Thus,

$$Y' = m'K + w'L \qquad (11.1)$$

or $$Y' = mK + wL + [(m' - m)K + (w' - w)L] \qquad (11.2)$$

is the value of aggregate output in constant prices.[12] We know that Y' is less than Y if m' differs from m or if w' differs from w. Hence, the term in brackets is negative in disequilibrium and is zero in equilibrium. If K and L are given, $(m' - m)$ and $(w' - w)$ approach zero as resources are more efficiently allocated. Thereby the value of Y' is raised towards Y.

Since for the same aggregate inputs of capital and labor the real value of output has been increased as resources are more efficiently allocated, the statistician working with an aggregate production function would detect technological improvement. This technological improvement has occurred exclusively as a result of a more efficient allocation of resources and is included under g in Equation (1). There have been interregional differences in the extent of the misallocation of resources. For example, the marginal returns to labor in agriculture have been smaller than the returns in urban occupation in the United States. Hence, the potential growth from the correction of the misallocation of resources was greater in the agricultural states than in the nonagricultural states. In recent years, the intersectoral wage differential has narrowed. Consequently, this source of interstate differences in the rate of technological change has been reduced in importance. These matters will be developed fully in Chapter 2.

On the international level, Kuznets found that, "the relative disparity in product per worker between the A [agriculture, forestry, and fishing] sector and the nonagricultural sector tends to be wider in the low-income than in the high-income countries."[13] If the ratio of the marginal to the average product of labor is not significantly higher in the A sector, then the degree of resource misallocation is greater in the low-income than in the high-income countries. If the rate at which resource misallocation is being corrected were the same in all countries, we would observe a greater rate of "technological change" in the countries of low per capita income than in the countries of high per capita income.

To summarize this section, there are three sources of economic growth: first, the growth of the labor and the capital inputs; second, the elimination of resource misallocation; and third, the growth that occurs when the *maximum* rate of output, produced by a given combination of inputs, is increased through time. This is the strict definition of technological change.

The Measurement of Inefficiency. Since the second source of economic growth, the elimination of resource misallocation, is central to Chapters 2, 6, and 7, a further discussion of this phenomenon is desirable.

In practice, the types of inefficiency or resource misallocation with which we shall be concerned do not include all the possible varieties that a market economy might experience. We shall be concerned primarily with differences in factor payments. This concern raises an issue of comparability. There is no question of comparability in the case of capital. If a dollar's worth of capital permanently invested yields 5 percent in one sector and 6 percent in another, income could be increased through a transfer to the higher yield sector.[14] The comparability problem arises, however, in the case of labor. If, on the average, workers in one region earn $5,000 per annum and workers in another earn $8,000 per annum, inefficiency is suggested but not proven. Returns to the average worker may not indicate how much comparable workers might earn in each region. One reason is a difference in skills; a region with highly skilled workers is giving evidence of higher returns than another. Comparable workers might earn the same return in each region. Another reason, which may be less important in practice, is a difference in worker preferences for income as opposed to leisure. If labor voluntarily works fewer weeks per year in one region, incomes per annum will be lower even if comparable effort could secure the same return.

Finally, even if it is clear that comparable workers can earn less in one region than another, it is not proven that real income would be increased if workers moved to the high-wage region. For one thing, resources must be used up in migration. For another, the cost of living in a low-wage region may be so much lower than in a high-wage region that differences in the standard of living of comparable workers in the two regions are canceled out. The reason for the lower cost of living is the low wage itself, since many items in the consumer budget are produced in cooperation with local labor. Nevertheless, a wage differential of X percent between regions could not produce a difference in cost of living of X percent for two reasons: first, many items in the consumer budget are produced outside the low-wage region and consequently are influenced in price by the wage levels of other regions; second, many items in the consumer budget are produced by capital cooperating with labor. If capital is not receiving a lower rate of return in the low-wage region, the relative cost of living in the two regions will not be as low as the relative wages. Because of these considerations, differences in the cost of living can never completely offset the influence of wage differences. They may nevertheless reduce the impact of wage differences on the willingness of workers to migrate in response to economic opportunity. Barriers to migration of this type will slow down the rate at which regional wage differentials are eliminated. To the extent that these barriers represent either the costs of migration or the compensating differences in the cost of living, the wage differential itself is no indication of economic inefficiency as far as the return to labor is concerned.

There is, however, another criterion that must be brought to bear on this question of inefficiency and regional wage differentials to comparable workers. If comparable workers are earning less in one region than another, it may also indicate a lack of efficiency in the capital market. If we assume that regions have the same constant returns to scale production function and sell output at the same net price, then a money wage differential implies differences in the rates of return on capital. A model embodying this approach is investigated in Chapter 3. It is useful as a first approximation to the growth process because it permits us to describe two phenomena: regional differences in the returns to capital and labor arising from initial inequalities in the regional endowment of these resources, and regional movements of capital and labor in response to such differences. Such a framework also generates regional differences in output growth if one resource possesses greater mobility than the other. If capital is more mobile than labor, then the low-wage regions will grow more

| | Returns to capital | |
Returns to labor	Above average	Below average
Above average	A	B
Below average	C	D

FIGURE 1.1

rapidly than the high-wage regions; conversely, if labor is more mobile than capital, the high-wage regions will grow more rapidly than the low-wage regions.

These phenomena may be summarized most conveniently by referring to the relative levels of returns to capital and labor in the United States and are presented in Figure 1.1.

The simple aggregate framework described above would lead us to expect the bulk of U.S. regions to appear in cells *B* and *C*. It also leads us to expect that capital moves from *B* to *C* and labor from *C* to *B*, with the consequence that wages grow more rapidly in *C* than *B*.

In fact, the behavior we shall examine indicates that this simple process does not occur with the regularity needed to substantiate its usefulness. There have been periods when the high-wage states evidenced more rapid growth of wages than the low-wage states. At individual moments of time we may observe regions where the returns to both labor and capital are higher than the national level and other regions where both returns are below the national level. The former regions are observed to grow more rapidly than the latter. These regions exist beside others where the more familiar pattern prevails, namely, high wages combined with low returns to capital and low wages combined with high returns to capital. This situation suggests the existence of a more complex set of influences on growth patterns than those described above.

How is it possible that one region simultaneously evidences higher returns to labor and capital than others? How is it possible that a high return region grows faster than a low return region? Chapter 3 will attempt to answer these questions.

ECONOMIC MATURITY

Kuznets observed retardation in the rate of growth in a majority of the countries he examined. As a result, he would conclude that there would not be a tendency for per capita output among countries to diverge. Retardation, or maturity, is a fascinating concept which can be discussed in terms of the general model of growth presented above.

A number of specific explanations have been adduced to explain why the growth rates of certain regions decline after a period of development.

One popular explanation focuses on the age of the manufacturing industry in a particular region. While age would appear to have a fortuitous and even negligible effect on growth, it does appear to be associated in a statistical sense with the rate at which regions develop. The relation between age and growth is not hard to specify, although it does appear to depend on a misconception as to the workings of the economy. It is frequently asserted that an older region may get a head start in the development of a manufacturing complex, but this head start may cause its own decay for a number of reasons.

First, the vigor of entrepreneurship may decline over time. The initial driving force behind the growth of family-held manufacturing firms will lapse as the business passes into the hands of generations in which the drive to accumulate wealth has weakened. While it is true that the corporate form of business organization is a structure that permits entrepreneurship to reinvigorate itself, the fact remains that, in order to prevent outsiders from gaining control, closely held firms need not avail themselves of such opportunities.

Second, the products of an older manufacturing complex are themselves old in the sense that future demand will not gain as rapidly as it has in the past.[15] At the same time, commitment to older products and processes may hinder a shift of product lines rapid enough to take advantage of new opportunities for market expansion. An example may be found in the metal-working industries of New England. Sewing machines, vacuum cleaners, typewriters, watches and clocks, jewelry and silverware, electric light bulbs, textile machinery, hand tools, and machine tools are all products of New England industry. At one time, when these were new, they enjoyed growing national markets. While New England firms still have strong commitments to the production of these items, national demand for these goods is growing quite slowly at the same time that other sources of production have been established both in the United States and overseas to compete for the same markets. In a sense the failure of firms to shift product lines represents a failure of entrepreneurship.

This attribute of stagnant firms in declining areas may be part of the phenomena discussed above. While the above statements are hardly untrue historically, they nevertheless do not form an explanation for regional growth, for what we have observed are the consequences of a self-selection process among firms in different regions. The decay of an older region such as New England has been associated with the failure of new firms to enter and expand in industries faster than the older industries have declined. The result is that we observe the predominance of a group of old firms in old industries. There are no obvious barriers to entry in newer industries which would be a disadvantage to New England compared with the rest of the country. Consequently, the differential growth rate among regions has led to the observation cited above. It would be a mistake to use the failure of entrepreneurship as a causal factor in an economy where entrepreneurship is free to move among regions.

A second aspect of development that has been linked erroneously to age in the search for an explanation of regional growth patterns is found in the application of the concepts of external economies and agglomeration effects. It is frequently asserted that an older industrial area grows more slowly than a newer because it has exhausted the investment opportunities associated with external economies and agglomeration effects. When a region begins to develop an industrial core, it must reach a certain level of activity before certain investments become profitable. Social capital embodied in highways, drainage systems, electric power facilities, and railway lines are all characterized by certain indivisible minimum capital requirements. Such investments pay off only when the level of industrial activity reaches a certain size. After this size has been reached and after these facilities are constructed, an important type of investment opportunity is eliminated. The same phenomenon holds true within a given industry. When the industry is first established in a region, there are certain production and repair activities that a firm must perform for itself and certain intermediate products that must be purchased outside the region. Only when the industry reaches a minimal size can these functions be specialized in the hands of individual firms within the region. Once this disintegration of process and specialization of function has taken place, a source of investment opportunities has been eliminated.

Again we have a case where the arguments are true but misleading. The exploitation and exhaustion of external economies may explain the evolution of a region's industrial structure. It does not, however, explain why a region's growth slows down. When we say that the external economies of a region have been fully utilized, we mean that all possibilities of cost reduction from scale expansion have been exhausted. Therefore, it is easier for firms to enter an industry in such a region. All types of social capital and all types of service facilities are available to it, compared with a newer region. Such ease of entry occurs because the capital requirements for entry have been eased. With the eased conditions for entry of new firms, it is difficult to argue that growth is inhibited. It is also difficult to argue that opportunities for capital-using investments are exhausted, for these opportunities depend on the continued growth of a region. While these capital-using activities represent minimum input requirements and minimum profitable levels of use, there are no maxima implied. A region that continues to develop will continue to need new investments in public utilities and other types of social capital.

Still a third linkage between age and growth has been sought through the effects of government social welfare expenditures and trade unions. It might be argued that as a region develops and grows wealthier, these two forces begin to sap its vitality. The growth of an urban social conscience forces a rise in local and state government provision of social services and a rise in taxation. This development cuts the yield on investment as compared with other regions where local government activities are not so highly developed. In the case of Federal social programs, the argument is posed somewhat differently, since Federal receipts and expenditures need not match in each state. The rise of Federal programs with a redistributional bias (from rich to poor states) may stimulate the poor states.

In similar vein it is argued that the activities of trade unions are likely to discourage business enterprise through their pressure on wage rates and through their interference with the internal allocation of labor in business firms. Unions are likely to be strongest in heavily urbanized regions. Consequently, they induce the appearance of wage differentials which favor economic development in nonunionized sections of the country.

In our view, both these arguments are faulty. While they may or may not be accurate historical descriptions, there is, in fact, no necessary relation implied between age and growth. In the case of state and local government expenditure, we may be viewing the substitution of public for private investment with no over-all decline of total investment. It is not at all obvious that a well-developed system of public social programs, such as schools and highways, is a net deterrent to private investment even if some of the tax load falls on the private investor. In the case of Federal programs, their redistributional bias from high-income to low-income states is well known. There is, however, no obvious regional relation between the age of the region and the level of per capita income.

In the case of trade unions, wage-setting activities may result in higher wages than would be set in a competitive market. It is perfectly clear that a strong union can drive an industry out of a region if cheaper labor supplies are available in other regions, but this availability depends on a differential degree of unionization and the relative importance of other cost influences on industrial location. It also depends on the ability of a union to maintain a strong bargaining position in the face of declining employment opportunities for its members.

While these conditions may have been satisfied on occasion, there is no way to know whether the particular industry would have moved in the absence of unions. In the case of the textile industry, its move to the South began after World War I, a period when unions were relatively weak. In addition, the wage differentials that are accepted as causing this move were no larger than a free market would set. In addition, the pace and character of the movement suggest that the response to wage differentials was strongly influenced by technological changes. These changes made it profitable to use relatively unskilled labor in certain types of textile production.

A final comment on the role of unions is suggested by the observation that unionization appears related to the degree of urbanization in a region. Consequently, the appearance of growth differentials among urbanized regions cannot be explained by this factor. For these reasons it is not at all clear that older areas are likely to be more heavily unionized than newer. Second, if they are more heavily unionized, it does not necessarily follow that unions will drive industries into newer areas.

According to our analysis, there are a number of adjustments in the course of the growth process which tend to slow the process down. The most important of these is the exhaustion of the sectoral shifts of the labor supply from low-income to higher-income occupations. Once a region has eliminated the misallocation of resources by reducing the relative importance of the low-wage sector, the growth rate will be reduced. The value of g will be reduced to the national rate of technological change.

A second cause of the reduction in the rate of growth is the reduction in the rate of growth of the supply of labor. Once a region has increased its degree of urbanization by shifting workers from farm to nonfarm employments, the growth rate of population (n) will be dominated by the

I N d i a ?

lower urban net reproduction rates. A concomitant decline occurs in both measured technological change (g) and the rate of growth of the labor force, thus reducing the rate of growth.

Finally, the imposition of national immigration barriers exerts a depressive influence upon the growth of the labor-importing regions. Usually, these regions have limited agricultural sectors from which to draw labor or have lower rates of natural increase than the labor surplus regions. As a result, the imposition of national immigration barriers exerts a depressive effect upon the urban, high-wage, labor-importing regions.

We view economic maturity as that phase of the growth process where the rate of growth of the labor force and the measured rate of technological change are reduced relative to the levels formerly prevailing. This reduction in n and g is usually an inherent part of the growth process.

AN OUTLINE OF THIS BOOK

It was pointed out earlier that the analytical framework was too general to permit direct confrontation with empirical data for the purposes of statistical verification. In order that statistical hypotheses be drawn from the model, it is necessary that additional empirical restrictions be imposed and certain types of behavior ruled out on a priori grounds. It is obviously impossible to test a theory which is consistent with any type of behavior. The specification of additional empirical restrictions and the derivation and testing of statistical hypotheses will be carried out in the following chapters. In the final chapter we shall present a framework for the evaluation of social policy toward depressed and growing areas.

Chapter 2 describes the empirical regularities of behavior evidenced by regions of the United States over the last eighty years. We identify areas of persistent growth and decay; we investigate the growth and convergence of per capita incomes, the growth of employment, the narrowing of sectoral wage differentials, and the shift within regions in the allocation of resources between agricultural and nonagricultural sectors.

In Chapter 3 we investigate and show the limitations of a simple aggregative theory of growth in which demand factors are neglected. We show that the data do not support the implications of such a theory and that we must look in a new direction for fruitful statistical hypotheses. We must look at the various activities undertaken in a region and try to understand its growth in terms of the changes in economic structure. In particular, we must set up models that permit us to identify and separate the role of demand for exports and the role of labor migration.

The role of export demand is investigated in Chapter 3, and we find that it has played a powerful role in certain periods of the twentieth century. In Chapters 4 and 5 we identify the role of shifts of the labor force between sectors and regions in stimulating regional growth. We take into account the two sources of growth in the labor supply identified in our model, namely, the shift of labor from a low- to a high-paying sector and from low-wage to high-wage regions. It will be possible to show that in the very long run this factor is of crucial importance.

In Chapter 6, we examine the relationship between growth, reallocation, and the return to resources. This is an important link in the continuation of a stable growth process, for if the rents to capital fall in a growing region, the stimulus to continued growth may be hindered. Consequently, we examine in Chapter 6 the influences on the returns to capital and labor that arise from the reallocation of resources between labor-intensive and capital-intensive sectors. We also examine the way in which the elimination of inefficient allocation over time may affect the prospect for further growth. In Chapter 7 we present in some detail a growth model which shows the interactions between export demand, capital imports, and the return to resources.

In Chapter 8, we evaluate the regional growth patterns in the light of modern theories of growth. We identify and demonstrate a method of predicting growth differentials which is derived from the earlier theoretical sections. This predictive method in conjunction with modern theories of growth enables us to understand the sense in which U.S. regional growth patterns may be considered efficient. Chapter 9 suggests several decision rules to determine appropriate government policies affecting areas which experience social problems as a result of the growth process.

2. EMPIRICAL REGULARITIES IN THE PROCESS OF GROWTH AND DECLINE

The present chapter is concerned with the regularities to be explained by a theory of growth. We have observed the following:

1. There has been a convergence of per capita personal incomes among states since 1880. The difference among states is narrowing over time.

2. Among states there has been a stable pattern of growth of manufacturing employment since 1869. Some states have persistently grown more rapidly than others.

3. There is a stable pattern of growth of nonagricultural employment and of the capital employed in nonagricultural industries. Again some states have persistently grown more rapidly than others since 1919.

4. Certain states have experienced an absolute decline of employment. Many of the "depressed areas," as identified by various government agencies, are clustered in these states.

5. A group of states have persistently experienced a slower-than-average growth of earnings per worker in nonagricultural occupations.

The object of this book is to explain why these events have occurred. An explanation is logically similar to a prediction. Hence, a theory that explains a certain set of events could have predicted this set of events. A causal explanation consists of three parts: a set of events E, a set of antecedent, or initial, conditions C, and a transformation T from C into E. On the one hand, if we are given the set of antecedent conditions C and the theory, or transformation, T, we can *predict* the set of events E. On the other hand, an *explanation* consists of finding a theory, or transformation, T, such that C and T imply the set of events E. An *explanation* is directed towards *past* occurrences, whereas a *prediction* is directed towards *future* ones.[1] Our theory of growth consists of finding a transformation T which is both an explanation and a prediction, in the sense described above.

Economics as a science is concerned with the question: Why does a certain phenomenon happen? By that we mean: According to what general laws, or transformations, and by virtue of what initial conditions *C* does the phenomenon occur? An explanation, or theory, must be general and hence abstract. The view that each situation is unique explicitly denies the possibility of an explanation. It is the essence of a scientific explanation in economics that we adduce general laws; i.e., we use economic theory. Our interest is not in theory for its own sake, but for its ability to explain or predict. We have found that neoclassical price theory, suitably developed, provides the explanation of interstate differences in growth rates.

THE CONVERGENCE OF PER CAPITA INCOMES

Interstate differences in per capita personal incomes have narrowed, in relative terms, from 1880 to 1950. Table 2.1 summarizes the relevant information. It is reproduced from a study by R. A. Easterlin.

TABLE 2.1. CONVERGENCE OF PERSONAL INCOME
PER CAPITA, 1880–1950

	1880	*1900*	*1919–20*	*1949–51*
Coefficient of variation	57.9	42.5	30.4	23.4
Relative personal income per capita, unweighted average of states in each region (U.S. = 100):				
New England[a]	129	120	111	98
Middle Atlantic[b]	129	125	123	119
South Atlantic[c]	45	47	61	70
East South Central[d]	50	48	52	58
West South Central[e]	60	58	68	72
East North Central[f]	99	101	104	111
West North Central[g]	92	98	84	94
Mountain[h]	191	142	105	99
Pacific[i]	164	149	126	113

Source: Richard A. Easterlin, "Regional Growth of Income: Long-Term Tendencies," in Simon Kuznets, Ann Ratner Miller, and Richard A. Easterlin, *Analyses of Economic Change* (Vol. II of *Population Redistribution and Economic Growth, United States, 1870–1950*, Philadelphia, American Philosophical Society, 1960), p. 146. Reproduced by permission of the authors and the American Philosophical Society.

[a] Maine, New Hampshire, Vermont, Massachusetts, Connecticut, Rhode Island.

[b] New York, New Jersey, Pennsylvania.

[c] Maryland, Delaware, District of Columbia, West Virginia, Virginia, North Carolina, South Carolina, Georgia, Florida.

[d] Kentucky, Tennessee, Alabama, Mississippi.

[e] Arkansas, Louisiana, Oklahoma, Texas.

[f] Michigan, Wisconsin, Ohio, Indiana, Illinois.

[g] Minnesota, North Dakota, South Dakota, Iowa, Nebraska, Kansas, Missouri.

[h] Montana, Idaho, Wyoming, Colorado, Utah, Nevada, New Mexico, Arizona.

[i] Washington, Oregon, California.

The trend of per capita incomes toward the U.S. average is unmistakable. In every region but the East North Central, the average tendency is toward convergence. When individual states are examined, the ratio of the standard deviation to the mean (coefficient of variation) steadily declines. By 1950, no region had a per capita income more than 20 percent above the national average or less than 42 percent below the national average. Seventy years earlier, the range of variation was from 91 percent above the mean to as low as 55 percent below the mean. The forces making for convergence from above were clearly stronger than the forces making for convergence from below.[2]

A statistical description of the factors accounting for the convergence of per capita income sheds quite a bit of light upon the process of economic growth. The view that convergence has occurred solely as a result of factor price equalization within sectors is not quite accurate. Easterlin's data show that a strong force making for convergence is the shift of labor from agricultural to nonagricultural employment, where income per worker has been higher.[3]

He shows this in the following way: per capita income, the ratio of total personal income (Y) to population (P), is written as a sum of two terms—service income per capita and property income per capita. In turn, service income may be partitioned into nonagricultural and agricultural components.[4] Per capita income in a state will rise if there is a rise in any of these three components. In addition, service income per capita will rise if there is an increase in the relative importance of a high-return sector. Historically, service income per worker has been higher in nonagricultural than agricultural occupations. Therefore, per capita income has risen in response to a rise in the relative importance of the nonagricultural sector. These influences may be understood with the aid of the following definitions:

W_N = average income per nonagricultural worker
L_N/P = ratio of nonagricultural employment to population
W_A = average income per agricultural worker
L_A/P = ratio of agricultural employment to population
Q/P = property income per capita
Y/P = personal income per capita

Then

$$\frac{Y}{P} = W_N \frac{L_N}{P} + W_A \frac{L_A}{P} + \frac{Q}{P} \tag{1}$$

Table 2.2 presents Easterlin's data on the convergence of W_A, W_N, and Q/P over time. Three measures of dispersion were used: the coefficient of variation, the unweighted mean deviation, and the weighted mean deviation.[5] Examining Table 2.2, we see that there was hardly any convergence of agricultural service income per worker (W_A) during this 70-year period. There was some convergence of nonagricultural service income per worker (W_N) during this period, but it did not occur steadily or strongly.

TABLE 2.2. CONVERGENCE OF SERVICE INCOME PER WORKER, NONAGRICULTURAL EMPLOYMENT TO POPULATION, AND PER CAPITA PROPERTY INCOMES, 1880, 1900, 1920, AND 1950

	1880	1900	1920[a]	1950[b]
Agricultural service income per worker, percent:				
Coefficient of variation	41.4	40.4	36.6	37.2
Unweighted arithmetic deviation	35.3	40.8	38.9	34.2
Weighted arithmetic deviation	33.8	35.7	33.1	32.3
Nonagricultural service income per worker, percent:				
Coefficient of variation	27.9	24.2	14.2	14.3
Unweighted arithmetic deviation	20.7	18.6	11.2	12.2
Weighted arithmetic deviation	12.4	11.8	10.0	11.8
Property income per capita, percent:				
Coefficient of variation	65.4	59.6	50.6	40.9
Unweighted arithmetic deviation	49.6	44.4	37.9	29.6
Weighted arithmetic deviation	51.1	51.1	42.3	29.3
Nonagricultural as a percent of total labor force:				
Unweighted arithmetic deviation	37.8	27.6	19.6	9.8
Weighted arithmetic deviation	38.5	31.3	21.2	8.6

Source: Richard A. Easterlin, "Regional Growth of Income: Long-Term Tendencies," in Simon Kuznets, Ann Ratner Miller, and Richard A. Easterlin, *Analyses of Economic Change* (Vol. II of *Population Redistribution and Economic Growth, United States, 1870–1950,* Philadelphia, American Philosophical Society, 1960), pp. 152, 153, 155, 163. Reproduced by permission of the authors and the American Philosophical Society.
 [a] Average of 1919–21.
 [b] Average of 1949–51.

With respect to the first variable, W_A, the arithmetic deviation rose from 1880 to 1900 and fell from 1900 to 1950. The magnitude of decline from 1880 to 1950 was small. The weighted arithmetic deviation fell from 33.8 percentage points in 1880 to 32.3 percentage points in 1950. During this period, the unweighted arithmetic deviation went from 35.3 percentage points in 1880 to 40.8 in 1900 to 34.2 percentage points in 1950— a negligible decline. The coefficient of variation declined from 41.4 in 1880 to 36.6 in 1920 and rose to 37.2 in 1950.

With respect to nonagricultural service income per worker, W_N, the coefficient of variation fell *from 27.9 in 1880 to 14.2 in 1920*, a 50 percent reduction. From 1920 to 1950, the coefficient of variation was constant. If the weighted arithmetic deviation is examined, convergence is not so clear. The weighted arithmetic deviation fell from 12.4 in 1880 to 11.8 in 1900, but the weighted deviation was 11.8 in 1950. Over the entire 70-year period, the arithmetic deviation declined by only 0.6 percentage point.

It is important to point out that service income per worker is not the same as wages and salaries per employee. Service income includes proprietor's income, which is a return to both labor and capital. It is possible that nonagricultural wages and salaries per employee did converge, while nonagricultural proprietor's income did not. This possibility will be examined below.

The W_A and W_N terms in Equation (1) were not very important in producing the steady convergence of per capita income from 1880 to 1950. Instead, it is clear that per capita incomes converged mainly as a result of the convergence in property income per capita and in the ratio of nonagricultural to total employment. Regardless of which measure of dispersion is used in Table 2.2, it is clear that the interstate differences in property income per capita narrowed from 1880 to 1950. The coefficient of variation declined *steadily* from 65.4 to 40.9. The unweighted arithmetic deviation declined steadily from 49.6 to 29.6 points. Similarly, the weighted arithmetic deviation fell from 51.1 in 1880 to 29.3 in 1950.

Similarly, the ratio of nonagricultural to total employment converged *steadily* and *markedly* among states in this 70-year period. The unweighted deviation fell from 37.8 to 9.8 percentage points. The weighted deviation fell from 38.5 to 8.6 percentage points.

On the basis of Easterlin's data, one concludes that the convergence of per capita personal income among states was the statistical result of two main forces: convergence of the ratio of nonagricultural to total employment and convergence of property income per capita. In each year—1880, 1900, 1920, and 1950—per capita state income was positively associated with property income per capita in the state and with the state ratio of nonagricultural to total state employment; that is, states with high per capita income enjoyed high property income per capita and had a high proportion of their labor force in nonagricultural pursuits. Furthermore, as states moved closer to the average in terms of these two variables, their per capita personal incomes also moved closer to the average.

Easterlin's findings for the later period may be supplemented by new data which have been prepared on returns to capital and labor by state.

These data are prepared on a produced income basis; that is, they show the payments to those states in which the resources are employed.[6] Easterlin's income data are on a received basis. Table 2.3 summarizes the distribution of payments to capital outside of agriculture, on a per employee basis for 1929 and 1953. Also shown are the nonagricultural wages and salaries per employee and per worker for 1919, 1929, and 1953. For each entity, we show the simple arithmetic state mean and the

TABLE 2.3. DISTRIBUTION OF COMPONENTS OF STATE INCOME PAYMENTS

	1919		*1929*		*1953*	
	Mean	*Coefficient of variation*	*Mean*	*Coefficient of variation*	*Mean*	*Coefficient of variation*
Nonagricultural wages and salaries:						
Per non-agricultural worker	$1,011	0.1453	$1,134	0.1953		
Per non-agricultural employee	$1,139	0.1282	$1,266	0.2449	$3,461	0.1196
Payments to non-agricultural capital per non-agricultural employee:						
Produced	. . .	. . .	$839	0.3037	$1,632	0.1335
Received	. . .	. . .	$695	0.4660	$1,651	0.2544

unweighted coefficient of variation. In Table 2.3, nonagricultural workers include both the employed and self-employed, while nonagricultural employees exclude the self-employed. For 1919 and 1929, the self-employed were eliminated from the data by the use of estimates of their presence in certain occupations.

The convergence of income payments to capital is borne out by these data. Between 1929 and 1953, the coefficient of variation declined by 45 percent for received payments to capital per employee. That this is a sharper convergence than that shown by Easterlin is most likely attributable to the fact that these data are on a per employee basis rather than a per capita basis and that they refer to the nonagricultural sector alone, while Easterlin's data include both agricultural and nonagricultural property.

An even stronger convergence pattern is in evidence for produced payments to capital. Here the coefficient of variation declines by 56 percent between 1929 and 1953. This decline is hardly surprising, for, if the convergence patterns are the result of a long-run economic process, as we believe to be the case, then they should operate more directly on produced income. The reason is that the distribution of received property income is partly influenced by the decisions of property owners to live in regions apart from the location of their assets.

There is also a convergence pattern in nonagricultural wages and salaries, although it is somewhat weaker than the pattern operating on the payments to capital. Between 1929 and 1953, the coefficient of variation of nonagricultural wage income declined by 51 percent. This decline stands in contrast with Easterlin's findings that nonagricultural service income per worker did not converge between 1920 and 1950. Most of the difference is due to the divergence in wages and salaries that occurred between 1919 and 1929. Using the findings on wages and salaries per nonagricultural employee, we see that between 1919 and 1953, the coefficient of variation declines by 7 percent.

While these data tend to confirm Easterlin's findings that nonagricultural service income failed to converge, they also point up the lack of homogeneity during the time period examined. During the period 1919–29, wage and salary income diverged strongly. In the succeeding period, they converged. In the next chapter, we shall examine the forces making for convergence and divergence.

ECONOMIC REASONS FOR THE CONVERGENCE OF PERSONAL INCOMES PER CAPITA

The convergence of per capita incomes among states may be explained by the hypothesis that resources *within* states have become more *efficiently* allocated over time. An *efficient* allocation is defined here as one that maximizes income per capita in the sense that returns are equalized at the margin (Figure 2.1).

Suppose that state employment were divided between the nonagricultural sector N and the agricultural sector A, so that $0r_1$ of the labor force were in nonagriculture and $(1 - 0r_1)$ were in agriculture. Assume that the ratio of the labor force to population, h, is given. The NN schedule in Figure 2.1 is a relation between the service income per nonagricultural employee and the proportion of total employment in nonagricultural pursuits; the AA schedule is the corresponding function for agriculture. Each schedule is negatively sloped with respect to its own coordinates. As we move from 0 to 1, the employment outside of agriculture increases and the service income per nonagricultural employee declines. The reason for the decline is the fall in the relative price of products produced in the non-agricultural sector as their rate of output increases. By the same token, if employment in agriculture rises, there will be a fall of service income per employee in agriculture. Diminishing returns on a fixed supply of agricultural land in the state will yield the decline of service income implied by the AA schedule. When Or_1 of the labor force is engaged in nonagriculture, the service income per employee in nonagriculture is W_N and

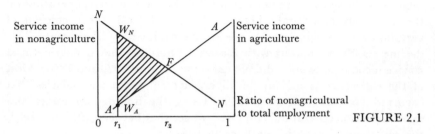

FIGURE 2.1

in agriculture it is W_A. A transfer of one worker from agriculture to nonagriculture would raise the value of personal income by $W_N - W_A$; and personal income per capita would rise by $W_N - W_A$ divided by the population.

The potential increase in income per capita from a more efficient allocation of labor depends upon three variables: first, the initial service income differential, $W_N - W_A$, in the two sectors; second, the ratio of nonagricultural employment (Or_2) which would make service incomes equal in the two sectors; and third, the extent to which employment in the low-wage sector exceeds $1 - Or_2$, the efficient allocation.

According to Figure 2.1, an increase in the ratio of nonagricultural employment from Or_1 to Or_2 would raise total personal income per capita by the shaded area multiplied by h—the ratio of employment to population. Note that we are assuming that economic equilibrium is consistent with the complete equalization of service incomes per worker in the two sectors; that is, workers in the two sectors employ the same amounts of capital. In a later section we shall reexamine this assumption and indicate that complete equalization is not required for competitive equilibrium or for economic efficiency. In fact, with the typically higher relative capital requirements in U.S. agriculture, the appropriate condition is that service income per worker be higher in agriculture.

In Figure 2.2 two hypothetical states are described that are identical except in size. Again the service income per employee in each sector depends upon the ratio of employment in this sector to total employment; and the ratio h of employment to population is the same in each state. The letter W refers to the service income, N refers to the nonagricultural sector, A refers to the agricultural sector, I refers to the first state, and II refers to the second state. For example, W_{AI} refers to the agricultural service income per employee in the first state.

The service income schedule in nonagriculture is NN in both states, and it is AA in the agricultural sector of both states. There is an inefficient

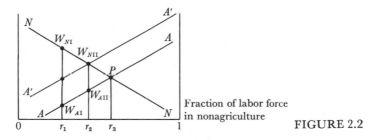

Fraction of labor force in nonagriculture

FIGURE 2.2

allocation of labor in each state, for equality of service income exists in neither state; but the extent of the misallocation is greater in state I. Personal income per capita could be increased by h times the area $W_{NI}W_{AI}P$ if the ratio of nonagricultural employment in state I were raised from $0r_1$ to $0r_3$. Since the extent of the misallocation is less in state II, personal income per capita could be raised by h times the area $W_{NII}W_{AII}P$ through a reallocation of labor, which would raise the ratio of nonagricultural employment from $0r_2$ to $0r_3$.

If the second state had a comparative advantage in agriculture, it would have a marginal revenue product of labor schedule in agriculture of $A'A'$ and a nonagricultural schedule of NN. Then, there would be no misallocation of resources in state II when the ratio of nonagricultural employment was $0r_2$.

Finally, consider states III and IV in Figure 2.3. The service income schedule for agriculture in state i is A_i, and for nonagriculture in state j is N_j. The extent to which personal income per capita could be raised through a reallocation of resources is constructed to be the same in each state. Area BCP is constructed equal to area DEP. In so far as the ratio of labor force to population h is assumed to be the same in the two states, we may focus exclusively upon the triangular areas BCP and DEP to measure the potential increases in personal income per capita, from a reallocation.

Figure 2.3 indicates that the potential increase in personal income per capita depends upon (1) the initial service income differential and (2) the

ratio of employment in the low-income sector. There is a greater differential in state IV (equal to DE) than exists in state III (equal to BC). The
extent of employment in the low-income sector is greater in State III
(equal to $1 - 0r_1$) than exists in state IV (equal to $1 - 0r_2$). Nevertheless,
the same increase in per capita personal income could occur in each state,
if the ratio of nonagricultural employment were raised to $0r_3$. Our theory
is that the growth of per capita income depends upon the initial extent
of resource misallocation. The greater the misallocation, the greater the

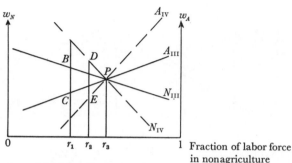

$0r_1$ = initial fraction in state III
$0r_2$ = initial fraction in state IV

FIGURE 2.3

potentialities for growth by correcting this misallocation; and mis-
allocations are corrected.

The evidence strongly suggests that the convergence of per capita
incomes among states from 1880 to 1950 can be explained, to a large
extent, by the improved allocation of resources within states. Three
sources of evidence may be cited.

First, we observed that the convergence of per capita income among
states was attributable to the convergence of service income per worker
and of property income per capita. Service income per worker did not
converge much as a result of a convergence of either nonagricultural or
agricultural service income per worker. What occurred was a convergence of the percentage of the labor force in nonagricultural employment.

Second, in each year (1880, 1900, 1919–21, 1949–51) there was a
positive association between state personal income per capita and the
ratio of nonagricultural to total state labor force.[7] States with a ratio of
nonagricultural employment above the average tended to have personal
incomes per capita above average.

In addition to the evidence examined earlier, a more direct test of this
theory can be made. On the average, service income per worker has been

lower in agriculture than in nonagriculture. A statistical hypothesis can
be formulated on the basis of our theory. Our hypothesis is that the rate
of growth of personal income per capita in a state, from period t to period
$t + 1$, depends upon the ratio of agricultural service income per worker to
nonagricultural service income per worker and the ratio of nonagricultural to total employment.

Our predictions are that the smaller the ratio W_A/W_N, i.e., the greater
the service income differential, the greater will be the percentage growth
in per capita personal income, and the smaller the ratio of nonagricultural to total employment, the greater are the potentialities for an
increase in income through a reallocation of labor.

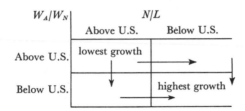

FIGURE 2.4

Tables 2.4, 2.5, and 2.6 present the relevant information. W_A/W_N is
the ratio of agricultural service income per worker to nonagricultural
service income per worker. States in the upper part of the table have
ratios greater than the U.S. average, and states in the lower part have
ratios below the U.S. average. According to our theory, there was a
greater misallocation of labor in the lower section. There was a larger
income differential within the states in the lower section, and hence a
greater growth in per capita income could be expected from a reallocation.
A higher growth rate should be found among the states in the lower
section.

Columns refer to the ratio of nonagricultural to total state employment
(N/L). States in the first column have higher ratios of the labor force in
nonagriculture than do states in the second column. There was a smaller
concentration of the labor force in the low-wage agricultural sector
among the states in the first column than in the second column. A greater
rate of growth of income from a reallocation of labor should occur in the
second column than in the first column.

Our conditional predictions are summarized by the direction of the
arrows in Figure 2.4. States in the second row and the second column have
the least efficient allocations of labor, and they will have the greatest
growth rates. States in the first row and the first column have the most
efficient allocations of labor, and they will have the lowest growth rates.

The data are quite consistent with the theory that the rate of growth

TABLE 2.4. GROWTH OF PERSONAL INCOME PER CAPITA, 1880–1900, IN RELATION TO WAGE DIFFERENTIAL BETWEEN SECTORS AND CONCENTRATION OF EMPLOYMENT IN LOW-WAGE SECTOR

	N/L above U.S. average[a]		*N/L below U.S. average*[a]	
	State	*Percent*	*State*	*Percent*
W_A/W_N above U.S. average:[b]	Maine	48	Vermont	34
	New Hampshire	27	Virginia	53
	Massachusetts	23	North Carolina	31
	Rhode Island	24	South Carolina	21
	Connecticut	22	Tennessee	46
	New York	36	Mississippi	21
	New Jersey	29	Arkansas	33
	Pennsylvania	33	Indiana	43
	Delaware	30	Michigan	25
	Maryland	40	Wisconsin	35
	Ohio	48	Minnesota	39
	Illinois	47	Iowa	42
	Idaho	− 7	Oregon	25
	Nevada	−23		
	California	10		
Average growth rate		26		34
Percent of states which grew faster than U.S. average		33		38
W_A/W_N below U.S. average:[b]	Montana	7	West Virginia	56
	Wyoming	14	Georgia	18
	Colorado	1	Florida	68
	Arizona	−5	Kentucky	33
	Utah	60	Alabama	25
	Washington	49	Louisiana	9
			Texas	65
			Missouri	41
			North and South Dakota	24
			Nebraska	60
			Kansas	83
			New Mexico	66
Average growth rate		21		46
Percent of states which grew faster than U.S. average		33		58

[a] N/L = ratio of nonagricultural to total employment in 1880
[b] W_A/W_N = ratio of agricultural to nonagricultural wage in 1880

TABLE 2.5 GROWTH OF PERSONAL INCOME PER CAPITA, 1900–1920, IN RELATION TO WAGE DIFFERENTIAL BETWEEN SECTORS AND CONCENTRATION OF EMPLOYMENT IN LOW-WAGE SECTOR

	N/L above U.S. average[a]		N/L below U.S. average[a]	
	State	Percent	State	Percent
W_A/W_N above U.S. average:[b]	Maine	41	Vermont	32
	New Hampshire	33	Virginia	65
	Massachusetts	30	North Carolina	115
	Rhode Island	26	South Carolina	95
	Connecticut	23	Oklahoma	92
	New York	38	Indiana	39
	New Jersey	27	Wisconsin	48
	Pennsylvania	29	Minnesota	20
	Delaware	40	Iowa	21
	Maryland	55	North Dakota	−5
	Ohio	38	South Dakota	27
	Illinois	39	Nebraska	14
	Michigan	69	Kansas	36
	Montana	−34	Idaho	17
	Wyoming	26	Oregon	30
	Colorado	−1		
	Utah	32		
	Nevada	3		
	Washington	13		
	California	19		
Average growth rate		27		43
Percent of states which grew faster than U.S. average		10		33
W_A/W_N below U.S. average:[b]	Arizona	−5	West Virginia	90
			Georgia	77
			Florida	69
			Kentucky	45
			Tennessee	56
			Alabama	56
			Mississippi	45
			Arkansas	60
			Louisiana	45
			Texas	70
			Missouri	35
			New Mexico	40
Average growth rate				57
Percent of states which grew faster than U.S. average				83

[a] N/L = ratio of nonagricultural to total employment in 1900
[b] W_A/W_N = ratio of agricultural to nonagricultural wage in 1900

TABLE 2.6. GROWTH OF PERSONAL INCOME PER CAPITA, 1920–1950, IN RELATION TO WAGE DIFFERENTIALS BETWEEN SECTORS AND CONCENTRATION OF EMPLOYMENT IN LOW-WAGE SECTOR

	N/L above U.S. average[a]		*N/L below U.S. average*[a]	
	State	*Percent*	*State*	*Percent*
W_A/W_N above U.S. average:[b]	Maine	36	Vermont	41
	New Hampshire	36	Virginia	86
	Massachusetts	24	North Carolina	88
	Rhode Island	26	Florida	92
	Connecticut	64	Oklahoma	50
	New York	30	Texas	72
	New Jersey	43	Wisconsin	75
	Pennsylvania	43	Minnesota	65
	Delaware	96	Iowa	75
	Maryland	45	North Dakota	90
	Ohio	63	South Dakota	70
	Illinois	57	Nebraska	82
	Michigan	61	Kansas	62
	Nevada	47	Montana	71
	Washington	48	Idaho	51
	Oregon	45	Wyoming	25
	California	29	Colorado	35
			New Mexico	72
			Arizona	31
			Utah	66
Average growth rate		47		65
Percent of states which grew faster than U.S. average		29		70
W_A/W_N below U.S. average:[b]	West Virginia	44	South Carolina	76
			Georgia	96
			Kentucky	61
			Tennessee	83
			Alabama	84
			Mississippi	66
			Arkansas	71
			Louisiana	69
			Indiana	83
			Missouri	69
Average growth rate				76
Percent of states which grew faster than U.S. average				100

[a] N/L = ratio of nonagricultural to total employment in 1920
[b] W_A/W_N = ratio of agricultural to nonagricultural wage in 1920

of personal income per capita is positively related to the extent of the initial misallocation of resources. Resource misallocation is measured by the initial service income differential in the two sectors and by the concentration of employment in the low-wage sector at the initial date. The agricultural service income is generally lower than the nonagricultural service income. Hence, the lower the initial ratio of the agricultural to the

TABLE 2.7. SUMMARY OF TABLES 2.4, 2.5, AND 2.6

	1880–1900		1900–1920		1920–1950	
	N/L above U.S. average[a]	N/L below U.S. average[a]	N/L above U.S. average[a]	N/L below U.S. average[a]	N/L above U.S. average[a]	N/L below U.S. average[a]
W_A/W_N above U.S. average:[b]						
Average growth rate, percent	26	34	27	43	47	65
Percent of states which grew faster than U.S. average	33	38	10	33	29	70
W_A/W_N below U.S. average:[b]						
Average growth rate, percent	21	46	−5	57	44	76
Percent of states which grew faster than U.S. average	33	58	...	83	...	100
	($n = 6$)		($n = 1$)		($n = 1$)	
F ratio	3.04		4.69		6.68	
Level of significance, percent	5		1		1	

[a] N/L = ratio of nonagricultural to total employment at initial date
[b] W_A/W_N = ratio of agricultural to nonagricultural wage at initial date

nonagricultural service income, the greater the initial degree of misallocation. Only in 1920 and 1950 was the agricultural service income higher than the nonagricultural service income in several states. This phenomenon will be discussed below. A higher growth rate is expected in the states with high concentrations of employment in the low-income agricultural sector than in states with low concentrations.

Table 2.7 is a brief summary of Tables 2.4, 2.5, and 2.6. The growth rate is predicted to move in the direction of the arrows in Figure 2.4, that is,

from left to right and from top to bottom for each time period. Two cells
have only one observation ($n = 1$). An analysis of variance was carried
out on the four growth rates in each period, and the F ratio, i.e., the ratio
of the subsample mean square to the individual mean square is given for
each period.[8] The hypothesis tested is that F does not differ from unity;
that is, we tested whether the observations in the cells were samples from
the same population of growth rates. In each case, F was significantly
different from unity at the 5 percent level or at the 1 percent level.
Hence, the four subsamples in each box are probably not drawn from a
common population; and whatever population means are involved are

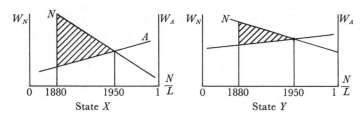

State X State Y FIGURE 2.5

estimated in an unbiased manner by the four subsample means. Except
where the number of observations in a cell is very small, the data behave
in accordance with the theory. We conclude that one must *reject* the
hypothesis that the variables W_A/W_N and N/L have *no effect* upon a
state's growth rate.

Our theory did not claim that *interstate* differences in W_A or W_N would
narrow. All that is claimed is that *intrastate* differences in W_A/W_N would
narrow as labor becomes more efficiently allocated among sectors of a
state. It may still be possible to raise per capita national income by
moving labor from low-wage to high-wage states.

States X and Y are described in Figure 2.5. Suppose that the ratio, h,
of labor force to population is the same in each state. Then from 1880 to
1950, per capita income rose by h times the shaded area—merely as a
result of better resource allocation. According to the example, by 1950
resources were optimally allocated *within* each state but not *among* states.

Convergence of W_N and W_A *among* states need not have occurred to any
considerable extent in terms of our analysis. According to Table 2.2, any
convergence (of W_N or W_A) that did occur was quite weak.

As states have become more similar over time in terms of their ratios
of agricultural to total employment, the intersectoral service income
differential has *in fact* narrowed. In terms of Figure 2.3 as the ratio of
agricultural to total employment among states has converged to $1 - 0r_3$,
the service income differential W_A/W_N between sectors of a state has

narrowed. Resource allocation has become more efficient, in terms of maximizing per capita personal income. Table 2.8 presents the intertemporal frequency distributions of the intersectoral service income differentials; and Table 2.9 gives the frequency distributions of the percentage of the labor force in agriculture.

There can be no doubt concerning the convergence of the ratios of agricultural employment. The average deviation of the ratio of agricultural to total employment fell from 19 percentage points in 1870 to

TABLE 2.8. FREQUENCY DISTRIBUTION OF STATES BY RATIO OF THEIR AGRICULTURAL TO NONAGRICULTURAL SERVICE INCOME PER WORKER, 1880, 1900, 1919–21, AND 1949–51

Agricultural service income per worker divided by nonagricultural service income per worker	Number of states			
	1880	*1900*	*1919–21*	*1949–51*
0.0–0.19 . . .	3			
0.20–0.39 . . .	18	14	1	
0.40–0.59 . . .	24	29	14	10
0.60–0.79 . . .	1	5	14	13
0.80–0.99 . . .			9	12
1.00–1.19 . . .			9	8
1.20–1.39 . . .			1	3
1.40–1.59 . . .				1
1.60–1.79 . . .				1
Total	46	48	48	48

Source: Richard A. Easterlin, "Regional Growth of Income: Long-Term Tendencies," in Simon Kuznets, Ann Ratner Miller, and Richard A. Easterlin, *Analysis of Economic Change* (Vol. II of *Population Redistribution and Economic Growth, United States, 1870–1950*, Philadelphia, American Philosophical Society, 1960), Table A4.3. Reproduced by permission of the authors and the American Philosophical Society.

8 percentage points in 1950. Similarly, there has been a narrowing of the service income differential between sectors over time. During the years 1880 and 1900, the service income differential between the agricultural and nonagricultural sector was quite large, in percentage terms. The agricultural service income was always less than 80 percent of the nonagricultural level; in 43 out of 48 states, it was less than 60 percent of the nonagricultural figure. By 1920, however, there were only 15 states where the agricultural service income was less than 60 percent of the nonagricultural figure. Agriculture was actually the high-income sector in seven states,[9] and in three states[10] incomes were equal in both sectors. With the passage of time, the differential narrowed even more. By 1950,

the differential between sectors did not exceed 20 percent in 20 out of 48 states, and in 13 states agriculture was the high-income sector.

The fact that service income in agriculture exceeds that outside of agriculture is due to the nature of the data. Service income is composed of wages, salaries, and self-employment income. A large fraction of self-employment income is actually a return to the capital invested in the

TABLE 2.9. FREQUENCY DISTRIBUTION OF STATES BY PERCENT OF EMPLOYMENT IN AGRICULTURE, 1870–1950

Percent in agriculture	*Number of states*								
	1870	*1880*	*1890*	*1900*	*1910*	*1920*	*1930*	*1940*	*1950*
Over 80.0	5	4	1	1					
60.0–79.9	14	12	10	10	6	3	1		
40.0–59.9	14	14	16	14	12	12	8	3	2
20.0–39.9	7	10	14	16	18	17	23	23	13
0.0–19.9	6	6	6	6	11	15	15	21	32
Total[a]	46	46	47	47	47	47	47	47	47
U.S. proportion, percent	51.5	49.4	40.6	38.8	32.5	25.6	21.4	17.5	11.6
Average deviation from U.S. average[b]	19.0	19.1	16.7	16.6	15.5	14.3	13.3	11.6	8.2

Source: Ann Ratner Miller, "Labor Force Trends and Differentials," in Simon Kuznets, Ann Ratner Miller, and Richard A. Easterlin, *Analyses of Economic Change* (Vol. II of *Population Redistribution and Economic Growth, United States, 1870–1950*, Philadelphia, American Philosophical Society, 1960), pp. 40, 46. Reproduced by permission of the authors and the American Philosophical Society.

[a] North and South Dakota are combined. Oklahoma data are not available for earlier dates.

[b] Measured in percentage points.

business. It is reasonable to expect this property income component to be a larger fraction of agricultural self-employment income than in such nonagricultural sectors as trade, services, or construction. The reason is the large capital requirements in agriculture compared with these other nonagricultural sectors.

Our earlier theoretical explanation implied that efficiency is realized when service incomes are equalized in the two sectors. In fact, this is a simplification, as the above considerations suggest. Efficiency would be realized when wages are equalized in the two sectors and when the rates of return on capital are equalized. Because of agriculture's heavy capital requirements, the efficiency condition in fact requires that service income per employee be higher in agriculture.

In summary, we may say that with the narrowing of the intersectoral income differential the relationship between per capita income and the ratio of nonagricultural to total employment should be attenuated. A low ratio of nonagricultural to total employment implies a large misallocation of resources only when there is a wide earnings differential between sectors. Table 2.8 indicated how the percentage differential has narrowed. A reduction has also occurred in the absolute differential between the U.S. average values of W_N and W_A, in 1929 prices. The differential, $W_N - W_A$, was \$680 (1880), \$722 (1900), \$563 (1919–21), and \$554 (1949–51). It should follow from the theory developed above that the positive association between Y/P and N/L should be weakened over time—since the income differential has narrowed. This, in fact, occurred. Easterlin calculated a coefficient of rank-order correlation τ between (1) state personal income per capita, Y/P, and (2) the state ratio of non-agricultural to total labor force N/L. This coefficient was 0.73 for 1880, 0.62 for 1900, 0.69 for 1920, and 0.45 for 1950.[11]

There is clear evidence that the theory advanced above is not inconsistent with the data. The growth of personal income per capita can be explained by the improved allocation of resources.

ECONOMIC MATURITY AND THE CONVERGENCE OF PER CAPITA INCOMES

The data examined above are our first indication that a long-term process is at work on the economies of U.S. regions. The convergence of per capita income has occurred through a transfer within states from low-income to high-income sectors. Labor and capital have moved to sectors that promise the highest return. They have entered nonagricultural pursuits and have left agriculture. Agricultural employment reached a peak earlier this century and has since declined.

Eight states had already reached their peak employment in agriculture during the nineteenth century. Another 26 reached their peaks at 1900 or 1910, and the remaining 14 reached their peaks at 1920 or 1930. Every state but two has had a steady decline in agricultural employment from the peak. In the remaining two states, California and Florida, there was a rise in agricultural employment from 1940 to 1950. Agricultural employment failed, however, to reach its previous peaks in these two states; and the increases in agricultural employment from 1940 to 1950 in California and Florida were negligible fractions of their increments of total employment.[12] There is no doubt that employment growth in each state is

TABLE 2.10 OCCURRENCE OF SUCCESS AND FAILURE AMONG 45 STATES, IN EIGHT DECADES, 1869–1949[a]

	1869 –1879	1879 –1889	1889 –1899	1899 –1909	1909 –1919	1919 –1929	1929 –1939	1939 –1949	Total successes
New Hampshire	–	–	–	–	–	–	–	–	0
Rhode Island	–	–	–	–	–	–	–	–	0
Vermont	–	–	–	–	–	–	–	–	0
Massachusetts	–	–	–	–	–	–	–	–	0
Pennsylvania	–	–	x	–	–	–	–	–	1
Maine	x	–	–	–	–	–	–	–	1
New York	–	–	–	–	–	–	x	–	1
Connecticut	–	–	x	–	x	–	–	–	2
Maryland	x	–	–	–	–	–	x	–	2
Delaware	x	x	–	–	–	–	–	–	2
Minnesota	x	x	–	–	–	–	–	x	3
Iowa	–	x	–	–	–	x	–	x	3
Kentucky	–	–	–	–	–	x	x	x	3
Montana	–	x	x	–	–	x	–	–	3
Mississippi	–	x	x	x	–	–	–	–	3
Nevada	–	–	–	x	–	–	x	x	3
Louisiana	–	x	x	x	–	–	–	–	3
Florida	x	x	x	x	–	–	–	–	4
Kansas	x	x	x	x	–	–	–	–	4
West Virginia	–	–	–	x	–	x	x	x	4
Missouri	–	x	–	–	x	x	–	x	4
Nebraska	x	x	–	–	–	–	x	x	4

State								Total
New Jersey	x	–	x	x	–	x	–	4
Wisconsin	x	–	–	x	x	–	x	4
Washington	x	x	x	x	–	–	x	5
Wyoming	x	x	–	–	x	–	x	5
Arizona	x	x	x	–	x	–	x	5
Arkansas	x	x	x	x	–	–	x	5
Indiana	–	x	–	–	x	–	–	5
Virginia	–	x	x	–	x	x	x	5
New Mexico	x	x	x	–	x	x	–	5
South Carolina	x	x	x	–	x	x	–	5
Tennessee	–	x	x	–	x	x	–	5
Georgia	x	x	–	x	x	x	x	6
Alabama	–	x	–	x	x	x	x	6
Colorado	x	–	x	x	x	–	–	6
Idaho	x	x	x	x	x	–	–	6
Illinois	x	x	–	–	x	–	x	6
North Carolina	x	x	x	x	x	x	–	6
Ohio	x	–	x	x	–	–	x	6
Utah	x	x	x	x	x	–	x	6
Oregon	x	–	x	x	x	x	x	6
California	x	–	x	x	x	x	x	7
Michigan	x	–	x	x	x	x	x	7
Texas	x	x	x	x	x	x	x	8

[a] x denotes a success; – denotes a failure.

explained, in a statistical sense, by the growth of the nonagricultural sector. For this reason, we have focused our attention upon this sector in explaining differential growth rates.

In addition to intrastate resource movements, the growth process has produced movements between states. The consequence is that some states are growing in economic output more rapidly than others. Two aspects of the growth process are notable. The first is that it has persisted as long as the equalization process noted above. The second is that it is related to the equalization process, as we shall see.

The persistence of the growth process may be seen in Tables 2.10 and 2.11. We have computed the percentage rate of growth of wage earners in manufacturing for each decade between 1869 and 1949.[13] This information is available for 45 states. For each decade we have compared the rate of growth in the state with the national average. If the state rate is greater than the national average, we call this a success; and if it is less, it is called a failure. Each state may have at most eight successes or eight failures (there are eight decades) or some combination of successes and failures that totals eight. The experiences of the states will form a frequency distribution of number of states with the number of successes. The experience of each state in terms of success (X) and failure ($-$) is shown in Table 2.10 and summarized in Table 2.11. There appears to be a definite growth pattern among the states. Ten of the states never had more than two successes each, and 12 of the states never had more than two failures each. This remarkable stability of performance is an indication that the growth and decline of states are subject to forces that take a long period of time to work themselves out and that may be said to be permanent influences on the growth position of the different regions.[14]

What is the relation between the growth pattern and the equalization process observed earlier? This may be seen by examining the extremes of the frequency distribution in Table 2.11. There are 10 slowly growing states with less than three successes, and there are 12 rapidly growing states with more than five successes.[15] The 10 slowly growing states are shown in Tables 2.4, 2.5, and 2.6 as experiencing slow growth of per capita income as compared with the nation or as compared with 12 rapidly growing states. In the same fashion as Tables 2.10 and 2.11, we may score a success when the per capita income of a state grows more rapidly than the national average and a failure when it grows more slowly. The 10 slowly growing states might have scored 30 successes in the three periods depicted by Tables 2.4, 2.5, and 2.6. Actually, they scored seven successes. On the other hand, the 12 rapidly growing states scored 17 out of 36 possible successes.[16] Thus, there appears to be a relation between the growth of employment in manufacturing and the growth of per capita income. This relation is not surprising in view of the earlier analysis regarding sectoral changes between agricultural and non-agricultural pursuits, but these findings provide additional and important

TABLE 2.11. SUMMARY OF SUCCESSES AND FAILURES, 45 STATES IN EIGHT DECADES, 1869–1949

Successes	Failures	States	Frequency
0	8	New Hampshire, Rhode Island, Vermont, Massachusetts	4
1	7	Pennsylvania, Maine, New York	3
2	6	Connecticut, Maryland, Delaware	3
3	5	Minnesota, Iowa, Kentucky, Montana, Louisiana, Mississippi, Nevada	7
4	4	Florida, Kansas, West Virginia, Missouri, Nebraska, New Jersey, Wisconsin	7
5	3	Wyoming, Washington, Arizona, Indiana, Virginia, New Mexico, South Carolina, Tennessee	9
6	2	Alabama, Colorado, Georgia, Idaho, Illinois, North Carolina, Ohio, Utah, Oregon	9
7	1	California, Michigan	2
8	0	Texas	1

information. They are not implied by the earlier analysis. We now know that the growth of the manufacturing sector in a state is related to per capita income growth, without taking into explicit account events in the agricultural sector. The nature of the agricultural labor market plays a vital role in our explanations of this phenomena, as we shall see below. The significance of these findings is that they provide a clue to the relation between per capita income growth and the over-all growth of the state's economy.

Historically, the manufacturing sector has been the most important growing export sector. It may be regarded as the multiplicand of an expansion process which raises the demand for the outputs of the domestic sector. While other sectors have provided a growth stimulus in specific regions, the above findings indicate the key role of manufacturing. Where manufacturing employment has grown, per capita income has grown, and conversely.

The 10 slowly growing states provide our first glimpse into the phenomenon of economic maturity, for they represent areas where growth has been persistently less than average for a long period of time in terms of significant measures of economic performance. Maturity is significant as a prelude to decline, for, as we shall see, the *chronic labor surplus areas* are geographically concentrated among these states.

Are the 10 slowly growing states economically mature? Are they the only states out of the 48 considered in this study which are economically mature? The first question may be answered unambiguously, but not the second. Although the 10 states or a subset of the 10 are mature in the sense that they evidence a persistently slower growth which has shaded off into actual economic decline, there is no sharp line at which the mature may be set off from the growing. Maturity is a relative concept which is useful as an indicator of future difficulties; it is not a perfect indicator of future decline, since events may interpose that alter the process we observe. There is nothing immutable about maturity, and the very reawakening of public policy may itself interfere with the accuracy of our predictions. Nevertheless, we feel confident that the regions we identify as mature are going through a process that leads to decline.

We investigated our 10 candidates for maturity in terms of five economic variables. They were identified by the first variable, the number of occasions they grew more rapidly than the nation since 1869 in terms of manufacturing employment. They had already been investigated in terms of the second variable, namely, the growth of relative per capita income. These analyses are summarized in the first two columns of Table 2.12. In addition, we have investigated three other characteristics: the relative growth of nonagricultural employment, the relative growth of nonagricultural capital, and the relative growth of nonagricultural wages per employee. These are summarized in the last four columns of Table 2.12.

On the basis of Table 2.12, we would classify the first seven candidates as mature. The recent performance of Connecticut, Maryland, and Delaware indicates that they are not approaching the situation facing the seven. The mature states are characterized by slower than average growth of

TABLE 2.12. CRITERIA OF ECONOMIC MATURITY IN TERMS OF THE GROWTH OF INCOME, EMPLOYMENT, AND CAPITAL

Candidates for maturity—fewer than three successes (Table 2.11)	Relative per capita income falling since 1880	Area of less than median nonagricultural growth					
		Employment since		Capital since		Wages per employee since	
		1919	1929	1919	1929	1919	1929
New Hampshire	Yes	Yes	Yes	No	Yes	No	Yes
Rhode Island	Yes	Yes	Yes	Yes	Yes	No	Yes
Vermont	Yes	Yes	Yes	Yes	Yes	No	No
Massachusetts	Yes	Yes	Yes	Yes	Yes	No	Yes
Pennsylvania	Yes	Yes	Yes	No	No	No	No
Maine	No[a]	Yes	Yes	No	Yes	No	No
New York	Yes	No	Yes	No	Yes	No	Yes
Connecticut	No[b]	No	No	No	No	No	No
Maryland	No[a]	No	No	No	No	No	No
Delaware	No[c]	No	No	No	No	No	No

[a] Relative per capita income rose 1880–1900, 1900–1920.
[b] Relative per capita income rose 1920–1950.
[c] Relative per capita income rose 1900–1920, 1920–1950.

manufacturing employment, per capita income, nonagricultural employment, and nonagricultural capital. Since 1929, there is some evidence that they are beginning to lag behind the average in wage payments. The mature states are located, not surprisingly, in the "old" industrial section of the United States, the Northeast. The conclusion that these states are mature is confirmed by additional evidence which may be brought to bear.

First, with two exceptions, there has been a net emigration of population from these states in the periods 1910–20 and 1930–50. The exceptions are New York and Rhode Island. The latter experienced a small amount of immigration, which may be explained by the important military installations located there. New York experienced a small degree of net immigration in both periods.[17]

Second, manufacturing employment has declined absolutely in four of the states, Rhode Island, Massachusetts, Pennsylvania, and Vermont, between 1948 and 1957. Both of these years are business cycle peaks and therefore provide an indication of the maximum employment during the relevant cycles.

Third, the chronic labor surplus areas are heavily represented in these states. In 1959, 40 percent of the total unemployment in chronic labor surplus areas was produced by the mature states of Massachusetts, Rhode Island, and Pennsylvania.

The U.S. Bureau of Employment Security listed 17 major labor markets as chronic labor surplus areas in 1959. These are defined as areas having unemployment rates at least 50 percent above the national average during four of the past five years. Ten of these major labor markets are in the seven mature states listed above. Table 2.13 summarizes the information on areas of chronic labor surplus. In addition to the 17 major areas of chronic labor surplus, the Bureau has identified smaller areas of substantial labor surplus. "Smaller areas" have a labor force of 15,000 or more, with at least 6 percent of the area's labor force unemployed. Many of these smaller areas may in fact be considered areas of chronic labor surplus. Smaller areas included in the seven mature states are Pottsville, Sunbury, Uniontown, Clearfield, Lock Haven, Berwick, and Lewistown, Pennsylvania; North Adams, Massachusetts; and Newport, Rhode Island.[18]

ECONOMIC MATURITY AND INDUSTRIAL COMPOSITION

It is widely believed that patterns of economic growth among U.S. regions are explainable in terms of their economic or industrial composition. It seems natural to think of a region as the weighted representation of a set of national industries. In this view, a region that contains a preponderance of rapidly growing industries will itself grow rapidly, for its industrial components are expanding at the same pace as their national counterparts.

TABLE 2.13. CHRONIC LABOR SURPLUS AREAS, MAY, 1959

State and area	Total unemployment	Annual average unemployment rates as a percent of labor force				
		1954	*1955*	*1956*	*1957*	*1958*
Massachusetts:						
Fall River	4,100	9.3	6.1	6.3	10.6	12.2
Lawrence	3,700	23.9	16.4	10.2	8.9	10.3
Lowell	4,750	10.5	8.8	6.7	7.0	11.0
New Bedford	5,500	11.3	8.6	6.1	6.6	11.2
Rhode Island:						
Providence	30,600	12.1	8.7	8.0	9.8	13.1
Pennsylvania:						
Altoona	4,900	17.4	11.9	9.2	10.4	16.5
Erie	12,300	8.8	7.5	5.0	6.2	13.3
Johnstown	12,200	16.0	10.6	8.0	6.6	15.4
Scranton	14,500	13.9	13.9	11.9	11.2	16.4
Wilkes-Barre–						
Hazleton	19,200	15.3	13.9	13.0	11.4	16.8
Indiana:						
Evansville	5,200	8.6	7.3	8.9	6.8	10.2
Terre Haute	3,000	12.1	12.8	11.3	7.7	8.5
Michigan:						
Detroit	140,000	8.8	4.3	7.7	7.3	16.1
Muskegan–						
Muskegan Heights	3,400	9.0	4.3	6.4	8.7	13.1
New Jersey:						
Atlantic City	5,300	9.5	10.1	9.3	9.4	11.5
North Carolina:						
Asheville	2,600	8.1	7.6	6.8	6.9	8.2
West Virginia:						
Charleston	11,100	11.9	11.5	8.7	8.2	11.6

Source: U.S. Department of Labor, Bureau of Employment Security, *Chronic Labor Surplus Areas* (Washington, D.C., July, 1959), Table 2.

The belief is not, however, borne out by the evidence. Apparently, state industries do not expand at the same pace as their national counterparts. In fact, in mature regions, state industries are more sluggish than their national counterparts. These conclusions are derived from a statistical standardization procedure that permits us to estimate the impact of

industrial composition on the growth of the region. Briefly, the stand-
ardized or hypothetical growth rate shows the rate that would occur if
each industry in the state grew as fast as its national counterpart.

The *actual* (*A*) growth rate in a state may then be viewed as the sum
of the *hypothetical* (*H*) growth rate and an *internal* (*I*) growth rate. The internal growth rate is defined as the difference between the actual and
hypothetical growth rate, $I = A - H$. It measures the importance of state
factors in producing a divergence between the actual state growth and
that expected upon the basis of industrial composition. When *A* is less than
H, *I* is negative.

We calculated the actual and hypothetical growth rates for the 48
states during four periods: 1919–29, 1929–47, 1948–53, and 1948–57.
Note that all initial and terminal dates are business cycle peaks. Except
for the period 1948–53, there was no significant association between the
actual and hypothetical growth rates. Interstate differences in growth
rates of manufacturing production worker employment do *not* arise
because states have different compositions of industries. These differences
arise because, in the industries they contain, states grow at rates different
from the national average in those same industries. Actual growth rates
are associated positively with *internal*, rather than with *hypothetical*, growth
rates.

Table 2.14 presents actual and hypothetical growth rates in the seven
mature states during the four cycles cited above. In 25 out of 28 cases, the
internal growth rates were negative. In 14 out of 28 cases, the *actual* growth
rates were negative. Every time a state had a negative *actual* growth rate,
its *internal* growth rate was negative. We conclude from Table 2.14 that
maturity and decline have *not* resulted from a state's concentration in
declining industries. In only 5 out of the 28 cases was the hypothetical
rate negative. On the contrary, decline and maturity were produced by
negative internal rates: the industries in the mature states did not grow
as rapidly as their national counterparts.

A major conclusion from Table 2.14 is that an explanation of interstate
differences in growth rates can neglect the industrial composition of
states (except for the 1948–53 period), since the actual and hypothe.ical
growth rates were not significantly associated with each other. *Actual*
growth rates are almost completely explained by *internal* growth rates.

We have seen that chronic labor surplus areas are concentrated in the
declining states of Rhode Island, Pennsylvania, and Massachusetts. That
these states are declining can be seen from Table 2.14, where the actual
growth rates from 1948–57 were negative. Except for Rhode Island, their
hypothetical growth rates were positive, indicating that there would have

been an expansion of employment if each industry in the state grew as rapidly as its national counterpart. Substantial negative internal rates produced this decline. The hypothetical growth rate in Rhode Island was −4 percent and the actual rate was −22 percent. The major problem in Rhode Island was the internal growth rate.

TABLE 2.14. CAUSES OF MATURITY AND DECLINE IN TERMS OF THE GROWTH OF MANUFACTURING PRODUCTION WORKER EMPLOYMENT IN FOUR BUSINESS CYCLES

State	*1919–29*		*1929–48*		*1948–53*		*1948–57*	
	A^a	H^b	A^a	H^b	A^a	H^b	A^a	H^b
Maine	80	98	129	133	101	102	95	99
New Hampshire	80	102	99	121	100	98	101	93
Rhode Island	91	102	100	119	95	100	78	96
Vermont	84	105	105	135	107	103	97	100
Massachusetts	78	104	105	135	103	106	96	104
Pennsylvania	91	103	125	139	105	111	98	109
New York	90	105	128	146	107	113	102	115

[a] A = ratio of actual employment at later date to actual employment at earlier date
[b] H = ratio of hypothetical employment at later date to actual employment at earlier date

In so far as this decline continued from 1948 to 1957, it is no surprise that there are major labor markets in these states which have had unemployment rates at least 50 percent above the national average during the period 1954 to 1959.

Some important conclusions emerge from this section. Maturity and decline are long-run phenomena and are not products of the business cycle. These phenomena are not produced to any significant degree by states having heavy concentrations in declining industries. Maturity and decline arise (as a rule) because the state's industries have grown at lower rates (in fact, negative rates) than their national counterparts. Our explanations of interstate differences in growth rates must explain interstate differences in *internal* rates. A theory of growth may usually[19] disregard this aspect of the composition of a state's industries, in explaining growth rates.

3. A CRITIQUE OF A SIMPLE AGGREGATIVE THEORY OF GROWTH

Can a simple theory be formulated to explain the phenomena of growth, maturity, and decline, such that we may have confidence in its usefulness as a tool of prediction? There exists a popular theory of growth which is constructed in terms of aggregates such as income, employment, and capital. This theory abstracts from the diversity of economic activities that are carried on within a state. Nevertheless, it may be capable of exposing the basic phenomena that generate growth, maturity, and decline. The patent unrealism of an aggregative model of economic growth should not be regarded as a condemnation. Every theory (model) is a simplified description of reality. Assumptions are not exact descriptions of reality. They are made to expose the basic forces which produce the phenomena we observe. The introduction of "more realistic" assumptions may merely complicate the analysis and cloud over the nature of the forces at work.[1] The art of theorizing consists of finding the crucial variables that produce the phenomena to be explained and not getting involved with a myriad of variables that are of secondary importance. The crucial tests of a theory are (1) whether its predictions are compatible with the data to be explained and (2) whether it helps us to understand the workings of our economic system. The theory of growth developed should be evaluated in terms of its ability to explain the empirical phenomena and not in terms of the verisimilitude of the assumptions made.   *Friedman.?*

The explanatory power of a simple and widely used aggregative model is examined in this chapter.[2] Some of the crucial variables involved in the growth process are thereby identified. We find, however, that the model fails to explain the observed patterns of economic growth. In particular it fails to explain the growth of capital and wages among states. For this reason, the aggregative model is supplemented in later chapters by microanalysis. Analysis at the sectoral level is necessary to explain much of the aggregative behavior of states or regions.

AN AGGREGATIVE MODEL OF REGIONAL GROWTH

A simple model of regional growth can be constructed wherein certain observable patterns of growth are generated by initial disparities in resource endowment.

If we assume that each region produces the same single output with the same production function, those regions with the highest proportion of capital to labor will evidence the highest real wage and the lowest marginal product of capital. In a free market we would observe capital moving from high-wage to low-wage areas, with the consequence that the low-wage areas experience higher rates of growth of capital and of the return to labor. If the regional wage differentials are large enough initially, we may also observe labor migrating from the low-wage to the high-wage areas. This migration will yield the same equilibrating effect on the return to capital and labor, although the effects on the growth of output in each region will be somewhat different. Whether or not labor migrates, capital movements will produce an eventual elimination of regional differences in resource endowment, in the real wage, and in the marginal product of capital. The adjustments that this model describes are movements along the production function of each region. The following assumptions underlying the model are sufficient, though not strictly necessary, to produce the conclusions:

1. A single homogeneous output is produced in each region. The production function, which maps inputs of homogeneous units of labor and capital into homogeneous units of output, is the same in each region and subject to constant returns to scale.

2. Capital consists of reinvested units of output; that is, the capital stock is the accumulation of past unconsumed outputs. Hence, the capital good input is measured in the same physical units as the output.

3. Pure competition prevails in each region.

The regionally uniform production function $X = f(C, L)$ is subject to constant returns to scale. This implies that the marginal physical product of labor, f_L, is a function of the ratio of capital to labor. A higher C/L implies a higher value of the marginal physical product of labor. Similarly, the marginal physical product of capital, f_C, is a function of the capital-to-labor ratio. A higher C/L implies a lower value of the marginal physical product of capital (Figure 3.1).

The upper half of Figure 3.1 depicts the marginal physical product of capital function, which is negatively sloped. As C/L rises, the marginal physical product of capital declines. In region A, with a capital-labor ratio of R_A, the marginal physical product of capital is i_A. In region B, with a ratio of R_B, the marginal physical product of capital is i_B.

The marginal physical product of labor function is illustrated in the lower half of Figure 3.1. With a ratio R_A, the marginal physical product of labor is w_A; and with a ratio of R_B, the marginal physical product of labor is only w_B.

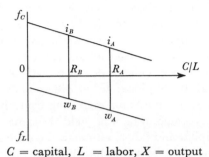

FIGURE 3.1

C = capital, L = labor, X = output

According to assumption (1), the production function is the same in each region. As a result, the region with the higher marginal physical product of capital must be the region with the lower marginal physical product of labor.

Since pure competition has been assumed to prevail, the marginal physical product of labor will be equal to the (real) wage, where the wage is measured in units of the physical output. Hence, there will be a negative correlation between the real wage and the marginal physical product of capital among a set of regions satisfying the above assumptions.

Let us assume in addition that:

4. The rate of growth of capital in the region is positively related to the level of the marginal physical product of capital of the region.

5. The labor force will tend to flow from low-wage to high-wage areas.

As a consequence, capital will flow from region A to region B, and labor will tend to flow from region B to region A.

The above model presents a simple theory of regional growth differences. It abstracts from differences in demand, differences in production techniques due to the quality and location of natural or human resources, and differences in the composition of output. Nevertheless, it provides a movement towards equilibrium and suggests two testable hypotheses. They are:

1. Low-wage regions will experience the highest rates of growth of capital and of the ratio of capital to labor because of the inflow of capital and the outflow of labor.

2. Low-wage regions will experience the highest rates of growth of wages because of the relation between the growth of the marginal product of labor and the growth of the capital-labor ratio.

The implications of the model will be contradicted if certain of the assumptions are contradicted. For example, in the long run the growth of labor supply will differ among regions. If the supply of labor grows faster in low-wage regions and if labor is not sufficiently sensitive to regional wage differentials, different conclusions are suggested. Low-wage regions will experience the highest rates of growth of capital, but they may not experience the highest rate of growth of wages. The reason is that the internal growth of the labor supply prevents a rise in the ratio of capital to labor.

This problem also arises if we examine one sector of a region's economy. If we are looking at the nonagricultural sector of low-wage regions, we know that the supply of labor may be increased through transfer of the region's labor force from agriculture. Again, the nonagricultural sector of a low-wage region may experience a very high rate of capital accumulation. The attraction of labor to this sector, however, prevents a rise in the ratio of capital to labor and in the real wage. These qualifications are suggested to indicate the conditions under which the narrower implications of this model might be contradicted by evidence. In a model which abstracts from demand conditions, however, it would still be true that low-wage regions experienced the greatest growth of capital. Further, if they did not experience the the greatest growth of wages per worker, it would be due to differences in the growth of employment.

THE MEASUREMENT OF CAPITAL, LABOR, AND WAGES

In order to subject the above hypotheses to test, it is necessary to measure the changes in capital, labor, and wages among regions.

In all cases, the regions examined are the 48 states of the time period from 1919 to 1953. This period is broken into shorter intervals marked by business cycle peaks as the initial and terminal dates. The purpose is to measure growth during the interval as the change between the initial and terminal dates. Such changes are independent of cyclical movements during the interval, in the sense that intervening cyclical troughs do not influence the statistical measurement of growth, from one peak date to the next. The intervals chosen are 1919–29, 1929–48, and 1948–53.

Capital. The growth of capital in each state will be measured by the growth of the income to capital. The owner of any concrete property owns capital to the extent that his property has market value.[3] In competitive markets, the value of his property is arrived at by capitalizing the rents expected to be received from the property. Let R denote property income (the rent received after subtracting the payments to labor), K the value of capital,[4] and r the capitalization factor. Then, $rK = R$.

Denote percentage changes by $*$. Then, $r* + K* = R*$: the percentage change in property income is equal to the percentage change in capital plus the percentage change in the capitalization factor. Suppose that the capitalization factor changes by the same percentage in each region. Then, $K_1* - K_2* = R_1* - R_2*$, where the subscripts denote regions. The rate of growth of capital in region 1 minus the rate of growth of capital in region 2 is equal to the rate of growth of proprietary income in region 1 minus the rate of growth of proprietary income in region 2. The growth of proprietary income is positively correlated with the growth of capital. Hence, the growth of capital in each state can be measured by the growth of income to property.

We may think of the total income produced in the state as the sum of payments to wage and salary earners and to property owners. The percentage change in the income to property owners is used to measure the change in the total return to capital in the state for the reasons described above. This percentage change has been computed for the non-agricultural sector of each state in the time intervals 1919–29, 1929–48, and 1948–53.

Labor and Wages. Estimates of the changes in labor are derived from the Census of Population and from the publications of the Bureau of Labor Statistics. We have restricted the inquiry to nonagricultural employment in each state. Percentage changes in nonagricultural employment in each state are computed for the intervals 1919–29, 1929–48, and 1948–53. For 1919 and 1929, the employment estimates are derived from the Census of Population. The employment data for 1948 and 1953 are estimates of the Bureau of Labor Statistics.

These sources were also used to derive estimates of the state employment in two nonagricultural sectors, mining and manufacturing, and a composite sector, which we have called "services." These data are used in later chapters. The service sector includes wholesale and retail trade; finance, insurance, and real estate; service and miscellaneous; and construction. These categories excluded employees in transportation, communication, public utilities, and government. In 1950, these excluded sectors made up approximately 23 percent of the employed nonagricultural workers.

The wage per employee in the nonagricultural sector is computed from the income and employment data previously mentioned. Leven[5] provides total nonagricultural wage payments by state for 1919; the Department of Commerce[6] provides it for 1929, 1948, and 1953. The wage change used is the percentage change in the wage income per employee between 1919 and 1929, between 1929 and 1948, and between 1948 and 1953.

STATISTICAL TEST OF THE SIMPLE AGGREGATIVE THEORY

A theory is refuted if its predictions are contradicted by the data. The aggregative model of growth described above implied two predictions: capital will grow at a higher rate in the low-wage areas than in the high-wage areas; the average wage will grow at a higher rate in the low-wage areas than in the high-wage areas.

The predictions were compared with actual behavior during three periods. For each period, the 48 states were divided into those where the average wage at the initial period was above the national average and those where it was below the national average. Several statistics were calculated for each set of states:

1. Percentage growth of nonagricultural capital (C^*).
2. Percentage growth of nonagricultural employment (L^*).
3. Percentage growth of nonagricultural wage per employee (w^*).
4. Percentage growth of nonagricultural ratio of capital to labor ($C^* - L^*$).
5. Percentage rate of migration in the preceding period per capita of base population (M^*).[7]
6. Rate of growth of population in the preceding period as a percentage of base year (P^*).

The relevant data are summarized in Table 3.1.

The explanatory power of the aggregative model is quite weak. In the first and third periods, capital (C^*) grew at a greater rate in the high-wage areas than in the low-wage areas. Moreover, the wage (w^*) grew faster in the high-wage areas during the same periods. Finally, employment (L^*) grew more rapidly in the high-wage areas only during the middle period. The theory is refuted for the periods 1919–29 and 1948–53, but is compatible with the data during the 1929–48 period.

The strength of these convergence and divergence patterns may also be seen in Table 3.2, which covers the three cycle periods examined. Each contingency table classifies the states according to initial wage level and wage growth. Shown for each period is the value of χ^2 which has been computed as a measure of association.[8]

TABLE 3.1. RELATIONSHIP BETWEEN WAGE LEVEL AND PERCENTAGE GROWTH OF CAPITAL, LABOR, AND THE WAGE: 1919–29, 1929–48, AND 1948–53[a]

	High-wage areas[b]	Low-wage areas[c]
1919–1929:		
$C*$	60	53
$L*$	22	23
$C* - L*$	38	30
$w*$	43	36
$M*$ (1910–1920)	5.49	−3.99
$P*$ (1910–1920)	21.19	10.66
1929–1948:		
$C*$	86	139
$L*$	31	29
$C* - L*$	55	110
$w*$	168	220
$M*$ (1930–1950)	12.05	−10.16
$P*$ (1930–1950)	33.52	18.98
1948–1953:		
$C*$	37	32
$L*$	13.4	13.7
$C* - L*$	24	18
$w*$	29	28

a Symbols are defined in the text.
b Wage not less than the U.S. average in the initial year.
c Wage below the U.S. average in the initial year.

TABLE 3.2. INITIAL WAGE LEVEL VERSUS WAGE GROWTH

	Wages above average	Wages below average
Wage growth,		
1919–1929:		
Above average	14	10
Below average	6	18
$\chi^2 = 5.48$		
1929–1948:		
Above average	5	19
Below average	15	9
$\chi^2 = 8.58$		
1948–1953:		
Above average	11	9
Below average	15	13
$\chi^2 = 0.01$		

There is a strong divergence among wages in the first period, a strong convergence during the second period, and no pattern in the third. The net result is that wages were distributed as equally in 1950 as in 1920, as seen in Chapter 2.

Predictions (1) and (2) above are contradicted by the data in two of the three periods. Nevertheless, we may ask whether the rate of growth of the wage (w^*) is positively associated with the growth of the ratio of capital to labor ($C^* - L^*$).

There does seem to be a positive relation between these variables. Table 3.1 shows that, during each period, the set of states with the higher $C^* - L^*$ had the higher w^*. A more direct test of this hypothesis can be made. For each period we have 48 states with $C^* - L^* = x$ and $w^* = y$. The correlations between these variables are given for each time interval:

$$
\begin{array}{ll}
1919\text{--}29 & r_{xy} = +0.717 \\
1929\text{--}48 & r_{xy} = +0.692 \\
1948\text{--}53 & r_{xy} = +0.236
\end{array}
$$

The first two coefficients are significant, in the probability sense, at the 5 percent level; the third is not. For the 1948–53 period, however, the partial correlation between the change in capital and the change in wages, holding the change in employment constant, is much larger, yielding a significant coefficient of $+0.688$.[9]

The conclusion of this statistical section is that the popular aggregative theory has a very limited predictive accuracy and that one should place little confidence in it as an explanation of regional growth and maturity.

EXPLANATIONS TO ACCOUNT FOR THE WEAKNESSES OF THE THEORY

Several ad hoc explanations can be adduced to account for the failure of the aggregative theory to predict the growth of capital and the average wage in the periods 1919–29 and 1948–53. First, there was a greater rate of migration into high-wage areas than into low-wage areas in these periods. Moreover, population grew more rapidly in the high-wage areas in these periods. These migrations and population increases induced capital formation in housing and services. Second, in the 1919–29 and 1948–53 periods, interstate differences in industrial composition partly explain interstate differences in growth rates. It could be argued that there was a greater rate of growth in the demand for the products of high-wage areas than of low-wage areas.

These ad hoc rationalizations were constructed because the aggregative

theory failed to predict correctly. In Chapter 4, recourse is made to disaggregation: capital and wage growth are then determined by the experiences of the component sectors of a state's economy, not by an over-all
level of the wage. It must be stressed that the aim of a theory is to dispense
with ad hoc events because no one knows what ad hoc events will be
operative in subsequent periods.

   Migration and Capital Requirements. Migration occurs from low-wage to
high-wage areas. The higher the relative wage of an area, the greater the
rate of migration as a percent of the population. From 1880 to 1900, 1900
to 1920, and 1920 to 1950 a statistically significant positive relationship was
found between the average wage in a region and the rate of immigration
into a region.[10] ρ was 0.783 (significant at the 5 percent level) from 1880
to 1900, 0.967 from 1900 to 1920, and 0.804 (significant at the 1 percent
level) from 1920 to 1950, when the nine census regions were examined.
ρ is the Spearman coefficient of rank correlation.

   There is no surprise that from 1910 to 1920 and from 1930 to 1950
there was a greater rate of immigration into the states which had above
average wages in 1919 and 1948, respectively. Table 3.1 indicates that
from 1910 to 1920 the average rate of migration was 5.49 percent in the
states with above average wages in 1919 and -3.99 percent in the remaining states. The negative term indicates migration out of the state.
Similarly, from 1930 to 1950, the rate of migration was 12.05 percent
into the states which had above average wages in 1948 and -10.16
percent in the remaining states. Population also grew at a faster rate
during these periods in the states which had higher than average wages in
1919 and 1948.

   Migrants raise the demand for new capital formation in houses,
schools, and other services. In the short run, the demand for investment
is raised more by an influx of N migrants than by the birth of N babies to
the indigenous residents. Babies usually live with their parents and do not
start school immediately. Migrants demand additional housing units, and
their children demand school space immediately. There were restrictions
on the volume of urban construction as a result of wartime shortages of
materials and labor during the 1910–20 and 1930–50 periods. It is quite
possible that the higher growth of capital in the high-wage areas from
1919 to 1929 and from 1948 to 1953 simply represented a period of
"catching up" or working off the backlog in the stock of *urban* capital.

   This argument requires that the economy of a state be divided into
two sectors: the sector which provides services (housing services, schools,
highways, and trade) and the sector which provides products that are
traded among regions. The rate of return on capital invested in the former

sector may be quite high as a result of migration although the rate of return on capital invested in the second sector may be quite low as a result of high wages. From 1919 to 1929 and from 1948 to 1953 the growth of capital in the first sector may have accounted for the greater rate of growth of capital in high-wage areas.

Similarly, the greater growth of the wage in the high-wage area may be rationalized within the framework of a multisector model. The growth in the demand for housing, schools, highways, and other public services raised wages in the service sectors of the high-wage regions. An increase in the wage was the inducement for labor to migrate into the region or to transfer from the export sectors to the service sectors. The pull of demand in the service sectors could have produced both the greater growth of the wage and the greater growth of capital in the high-wage regions. We have shown how the simple aggregative theory of growth is contradicted by the data and why it must be supplanted by a less aggregative approach.

Disaggregation to Take Account of Interstate Differences in Demand. If we depart from a simple aggregative model and view a state as a composite of many sectors, then there is a second way to account for the higher rates of growth of wages and capital in the high-wage states from 1919 to 1929 and from 1948 to 1953. Let each state consist of an export sector and a home sector, which produces goods and services not entering into interregional trade. The export sector is not identical among regions: the high-wage region specializes in the export of *H* goods, and the low-wage region specializes in the export of *L* goods.

During a given period, the national demand for *H* goods may increase relative to the demand for *L* goods. There is an export boom in the high-wage area but not in the low-wage area. A rise would occur in money wages and income in the high-wage area as a result of the export boom. Hence, there could be a greater growth of wages in the high-wage area than in the low-wage area. Moreover, if the prices of *H* goods rise more rapidly than the prices of goods and services consumed by workers, real and money wages would both rise. If "wage goods" are imported from other regions, an improvement in the commodity terms of trade would raise real wages.

This export boom in *H* goods could also raise the marginal efficiency of investment and produce a greater rate of growth of capital in the high-wage region. The marginal efficiency of investment is the marginal physical product of a capital good multiplied by the ratio of the price of output to the price of the capital good. In so far as the export boom in *H* goods raises the prices of *H* goods relative to the imported capital goods, the marginal efficiency of investment is increased in the high-wage region. In a multicommodity world, the marginal efficiency of investment could rise simultaneously with a fall in the marginal physical product of the capital good. This would result from a rise in the ratio of the price of output to the price of the capital good which exceeded the percentage fall in the marginal physical product of the capital good. Such a phenomenon could never occur in an aggregate model with one good, since the price ratio is always unity.

The value of the marginal product of labor (equal to the wage) and the marginal efficiency of investment can move in the same direction if the rise in the price of output is sufficiently great to overcome the decline in the marginal physical product of the more rapidly growing input. In so far as the rate of growth of capital depends upon the marginal efficiency of investment, both wages and capital can grow at faster rates in the high-wage areas than in the low-wage areas. A sufficient condition for this phenemenon is an export boom and favorable terms of trade in the products of the high-wage area.

Do the data support the view that from 1929 to 1948 factor prices were primarily influenced by changing factor proportions and that from 1919 to 1929 and from 1948 to 1953 the more rapid growth of wages and capital in the high-wage states resulted from a greater increase in the demand for products produced by high-wage states than by low-wage states?

The analysis of the role of demand influences is carried out in two parts. In the first part, we shall investigate the influence of demand as it operates through industrial composition. In the second part, we shall investigate the movement of prices and their relation to economic changes.

Changes in the demand for a product will affect individual states differently. Those states will prosper which produce a large share of a product with a growing market. Those states will suffer which produce a large share of a product with a stagnant or declining market. In this view, the region is merely a weighted bundle of certain national activities, with each industrial element of the bundle growing as rapidly as the national total. To test this hypothesis, we constructed the growth rate each state would experience if its manufacturing elements grew at their national rates. If the actual state growth rates conform to these constructed hypothetical rates, we can be confident that state patterns are generated by national demand influences. If the actual growth rates do not conform, we have ground for rejecting the hypothesis.

In constructing the hypothetical rates, we used the actual growth rates of 20 national industry groups.[11] The projected growth rate of manufacturing employment is then the rate the state would experience if each of its industrial components grew at the national rate.[12]

The computation of hypothetical and actual growth rates in manufacturing employment was carried out for the 48 states over the three time intervals, 1919–29, 1929–47, and 1948–53. It will be noted that the terminal dates of all three intervals correspond roughly to peak business cycle dates. By measuring changes between similar phases of the business cycle, we can eliminate most cyclical influences, since these trends are consistent with any value of cyclical amplitude.

The actual and projected growth rates are compared through the use of Spearman rank correlation coefficient. These values of rank correlation between projected and actual growth rate of manufacturing employment in 48 states and in three time intervals are as follows:

1919–29	−0.0334
1929–47	+0.0601
1948–53	+0.4348 (significant at the 5 percent level)

It can be seen that only one of the correlations is significantly different from zero. In two of the three periods examined, the state industrial components grow at rates that bear little relation to their national counterparts. Only in the period 1948–53 do we find that industrial composition has a significant influence on state growth.

The Role of Price Changes. Investigators have discovered a high correlation between the industrial composition of a state and the average wage level.[13] A state with a larger proportion of nationally high-wage industries tends to have a higher average wage than a state with a large proportion of nationally low-wage industries. Therefore, a relative increase in the demand for the products of high-wage industries would primarily affect the states containing such industries.

The influence of demand conditions can be perceived partly through the change in prices and partly through the change in employment. If the demand for a certain class of goods rises more than for another class, we can expect the price of this class to rise by a greater proportion, given the elasticity of supply of the two classes. We would also expect the output and employment to rise more rapidly in the sector which has experienced the greatest growth in demand. Did this occur?

The Period 1929 to 1948.—There is no evidence to support the view that the greater rates of growth of capital and wage in the low-wage states during this period was due to an export boom in the products of these states. Instead, the movements of wages and capital should be explained by the aggregative theory of growth. Two sources of evidence support this view.

First, it was indicated above that there was no significant positive relationship between actual and hypothetical growth rates of states during this period. The hypothetical growth rate measures the rate of growth of manufacturing employment that would result if each industry in a state grew at the same rate as its national counterpart. A state with an above average hypothetical growth rate can be viewed as one that is producing goods the national demands for which are growing quite rapidly. Similarly, a state which had a below average hypothetical growth rate can be viewed as one that is producing goods the national demands for which are growing quite slowly. It was observed that the first set of states (with above average hypothetical growth rates) did not grow more rapidly than the national average, and the second set of states did not grow less rapidly than the average during this period. Hence, the national growth of demand for products fails to explain state growth rates during this period.

Second, there is no indication that products of low-wage industries rose more in price during this period than products of high-wage industries. The wholesale prices of 34 manufactured products were examined between 1929 and 1948. The wage level and the wage growth in the industries producing such commodities were also examined.[14]

1. No statistically significant (rank) correlation was found among industries between the wage level in 1929 and the relative price growth from 1929 to 1948.

2. There was a greater wage growth in the low-wage industries than in the high-wage industries.[15]

We must reject the hypothesis that the greater wage growth and capital growth in low-wage states was due to the greater rise in the demand for the products of low-wage industries (found in low-wage states). Instead, we may hold the view that the events in this period conform to the predictions of the aggregative theory of growth.

The Period 1948 to 1953.—The ad hoc explanation is compatible with available evidence. The greater rates of growth of wages and capital in the high-wage states during this period can be accounted for by interstate differences in demand.

First, there was a positive (and significant) association between actual and hypothetical growth rates during this period. States which were expected to experience above average growth rates because they were heavily weighted with industries which were growing rapidly nationally tended to have above average growth rates. National demand did exert a perceptible influence upon state growth rates.

Second, in this period there is a strong positive correlation among industries between the initial wage level and the subsequent growth of prices. There is also a strong positive correlation among industries between the initial wage level and the subsequent growth of wages. In this period, the high-wage industries experienced greater wage growth and greater relative price growth than the low-wage industries.[16] Thus, the regional growth patterns appear to be dominated by national demand conditions in the 1948–53 period.

The Period 1919 to 1929.—This was a period of wage divergence. Hence, the same explanation should be applicable. According to the criteria used above, however, there is no evidence that there was a greater growth in the demand for the products of high-wage industries and states than for the products of low-wage industries and states. Hence, the export hypothesis referred to above may not be applicable. First, it was shown above that there is no significant relation between the actual and hypothetical growth rates during this period. Second, there is no significant relation between the level of wages paid in an industry in 1919 and the subsequent growth in prices. Third, there is no relation between the initial industry wage and the subsequent growth of wages in the industry. Fourth, there is no relation between the wage growth in the industry and the price growth in the industry. Nevertheless, there are other bits of evidence which indicate that there may have been a greater growth in the demand for the products of high-wage industries, than was reflected in price and wage increases.

First, physical output of high-wage sectors grew by a greater proportion than the physical output of low-wage sectors. Output indexes and wage data for 59 manufacturing industry groups were examined. A significant positive association was found between the growth of output and the level of the wage. Table 3.3 classifies the 59 industry groups by percentage growth of physical output and wage level.

Second, the capital-labor ratios rose in high-wage industries relative to their change in low-wage industries. The growth of the capital-labor ratio in these manufacturing industries is measured by growth of the ratio of horsepower per worker. Table 3.4 shows, for those industries where horsepower data are available, the relation between wage level and growth of horsepower per worker. It is clear that the high-wage industries enjoyed a greater growth of the capital-labor ratio.

Third, the ratio of wage payments to value added fell more frequently in the high-wage industries than in the low-wage industries. The relation between the wage level in an industry in 1919, and the change in the ratio of the wage bill to value added from 1919 to 1929 is shown in Table 3.5.[17]

TABLE 3.3. WAGE LEVEL, 1919, VERSUS GROWTH OF OUTPUT, 1919–29, IN 59 INDUSTRY GROUPS

	Wages above median	*Wages below median*
Growth of output above median	21	8
Growth of output below median	8	22

$\chi^2 = 12.37$ (significant at 1 percent level)

Source: Manufacturing output indexes are taken from S. Fabricant, *The Output of Manufacturing Industries, 1899–1939* (New York, National Bureau of Economic Research, 1940).

TABLE 3.4. WAGE LEVEL, 1919, VERSUS GROWTH OF HORSEPOWER PER WORKER, 1919–29, IN 58 INDUSTRY GROUPS

	Wages above median	*Wages below median*
Growth of horsepower per worker above median	20	9
Growth of horsepower per worker below median	8	21

$\chi^2 = 9.94$ (significant at 1 percent level)

Source: Horsepower data are shown for most industrial classifications in *Census of Manufactures* (U.S. Department of Commerce, Washington, D.C., 1919, 1929).

TABLE 3.5. WAGE LEVEL, 1919, VERSUS CHANGE IN RATIO OF WAGE BILL TO VALUE ADDED, 1919–29, IN 69 INDUSTRY GROUPS

	Wages above median	*Wages below median*
Increase in ratio of wage bill to value added	3	15
Decrease in ratio of wage bill to value added	31	20

$\chi^2 = 10.35$ (significant at 1 percent level)

Source: *Census of Manufactures* (U.S. Department of Commerce, Washington, D.C., 1919, 1929).

This change indicates that the distribution of factor payments turned in favor of capital in high-wage industries. The change in distribution has a number of possible causes which cannot be investigated in detail. These are the emergence of labor-saving innovations in the high-wage industries and the existence of greater than unit elasticity of substitution in the high-wage industries.[18] Whatever the cause, the effect of the change in the distribution is a lower demand for labor than that which would otherwise occur.[19] This behavior is summarized in Table 3.6, a cross tabulation of the industry sectors by wage level and output growth.

In Table 3.6, n indicates the total number of industries in the cell, R_1 the number of industries with greater than median increases in the capital-labor ratios, and F_1 the number with less than median increases. R_2 indicates the number of industries experiencing a rise in the ratio of wage bill to value added; F_2 indicates those experiencing a fall. It is clear that the rise in the ratio of capital to labor occurred in high-wage industries. The wage level appears to be the chief statistical influence on

TABLE 3.6. WAGE LEVEL, 1919, VERSUS OUTPUT GROWTH, 1919–1929

	Wage level greater than median					*Wage level less than median*				
	n	R_1	R_2	F_1	F_2	n	R_1	R_2	F_1	F_2
Output growth greater than median	20	15	2	5	18	8	2	3	6	5
Output growth less than median	8	5	1	3	7	22	7	12	15	10

the movement of the capital-labor ratio. The wage level is also strongly associated with the change in the distribution of factor payments. The growth of output appears less influential as a determinant of these two variables.

These events lead to the following explanation of wage divergence during the 1919–29 period:

1. The demand for high-wage goods rose by a greater proportion than the demand for low-wage goods.

2. The output of high-wage industries grew by a greater proportion than the output of low-wage industries. Note that the prices of high-wage goods did not respond to demand growth.

3. The distribution of factor payments turned in favor of capital in high-wage industries.

4. The capital-labor ratio rose more in high-wage industries than in low-wage industries.

5. Investment rose in high-wage industries, and in those states containing high-wage industries.

These explanations would enable us to account for the more rapid growth of capital in high-wage states. A number of questions of interest do remain, however. If the distribution of income turned against labor in high-wage industries, why do we observe an increased demand for labor and an increase in the wage in high-wage states? This question cannot be answered with certainty without an explanation of the change in the distribution of factor payments. If, on the one hand, the only change during the period were a change of distribution of payments due, say, to technological change, then the demand for labor might remain unchanged or conceivably decline. On the other hand, if the changed distribution were due to a movement along a production function with a greater than unit elasticity of substitution, the demand for labor would still rise with a rise in demand for output.

Another question related to the first is why the prices of high-wage goods failed to increase with the change in factor proportions.[20] Two explanations are possible, although they are difficult to disentangle. One is the emergence of technological changes in high-wage industries, which was mentioned previously as a possible cause of the changing distribution of factor payments. If innovations are the cause of the two phenomena, it is clear that they were not sufficiently strong to wipe out the effect of increased demand for output on the demand for labor. The second possible explanation is the existence of increasing returns in the high-wage industries. The presence of increasing returns would allow these industries to expand in response to increased demands without the existence of price increases. It is not possible to give a final answer to these questions. These explanations indicate, however, the length to which one must go in order to explain the wage divergence of the 1919–29 period.

The weaknesses of the aggregative model stem from its failure to recognize the diversity of economic activities that are conducted in a region. As a rule, interstate differences in the composition of the manufacturing sector do not explain differences in growth rates of manufacturing employment. Only in the 1948–53 period do these differences account for the higher capital and wage growth in high-wage areas. During the period 1919–29, and to some extent 1948–53, developments in the nonmanufacturing sectors—such as housing and public and private services— further vitiated the predictions of the theory.

The influence of wage differentials in affecting the growth of capital should be greatest in manufacturing. In this sector one is most likely to find exportable commodities which are neither materials- nor market-oriented. In the mining and agricultural sectors, production function differences are likely to dominate any influence of wage differentials. In the service, transportation, and construction sectors, the growth characteristics of the market are likely to dominate the influence of wage differentials. A more powerful theory of growth which takes these differences into account is developed in the next chapter.

4. INTERSTATE DIFFERENCES IN RATES OF GROWTH OF MANUFACTURING EMPLOYMENT

The explanatory power of the simple aggregative model was weak. It assumed that each state produced one and the same good; consequently, interstate and intersector differences in demand were ignored. Contrary to the predictions of the theory, we observed that, during two of the three periods, capital grew more rapidly in the high-wage states than in the low-wage states. The contradiction cannot be resolved without sacrificing certain elements of the original theory. If, for example, we try to explain the behavior patterns by reference to migration between states, we must broaden the category of output to include elements of social capital such as schools and hospitals, thus violating the assumption that each state produces the same product. On the other hand, if we explain the behavior by reference to differential demand conditions, we are again forced to recognize the diversity of output composition.

In this chapter we shall present a theory of growth that focuses on the disaggregated components of a state's economy. As a result of using a disaggregated approach to the process of economic growth, the predictive accuracy (i.e., explanatory power) of our theory is considerably improved.

THE GROWTH OF MANUFACTURING EMPLOYMENT

Our theory of growth of manufacturing employment concentrates upon the factors affecting the supply of labor for manufacturing in the various states. In Chapter 3, we examined the force of demand and discovered that it was at best only a partial explanatory factor in the growth process. While it provided an adequate explanation for the period from 1948 to 1953, it played a minor role between 1929 and 1948 and at most a hidden role between 1919 and 1929. For this reason we concentrate on those forces affecting the supply of labor for manufacturing in different states. We shall examine the role of labor supply in explaining differences in growth rates of manufacturing employment.[1] Stated in its simplest terms, our theory relates state differences in growth rates of manufacturing employment to (1) the elasticity of labor supply facing a specific industry and (2) the factors shifting the labor supply function for the manufacturing sector.

Let there be two groups of firms in the same competitive industry in different localities. For the moment, ignore differences in transport cost, so that each firm sells its product at the same price in a national market and assume that the price of capital goods is the same for each firm. Moreover, assume that each firm has the same production function, homogeneous of the first degree, and that there is a limit to the size of firms sufficient to preserve competition.

It will be shown in a later section that these conditions imply that in long-run equilibrium every firm in the industry pays the same wage. This assumption has important implications for regional growth. It means that regional wage differentials in a given industry are inconsistent with long-run equilibrium of the industry. If we suppose for a moment that labor does not immediately move from low-wage to high-wage regions, then it is possible to conceive of a period of time in which the differential might persist. There will be two forces tending to eliminate the differential. The most familiar is the movement of labor, but equally important is the movement of capital to restore long-run industry equilibrium.

What is the role of the labor-supply curve in this growth process? Figure 4.1 shows two labor-supply curves, one for each region. The initial wage w_0 is paid in both regions, indicating that the industry is in equilibrium and that there is no inducement for labor to shift from one market to the other. Now suppose there is a rise in the demand for the product of this industry. The price of output will rise, and this rise will induce the existing firms to use their capital more intensively. There is also an increase in the money wage paid. When the industry has attracted new capital and has settled in its new equilibrium, it has increased the number of workers hired and the number of units of capital. The increase in both capital and employment is, however, greater in the region with the greater elasticity of labor supply. Thus, we see that employment growth among elements of the same industry is positively related to the elasticity of labor supply.

A second influence on employment growth arises from factors that might shift the labor-supply function. These shifts may occur concurrently with shifts in the demand for the final product. In any case, employment growth will be greatest in those industrial elements where the labor-supply function has increased most.

It should be noted here that shifts of the labor-supply function may play the role of distinguishing the short- and long-run responses of the labor market. For example, the short-run supply curve may show the response of workers to alternate wage rates paid in a given locality, where the employment alternatives consist only of other firms in the same industrial sector and locality. The shifting of this function then represents the movement of workers into and out of the region and into and out of the industrial sector. These shifts will occur in response to wage differentials

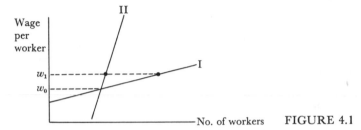

FIGURE 4.1

between this and other regions and between this and other industrial sectors. If this is the case, the shifts of the labor-supply curve trace out a long-run supply curve for labor.

In the following sections we shall subject these notions to statistical test. Finally, we shall present a formal theory of growth which integrates the empirical experience with the simple explanations presented above.

INFLUENCES ON STATE GROWTH

As a first step towards assessing the role of labor supply, let us examine the gross relations between the relevant variables among states. We shall focus on a long period of time which begins and ends with cyclical peaks of business activity—1919 to 1953.

We find that during this period the rate of growth of manufacturing employment in a state was (1) negatively related to the ratio of manufacturing employment to total state employment, (2) positively related to the rate of immigration into a state, and (3) not significantly related to the level of the wage prevailing in the state's manufacturing industries.

These variables were chosen because they represent possible influences on the elasticity of labor supply or factors which shift the labor supply function in a region. Their statistical influence on the growth of manufacturing employment is a partial verification of the hypothesis that they play an important role in state growth.

1. The ratio of manufacturing employment to total state employment is an indicator of the possible shift of labor within a state from other

sectors to manufacturing. The validity of this indicator is shown below. We shall see that manufacturing is a relatively high-wage occupation, especially in states where it does not absorb a large fraction of the labor supply.

2. The rate of immigration into a state is a clear indicator of the shift of the labor-supply function facing the manufacturing sector.

3. The wage level in manufacturing is also an indicator of the ability of the state to attract labor from other regions. While wage levels are correlated with immigration, they are apparently not an independent influence in the statistical sense on the growth of manufacturing employment. The reason is clear: the level of manufacturing wages has opposing effects on the growth of employment, and these cancel out its statistical importance. On the one hand, high wages attract migrants; on the other hand, high wages induce the exit of firms which are seeking the cheapest sources of labor supply.

The statistical relations between the above variables are as follows:

Let Y indicate the growth of manufacturing production worker employment between 1919 and 1953, expressed as the ratio of the value for the later date to the value for the earlier date and varied from 94 percent for Rhode Island to 402 percent for Nevada.[2]

Let X_1 indicate the ratio of manufacturing employment to total state employment. This ratio was computed for 1939, a census year falling between the initial and terminal dates of the inquiry,[3] and varied from 4.5 percent for Nevada to 45.8 percent for Rhode Island.

Let X_2 denote the migration of population age 15 to 64 into the state during the period 1920–50, expressed as a percentage of the average state population in the period.[4] This term varied from -18.40 percent for North Dakota to $+20.78$ percent for Nevada.

Let X_3 denote the 1939 level of production worker annual earnings in manufacturing. This term varied in value from \$681 for Georgia to \$1,520 for Nevada.

The statistical relations among these variables were investigated through the use of multiple regression techniques. The following significant relation was determined among Y, X_1, and X_2:

$$Y = -4.010X_1 + 2.842X_2 + 268.37 \qquad R^2 = 0.392$$
$$(0.8100) \quad (0.0872)$$

(The standard errors of the regression coefficients are shown beneath in parentheses.) It can be seen that both coefficients exceed their standard errors by more than threefold. This equation indicates that over the period examined, the manufacturing employment ratio was negatively related to manufacturing employment growth. A 10 percent difference of the manufacturing employment ratio was associated (negatively) with a 40 percent difference in the rate of employment growth.

In addition, the migration rate was positively related to manufacturing employment growth. A 10 percent difference of the migration ratio was associated with a 28 percent difference in the rate of employment growth.

It is not possible to predict manufacturing employment growth through the use of the variable which measures annual earnings of production workers (X_3). It is true that migration occurs predominantly from low-wage to high-wage states, but the earnings level has an ambiguous relationship with the growth rate. The multiple regression relation among Y, X_1, and X_3 is

$$Y = -3.441X_1 + 0.0349X_3 + 218.89 \qquad R^2 = 0.259$$
$$(0.8710) \quad (0.0440)$$

It can be seen that the regression coefficient of X_3 fails to exceed its standard error; and, therefore, it cannot be regarded as significantly different from zero. This equation again shows the negative relation between the manufacturing employment ratio X_1 and the rate of growth of manufacturing employment.

AN INDUSTRY-STATE ANALYSIS

The influence of industrial composition was ignored in the preceding section. We treated each state as if its manufacturing sector were homogeneous. We then identified two influences on the growth of the manufacturing sector—the manufacturing employment ratio and the rate of immigration.

In this section we shall probe deeper into the role of state differences in the composition of manufacturing employment. We examined this factor in Chapter 3 under the heading, "The Role of Demand Factors." We must examine this problem here again because of the possible influence of demand differences. In so far as differences in industrial composition exist, it is possible that state growth of manufacturing employment is affected by demand factors as well as the supply influences on the labor force, which are summarized under the headings of the manufacturing employment ratio and migration.

We must then pose the question: Do the variables X_1 and X_2 explain manufacturing growth after we have taken into account interstate differences in industrial composition? We may state this question as a statistical hypothesis in the following manner:

The probability that manufacturing industry X will grow more rapidly in state A than in the United States as a whole depends upon two variables: (1) the ratio of manufacturing employment to total employment in the state and (2) the rate of migration into the state. This is a repetition of the hypothesis we examined earlier on an aggregative level. We shall examine the influence of the two variables X_1 and X_2 on individual industries within each state.

In order to subject the hypothesis to test, we examined the growth of 14 manufacturing industries in 48 states in the period between 1947 and 1953. If each industry were represented in all states, we would have a total of 672 observations. It turns out, however, that the actual number of observations was 281. The difference arises from the failure of each industry to be represented in all states and from Census disclosure rules.

The fourteen industries examined were as follows:

S.I.C. No.	Industry
22	Textile mill products
23	Apparel and related products
25	Furniture and fixtures
26	Paper and allied products
27	Printing and publishing industries
28	Chemicals and allied products
30	Rubber products
31	Leather and leather products
33	Primary metal industries
34	Fabricated metal products
35	Machinery (except electrical)
36	Electrical machinery
37	Transportation equipment
38	Instruments and related products

There are in all 19 identifiable manufacturing industry groups in the two-digit classification. The above 14 were chosen for study, and five were rejected. The five industry groups were excluded because plant location in these activities is mainly determined either by the site of production of raw materials, by the cost of transporting raw materials, or by the location of consumers.[5] The likely influence of the regional labor-supply function on the expansion of such industrial sectors is small. The excluded industrial groups are as follows:

S.I.C. No.	Industry
20	Food and food products
21	Tobacco and tobacco products
24	Lumber and products
29	Products of petroleum and coal
32	Stone, clay, and glass products

While the dividing line between the excluded five and the 14 industries examined may appear arbitrary, it was believed that labor-supply conditions would have a sharper influence on the 14 industries that were analyzed. We are able to specify the general magnitude of our errors in prediction in various circumstances. The error of prediction in the excluded industries is expected to be greater than in the included industries. Such a specification is an essential part of a useful theory.[6]

We examined the 14 industries in 48 states. This produced 281 observations as explained previously. If the rate of growth of production worker employment was greater for the ijth observation (i is industry, j is state) than for the i industry nationally, we score a success. Otherwise, we score it as a failure. Within the 281 observations, 130 grew more rapidly than their 14 national counterparts. Thus, we may say that the probability of success in the entire sample is 130/281, or 0.4626.

The hypothesis subject to test claims that the probability of success is related to two variables, the ratio of manufacturing employment to total employment, and the rate of migration. To evaluate the influence of these characteristics, we constructed a 3×2 table (Table 4.1). The three rows of the table consist of a classification of the states in terms of the ratio of manufacturing to total employment. The ratio was computed for the year 1950. If we order the states from high to low in terms of the magnitude of the ratio, row 1 contains the top third, row 2 the middle third, and row 3 the bottom third.

The two columns of the table consist of a classification of states by the rate of migration. Column 1 contains the 20 states which experienced immigration of civilian population in the period 1945–54. Column 2 contains the 21 states which experienced emigration in the period.[7]

There is some correlation in this and other periods between the two variables used in the classification. On the average, labor migrated from nonmanufacturing to manufacturing states.[8] Hence, a good deal of caution is necessary in interpreting Table 4.1.

Our hypothesis implies that, as we descend from row 1 to row 2 to row 3, the probability of success is expected to increase. That is, we expect the manufacturing employment ratio to have a negative influence on the growth of manufacturing employment.

This influence in fact occurs whether we look at the states with net immigration or with net emigration. Among the states that had net immigration, the probability of success increased from 0.2824 to 0.6071 to 0.8571 as the ratio of manufacturing to total state employment decreased. Similarly, among the states that experienced net emigration, the

TABLE 4.1. PROBABILITIES OF STATES' GROWING MORE RAPIDLY
THAN THE NATIONAL AVERAGE, 1947–53[a]

	Net immigration			*Net emigration*			
	State	n	s	State	n	s	
Top third:[b]	New Hampshire	3	1	Maine	4	1	
	Massachusetts	13	4	Rhode Island	5	2	
	Connecticut	11	2	North Carolina	4	3	
	New York	14	4	South Carolina	3	2	
	New Jersey	13	5		16	8	
	Pennsylvania	14	4				
	Ohio	13	4				$n = 147$
	Maryland	9	4				$s = 45$
	Illinois	12	0				$p = 0.3061$
	Michigan	12	5				
	Wisconsin	12	2				
	Delaware	5	2				
		131	37				
	$p_{11} = 0.2824$			$p_{12} = 0.5000$			
Middle third:	Minnesota	4	1	Vermont	2	1	
	Maryland	11	5	Iowa	6	4	
	Oregon	4	2	Missouri	10	5	
	California	9	9	Virginia	9	5	
		28	17	West Virginia	5	1	$n = 106$
				Georgia	7	4	$s = 62$
				Kentucky	7	4	$p = 0.5849$
				Tennessee	9	4	
				Alabama	6	4	
				Arkansas	6	5	
				Louisiana	6	4	
				Washington	5	4	
					78	45	
	$p_{21} = 0.6071$			$p_{22} = 0.5769$			
Bottom third:	Florida	2	2	Nebraska	2	0	
	Texas	10	9	Kansas	4	4	
	Colorado	1	0	Mississippi	3	3	$n = 28$
	Arizona	1	1	Oklahoma	3	2	$s = 23$
		14	12	Utah	2	2	$p = 0.8214$
					14	11	
	$p_{31} = 0.8571$			$p_{32} = 0.7857$			
Totals		173	66		108	64	$n = 281$
							$s = 130$
	$p = 0.3815$			$p = 0.5926$			$p = 0.4626$

Source: For growth data, *Census of Manufactures, 1947*, and *Annual Survey of Manufactures, 1953*; for data on the ratio of manufacturing to total employment, *Statistical Abstract, 1954*; for migration, *Current Population Reports, Population Estimates* (U.S. Bureau of the Census, Washington, D.C.), Series P-25, No. 124, October 24, 1955, p. 7.

[a] n = number of industries examined in each state
  s = number of successes, that is, number of times an industry grew faster than its
    national counterpart
  p = probability of success, namely, s/n
[b] In terms of manufacturing to total employment.

probability of success increased from 0.50 to 0.5769 to 0.7857 as the ratio of manufacturing to total state employment decreased.

A test of statistical significance was applied to the rows. The probability of success in the entire sample is 0.4626. We may ask whether the differences in probabilities of success and failure among the rows arises solely from random sampling out of a common population with a probability of success of 0.4626, and of failure of 0.5374.

In order to test the distribution of successes and failures among the rows, we use Table 4.2.

TABLE 4.2

Row	Success	Failure	Total	Frequency of success
1	45	102	147	0.3061
2	62	44	106	0.5849
3	23	5	28	0.8214
Total	130	151	281	0.4626

The industries are classified by two criteria, (1) whether they grew faster than their national counterparts (a success) and (2) the manufacturing employment ratio in the state—the three rows.

We wish to discover whether the occurrence of success and failure is influenced by the manufacturing employment ratio. Phrasing the question as a statistical hypothesis, we wish to know whether the distribution of observations is independent of the two classifying variables. The test is performed by comparing the actual frequency of observation in each cell with the frequency that would be observed if the two classifying characteristics were independent of each other. The difference between actual and hypothetical frequencies yields a value of χ^2 of 35.25 with two degrees of freedom. This value is significantly different from zero at the 1 percent level. We may therefore reject the hypothesis that employment growth within an industry in a state is independent of the manufacturing employment ratio in that state.

The hypothesis also claims that the probability of success is positively related to the rate of migration. States having net immigration are expected to have a higher probability of success than states having net emigration. The data presented in Table 4.1 are not conclusive, partly because the rate of migration and the ratio of manufacturing to total employment are positively correlated. Except for row 1, the probability of success is greater in column 1 than in column 2. Given the ratio of manufacturing employment, states receiving net immigration did better than states having net emigration in two out of three cases. The states in row 1, column 1 are heavily industrialized compared with North

Carolina, South Carolina, and Maine in row 1, column 2. Hence, the poorer performance of states in row 1, column 1 compared with the states in row 1, column 2 may reflect merely the dominant effect of industrialization (i.e., the ratio of employment in manufacturing) in inhibiting growth. The multiple regression analysis used above is a finer test of the hypothesis than the probability test used here, owing to the presence of correlation between migration and industrialization.

The same method of analysis can be used to evaluate the influence of the state average wage upon the probability that a given industry will grow more rapidly in state A than in state B. The 48 states in this study were divided into four categories. In row 1, we placed the states that had greater than average ratio of employment in manufacturing in 1950. In row 2, we placed the states that had lower than average ratio of employment in manufacturing. We then classified states into high-wage and low-wage states. A high-wage state is one where the annual earnings of wage and salary workers, by occupation, are higher than the earnings of their national counterparts. A low-wage state is one where the annual earnings of wage and salary workers, by occupation, are lower than the earnings of their national counterparts. Interstate differences in occupational composition are explicitly taken into account by the use of Frank A. Hanna's data[9] on rate-constant and reported earnings. Hanna weighted the reported national average annual occupational earnings by the numbers in an occupation and state and computed a state average annual earnings that reflects the state's occupational composition. Since the occupational earnings rates are held constant, it is called by Hanna the state's "rate-constant occupational earnings." We computed for each state in 1949 the ratio of reported to rate-constant earnings. When this ratio exceeds unity, the state is called a "high-wage" state; when the ratio is less than unity, the state is called a "low-wage" state.

X_1 is the 1950 ratio of manufacturing employment to total employment, and X_2 is the 1949 ratio of reported to rate-constant earnings. These two variables were correlated, with $r = 0.2930$ (significant at the 5 percent level).

Each state has a certain number of industries, n. For each industry and state we calculated whether the *given* industry grew more rapidly in the state than it did in the United States as a whole. If it grew more rapidly in the state, we call it a "success" (s).

The high-wage states that have above-average ratios of manufacturing to total employment contained 143 industries, of which 43 grew more rapidly than their national counterparts.

On the whole, 281 industries were covered, of which 130 grew more rapidly than their national counterparts. The probability of success in the entire sample is again 0.4626. Previous results indicate that over all the probability of success, p, is higher among the states in row 2 than in row 1; i.e., the probability of success is higher among the states with low ratios of manufacturing to total employment than among the states with high ratios of manufacturing to total employment. Earlier findings also indicated that the wage level in a state did not have a clearcut effect upon the growth rate. Since variables X_1 and X_3 are positively correlated, care must be exercised in interpreting Table 4.3. To isolate the effects of each variable, we shall hold one variable constant and see how the probability of success changes with the other variable.

TABLE 4.3. PROBABILITIES OF STATES' GROWING MORE RAPIDLY THAN THE NATIONAL AVERAGE AS RELATED TO WAGES AND MANUFACTURING RATIOS

	Wages above mean			*Wages below mean*			*Total*		
	n	s	p	n	s	p	n	s	p
Manufacturing ratio above mean	143	43	0.301	44	23	0.523	187	66	0.3529
Manufacturing ratio below mean	17	16	0.941	77	48	0.625	94	64	0.6809
Total	160	59	0.3688	121	71	0.4848	281	130	0.4626

Whether we examine the high- or the low-wage states, we again find that the probability of success increases as the ratio of manufacturing to total employment decreases. Consider the high-wage states, column 1. The states with high ratios of manufacturing to total employment have a probability of success of 0.301, whereas the states with low ratios of manufacturing to total employment have a probability of success of 0.941. Then, consider the low-wage states, column 2. The states with high ratios of manufacturing to total employment have a probability of success of 0.523, whereas the states with low ratios of manufacturing to total employment have a probability of success of 0.623. *If the average wage is held constant, the probability of success increases as the ratio of manufacturing to total employment decreases.* This result is the same as the earlier findings.

Let us now hold X_1 (the ratio of manufacturing to total employment) constant and see if the probability of success varies with the wage level. Examination of Table 4.3 indicates that on a gross basis variations of the wage level are negatively associated with employment growth. The higher the wage level in the state, the lower is the probability that state industries grow more rapidly than their national counterparts. This finding is borne out by a test of significance on the frequency of occurrence of the observations. Using a contingency table to test the association between the wage level and the rate of growth, we obtain a value of χ^2 of 13.14, with one degree of freedom.[10] This value is significant at the 1 percent probability level.

This gross relation does not, however, hold up when we stratify the data by the manufacturing employment ratio. As we see in Table 4.2, high wages are negatively associated with employment growth in row 1, but are positively associated with employment growth in row 2. It will be recalled that row 1 consists of states with high manufacturing employment ratios. It is clear that the gross relation between wage level and employment growth is due to the correlation between the wage level and the manufacturing employment ratio.

In conclusion, the wage level has an ambiguous relationship with employment growth that arises from the two effects of high wages: first, it is a deterrent to the demand for labor; second, it is a stimulant to migration. Which of these relationships is dominant depends on forces which we shall examine below in a more complete model.

A REJECTION OF SIMPLISTIC RATIONALIZATIONS

It would seem that the above empirical findings could be rationalized with commonsense reasoning alone and without the use of economic theory. We shall see that a nontheoretical approach of this kind is misleading. Two simplistic views need examination:

The first simplistic view holds that growth from a small base looks large. Thus we find the highest percentage growth of manufacturing employment in states with a low proportion of manufacturing employment to the total. This view is automatically subject to some doubt, for in the previous analysis we always chose a midpoint year at which to measure the manufacturing employment ratio. Nevertheless, it does contain an argument that must be dealt with seriously. The simplistic view may be stated as a statistical hypothesis. Let ΔM_i indicate the growth of manufacturing employment in state i over the time interval; let M_i indicate the number of manufacturing employees in state i at the midpoint of the time interval; L_i indicates the size of the labor force in state i at the midpoint of the time interval. Our simplistic hypothesis is that $\Delta M/L$ is independently distributed with respect to M/L. As a consequence, $\Delta M/M$ (the growth of manufacturing employment) appears higher where M/L (the manufacturing employment ratio) is lower.

Statistical tests of the above hypothesis were carried out by splitting the 48 states into two groups: those with a higher than median manufacturing employment ratio (M/L) and those with a lower than median ratio. For these groups, the mean growth rate ($\Delta M/L$) was greater for the high M/L group.[11] Assuming that the two groups share a common variance, the t test was employed. The difference between the means is significant at the 5 percent level.

More intensive analysis of the variances of the two groups indicated, however, that they were significantly different, the groups with high M/L and $\Delta M/L$ having a significantly larger variance of $\Delta M/L$ than the other group. If the means of the two groups are corrected for the difference in variances, they are no longer significantly different from each other. This correction, however, serves merely to pinpoint the source of heterogeneity between the two groups. Their variances differ, and consequently the distribution of $\Delta M/L$ is not independent of M/L.

A second test of the simplistic hypothesis confirms the results of the first. A contingency table was formed between the two occurrences: $\Delta M/L$ exceeds or falls short of median; M/L exceeds or falls short of median. Again it is shown that the two characteristics are not independent.[12]

A second simplistic view provides an attempted explanation of the observed relation between migration and growth. Immigration is in itself evidence of good manufacturing job opportunities. People move to the jobs; hence, employment growth appears greatest in those areas where people are moving.

The surprising thing is that the rate of immigration (X_2) and the rate of growth (Y) are not correlated at the zero order. In the period 1919–53, the total correlation between X_2 and Y is $+0.2400$, not significantly different from zero at the 5 percent level. It is by no means obvious that the rate of migration is positively associated with the rate of growth. It is only in a partial correlation that the influence of migration upon growth manifests itself. The partial regression coefficient of X_2 (in the regression presented above) is statistically significant at the 1 percent level. The partial correlation $r(Y, X_2 \cdot X_1)$ is equal to $+0.4347$, which is significant at the 1 percent probability level.

One must explain why the total correlation $r(Y, X_2)$ is not significant, whereas the partial correlation $r(Y, X_2 \cdot X_1)$ is significant. The explanation must be based upon economics. Moreover, one must explain why the wage level (X_3) is not significantly associated with the rate of growth (Y). A simplistic theory fails to do these things.

A THEORY OF GROWTH

The failure of the simplistic rationalizations suggests the need for a theory of growth which can explain the empirical regularities described previously. The theory we shall present below is a formal exposition of the explanation presented earlier in this chapter. We shall indicate the role of the labor-supply function as a generator of regional growth differences.

1. Assume that the f.o.b. price of a product produced by a given manufacturing industry is the same for each firm, regardless of its regional location. Transport cost varies directly with the distance of the consumer from the factory concerned. The transport cost per mile may differ among firms. Consumers are assumed to buy from the firm for which the total price is cheapest. Well-defined market areas exist for the various firms under these assumptions.[13]

Moreover, let us assume that the producers in any single state cannot significantly affect the price of a given product by varying the state's rate of output. This assumption is convenient but not crucial for analysis. Let the f.o.b. price of output, p, be determined by national supply and demand conditions. The f.o.b. price p grows at p^* percent per year.

2. The price of capital goods to each firm in a given manufacturing industry is equal to $Z = Z_0 + ts$, where Z_0 is the uniform f.o.b. price and s is the distance from the producer. The variable t is transport cost per mile. The variable ts is assumed to have the same density function in each state for firms in a given manufacturing industry. Hence, the average c.i.f. price of capital goods to firms in a given industry will be the same for producers in each state.

Price Z_0 is determined by national supply and demand factors, and the c.i.f. price grows by Z^* percent for the average firm in each state in a given industry.

3. Production functions of firms in a given manufacturing industry are assumed to be identical among states and subject to constant returns to scale. The uniformity of production functions is based on the view that interstate differences in soil fertility and climate are not very important in affecting manufacturing output, given the inputs of labor and capital.

Since we assumed that there are constant returns to scale for each firm, we must prevent a single firm from monopolizing the industry. Let us assume a limit to the size of each firm such that competition is allowed to prevail. Entry into this industry is free.

4. Finally, assume that pure competition prevails, so that firms attempt to maximize profits.

The assumptions enable us to expose the fundamental role of labor-supply conditions in generating interstate differences in the rate of growth of manufacturing employment. The usefulness of the model and the assumptions are examined in terms of the explanatory value of the model.

Comparison of Long-Run Equilibria. Every firm in a given manufacturing industry will select a ratio q of capital to labor such that the value of the marginal product of capital goods is equal to the price of capital goods.[14] If f is the marginal physical product of capital function, p is the f.o.b. price of output, and Z is the c.i.f. price of capital goods, then

$$f(q) = \frac{Z}{P} \qquad f' < 0 \tag{1}$$

It was assumed that each firm in the industry has the same f, which is a function solely of q; and p was assumed to be the same for all firms regardless of their regional location. Although the c.i.f. price of Z varies according to the purchaser's distance from the factory, the average value of Z will be the same from state to state in the given manufacturing industry. Consequently, *in long-run equilibrium*, q will be the same for firms in the given industry regardless of their regional location.

The long-run equilibrium value of q determines the marginal physical product of labor and with the price of the product, p, determines the equilibrium wage, which is equal to the value of the marginal product of labor. Consequently, in long-run equilibrium, each firm in the industry will pay the same wage:

$$pF(q) = w \qquad F' > 0 \tag{2}$$

In so far as p, F, and q are, on the average, the same in each state in the given industry, the long-run equilibrium wage will be uniform among states. If the wage in this industry is not the same in each state, there is an incentive for firms to expand in some states and contract in others.

Since the long-run equilibrium wage is determined, the labor-supply function determines the quantity of labor that will be forthcoming and employed in each state. The labor-supply function may be defined as

$$w = \frac{1}{v} g\,(L) \tag{3}$$

where v is a shift factor and L is the quantity of labor supplied. When v rises, the labor-supply schedule shifts to the right along the quantity dimension and when v falls, the labor-supply schedule shifts to the left.

We can solve for the state rate of growth of employment in the given industry, $L^* = \dot{L}/L$ in terms of three parameters. The parameters are the rate of growth of the product price, $p^* = \dot{p}/p$; the rate of growth of the average c.i.f. price of capital goods, $Z^* = \dot{Z}/Z$; and the shift of the state labor-supply function, $v^* = \dot{v}/v$. Equations (1.1), (2.1), and (3.1) are derived by differentiating the logarithms of Equations (1), (2), and

(3) with respect to time:

$$Z^* - p^* = \frac{f'(q)}{f(q)} \dot{q} \tag{1.1}$$

$$w^* - p^* = \frac{F'(q)}{F(q)} \dot{q} \tag{2.1}$$

$$w^* + v^* = \frac{g'(L)}{g(L)} \dot{L} \tag{3.1}$$

The following four terms, u, e, s, and k^*, are defined as follows:

$$u = \frac{d \log q}{d \log f(q)} = \frac{f(q)}{f'(q)} \frac{1}{q} \tag{4}$$

is the elasticity of the marginal product of capital schedule with respect to q and is negative,

$$e = \frac{d \log q}{d \log F(q)} = \frac{F(q)}{F'(q)} \frac{1}{q} \tag{5}$$

is the elasticity of the marginal product of labor schedule with respect to q and is positive,

$$s = \frac{g(L)}{g'(L)} \frac{1}{L} \tag{6}$$

is the elasticity of labor supply with respect to the wage, and

$$k^* = z^* - p^* \tag{7}$$

is the growth of the "real" price of capital goods.

A substitution of Equations (4) through (7) into (1.1), (2.1), and (3.1) yields

$$L_i^* = s_i \left(p^* + \frac{u}{e} k^* \right) + s_i \cdot v_i^* \tag{8}$$

where i refers to the ith state.

The rates of growth of the product price p^* and the real price of capital k^* are assumed to be the same in all states in a given manufacturing industry. In so far as the production function is identical among firms in this industry, u/e is the same among states. Suppose that s, the elasticity of labor supply, were uniform among states. Then

$$\frac{L_1^*}{L_2^*} = \frac{p^* + (u/e)k^* + v_1^*}{p^* + (u/e)k^* + v_2^*} \tag{9}$$

Interstate differences in rates of growth of employment in a given manufacturing industry, *from one long-run equilibrium to another*, then arise solely from interstate differences in the growth of the labor-supply function. It should be noted that the elasticity of labor supply plays a role similar to that performed by shifts of the labor-supply function. In the analysis at the beginning of this chapter we implicitly assumed $v_1{}^* = v_2{}^*$, while $s_1 \neq s_2$. Differences in the rates of employment growth would then be attributable to differences in s. In practice it may be difficult to give content to s_i as distinct from $v_i{}^*$. In the conclusion we shall define the forces operating on these two crucial variables.

Disequilibrium and Growth. It is well known that interstate differences exist in the average wage paid in given manufacturing industries. According to our model, this difference means that firms are not at their long-run equilibrium positions.[15] Firms in low-wage states will yield higher marginal products of capital than firms (in the same industries) located in high-wage states. The length of time required to bring the wage up to the equilibrium value depends upon the speed at which capital flows into low-wage areas to benefit from the higher marginal product of capital.

Suppose that the equilibrium wage rises by $y = p^* + (u/e)k^*$ percent from 1919 to 1953. If the wage in the low-wage state rose to the new equilibrium, then the percentage increase in the wage in the low-wage state would be $d(1 + y) + y$ percent.[16] The variable d reflects the percentage difference between the initial equilibrium and the initial low-wage. In actuality, the wage may rise by only x percent of that amount, owing to the insufficiency of the capital inflow that occurred during the period. Consequently, the relative rates of growth of employment in the low-wage state to the high-wage state in a given manufacturing industry is[17]

$$\frac{L_1{}^*}{L_2{}^*} = \frac{y + xd(1 + y) + v_1{}^*}{y + v_2{}^*} \tag{10}$$

where x is between 0 and 1 and reflects the extent to which the disequilibrium has been decreased.

It thus appears that the rate of growth of employment in a given state in a given manufacturing industry depends upon (1) the percentage increase in the equilibrium wage, y, which is the same for each firm in the given manufacturing industry; (2) the rate at which the labor-supply schedule is shifting to the right in a given state, v^*; (3) the extent to which the wage was initially below the equilibrium wage, that is, d; and (4) the extent that the disequilibrium is eliminated, that is, x.

On the basis of (3), low-wage states would tend to have higher rates of growth of employment than high-wage states in the same industries, provided that migration did not occur from low-wage to high-wage states.

We shall now complete our model by discussing the determinants of v^*, the rate at which the labor-supply curve shifts. There is evidence that emigration occurs from low-wage to high-wage states. As a result, the low-wage states, on balance, need not have higher rates of growth of employment than high-wage states.

Determinants of the Regional Labor-Supply Function. The basic conclusion of the model is that interstate variations in rates of growth of manufacturing employment in a given industry stem from differences in the shift v^* of the labor-supply schedule, from deviations d between the initial wage and the initial equilibrium wage, and from differences in the elasticity of labor supply s facing a given industry. Attention will now be focused upon interstate differences in v^* and s.

There are three important influences on the labor-supply function facing the manufacturing industries of a region. These are the proportion of the region's workers outside manufacturing, the rate of growth of the region's labor force due to population fertility, and the migration of workers from other regions.

The growth of the labor-supply curve facing a particular manufacturing industry or facing all manufacturing in general will depend on the alternatives open to the labor force. The conditions under which labor will be attracted into the manufacturing sector depend upon the relative attractiveness of the two sectors. In practice a differential in favor of the expanding sector may be necessary to attract labor out of other occupations. If manufacturing is not the high-wage sector of a state it is not likely to expand through intersectoral shifts.

The attractiveness of the manufacturing sector, for production worker employment, may be measured by the value of the average production worker's annual earnings in manufacturing relative to state per capita income. These earnings represent the most likely amount that a production worker can earn in the manufacturing sector. This figure takes into account the average hourly earnings among the different manufacturing industries, the state composition of manufacturing industries, the opportunities for overtime work, and the steadiness of employment. State per capita income reflects the income received from all sources. The higher the ratio of the average production worker's annual earnings to state per capita income, the greater will be the incentive for the labour force to shift into the manufacturing sector.

As a matter of historical evidence, the ratio of average yearly production worker earnings to state per capita income is negatively correlated with the ratio of manufacturing to total employment. In 1940, the correlation between these two variables was −0.65, among the 48 states. This value is significantly different from zero at the 1 percent level. Thus, the incentive to shift into the manufacturing sector appears to increase as the ratio of manufacturing to total employment decreases.

This analysis is very similar to the one developed in Chapter 2. It was shown that the greater the misallocation of resources between the agricultural and nonagricultural sectors, in the initial period, the greater the growth of per capita income. Income rose precisely because labor migrated from the low-wage to the high-wage sectors.

The rate of migration from agriculture to nonagriculture is positively related to the income differential in the two sectors. Hence,

$$\frac{-\dot{A}}{A} = h(w) \tag{11}$$

where w is the wage in nonagriculture minus the wage in agriculture, A is agricultural employment, and $\dot{A}$ is the time rate of change of agricultural employment.

Labor moves from agriculture to nonagriculture, given total employment in a state. Let N be nonagricultural employment. Then

$$\dot{N} = -\dot{A} \tag{12}$$

$$\frac{\dot{N}}{N} = \frac{-\dot{A}}{A}\frac{A}{N} \tag{13}$$

$$= h(w)\frac{A}{N} \tag{14}$$

The rate of growth of nonagricultural employment $\dot{N}/N$ depends positively upon two variables: the wage differential w between the two sectors and the ratio (A/N) of agricultural to nonagricultural employment. Given the wage differential, nonagricultural employment will grow more rapidly in agricultural states than in nonagricultural states.

Now let the manufacturing sector (which is contained in the nonagricultural sector) gain $k\dot{N}$, $1 \geq k \geq 0$, of the growth in nonagricultural employment. Then

$$\frac{\dot{M}}{M} = k\frac{\dot{N}}{N}\frac{N}{M} \tag{15}$$

$$= k \cdot h\left(w\right) \cdot \frac{A}{M} = v^{*} \tag{16}$$

M is the manufacturing employment, and $\dot{M}$ is the time rate of change of manufacturing employment. Given w, $\dot{M}/M$ is precisely v^*, the growth of the manufacturing labor-supply curve. Substitute (14) into (15) to derive (16). Then, $v^* = \dot{M}/M$ depends positively upon the ratio of agricultural to manufacturing employment. The less industrialized a state, the greater is A/M. Thereby, v^* is greater in nonindustrialized states than in industrial states, given the wage differential w (see Figure 4.2).

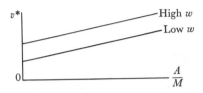

FIGURE 4.2

The natural increase of the population is typically greater in rural than in urban areas. Therefore, shifts of the labor supply function from this source are likely to be most pronounced in areas where manufacturing employment is not widely prevalent, since the degree of urbanization is itself strongly related to the development of manufacturing. It follows that the smaller the ratio of manufacturing employment to total employment, the greater the potentialities for the growth of the manufacturing labor-supply schedule through the natural increase of the population.

The above considerations explain why the ratio of manufacturing employment to total employment is such a powerful variable in explaining statistical variation in the growth of manufacturing employment, for there are two sets of economic forces working through this variable. One is the rate of natural population increase mentioned directly above. That is to say, the manufacturing employment ratio is a negatively correlated proxy for the growth of the state labor force through natural increase. The second set of forces work through the income inducements for labor to move into manufacturing employment from other sectors.

A third major influence on the regional labor-supply function is interstate migration. The greater the rate of immigration of people into the labor force, as a percentage of the state labor force, the greater will be the rightward shift of the labor-supply curve facing the manufacturing sector. Migration occurs, to a large extent, from low-wage to high-wage states.[18] Hence, v^* is affected by the ratio of the wage in one state to the average wage prevailing in the other states.

In summary, s and v^*, the elasticity and shift of the labor-supply curve facing the manufacturing sector of a given state, are affected by three major variables:

1. The natural rate of increase. The ratio of nonmanufacturing to total state employment is a proxy for this variable.

2. The relative attractiveness of the manufacturing sector to the other sectors within the state.

3. The rate of immigration, which is affected by the ratio of the wage in this state to that prevailing in other states. Immigration is also affected by climate and expectations of future growth in the state's economy.

The Explanatory Power of the Theory. The theory implies the phenomena described at the beginning of this chapter and may therefore be considered an explanation of interstate differences in growth rates:

1. The rate of growth of manufacturing production worker employment, in a given manufacturing industry, will be higher in states with low ratios of manufacturing to total employment than in states with high ratios. This is compatible with the results of the regressions and Table 4.1.

2. When the manufacturing ratio is taken into account, the rate of immigration will be positively associated with the rate of growth of employment. That this correlation actually occurs is shown above. It is likely that the *partial* correlation of migration and growth of employment reflects the fact that workers migrate from low-wage to high-wage areas. Consequently, in low-wage areas, v^* is less and in high-wage areas v^* is greater than one would expect on the basis of the rate of natural increase in the labor force.

3. The rate of growth of manufacturing production worker employment, in a given manufacturing industry, will not necessarily be higher in low-wage states than in high-wage states. The level of the state wage has two counterbalancing effects upon the rate of growth of employment:

The marginal rate of return on capital is higher in low-wage states, in a given industry, than in high-wage states. Capital is therefore attracted to the state. As capital flows in, it generates a demand for labor. Thus, low wages and high growth rates should be correlated positively.

On the other hand, emigration of labor occurs in low-wage states as labor flows from low-wage to high-wage states. As a result, emigration tends to reduce v^* (the shift of the labor-supply schedule facing manufacturing) in low-wage states. In high-wage states, immigration of labor from low-wage states tends to increase v^*. This implication is compatible with the finding that the regression coefficient of x_3 was not significant.

4. The stability of relative growth rates, as shown in Chapter 2, is

partially explained in terms of the invariance of the ranking of states by the percentage of employment in manufacturing. The composition of the 10 states with the greatest ratios of manufacturing employment was practically unchanged from 1920 to 1940. Similarly, the composition of the 10 states with the lowest ratios of manufacturing employment was practically unchanged during this period. The former group is dominated by states with no more than two successes, whereas there is no more than one state in the latter group which had fewer than four successes (see Chapter 2). Success indicates that manufacturing employment in the state grew more rapidly than the national rate.

5. INTERINDUSTRY REPERCUSSIONS OF GROWTH AND DECLINE

In this chapter we shall continue the development of sectoral models of regional growth. Here we focus attention on the interactions within a region which result from the growth process. These interactions arise through the alternative methods of expansion which are available to a growing sector. A sector may draw resources from outside the region, or it may draw resources from other activities within the region. If resources are withdrawn from other economic activities within the region, there will be repercussions on the economic forces making for continued growth as well as on the economic returns to the owners of productive resources.

The nature of these repercussions will depend on the allocation of resources in existence prior to the initiation of the growth process. On the one hand, this prior allocation may be highly efficient, in the sense that resources are fully employed and that economic gains are not possible through the redistribution of productive services to alternative employments. If such is the case, it is extremely likely that economic growth will proceed through migration of labor rather than through the redistribution of labor from one sector of the region's economy to another. On the other hand, the prior allocation may consist of considerable underemployment of labor and may suggest the possibility of gains in productivity though a transfer of labor to other employments.

This question of the prior allocation of resources is crucial to the understanding of the growth process for two reasons. First, the nature of the prior allocation is itself a variable in explaining the magnitude of economic growth in a region and the forms which this growth process assumes, as we have seen in earlier chapters. The ratio of manufacturing employment and the rate of migration are two variables that reflect the allocation of resources prior to the initiation of a growth process. The rate of migration reflects the allocation in the sense that the allocation is a determinant of the return to labor in a region. The return to labor in the region compared with its return in other regions is in turn a determinant of the migration rate. Second, the prior allocation will have a strong influence on the observable effects of the growth process in terms of the returns to capital and labor. The consequence is that our understanding of the growth process requires that we separate out the influence of initial allocation on the final results of the process.

In this chapter and the next we shall examine interactions between sectors for two classes of problems. First we shall be concerned with interactions between migration and economic growth for the period 1929–47. This investigation refines the simple relations that were exposed in Chapter 4 and indicates a wider variety of repercussions between the relevant variables.

In Chapter 6 we shall be concerned with the effects of growth on the reallocation of resources and in turn with the effects of reallocations upon the distribution of income and upon the prospects for continued growth.

RELATIVE IMPORTANCE OF HYPOTHETICAL AND INTERNAL GROWTH RATES

The differences in rates of growth of manufacturing production worker employment, among states, may stem from two causes. First, differences in the industrial composition of states may produce differential growth rates. Although a given industry may grow at the same rate in each state, each industry does not have equal influence. Some states may start with a preponderance of industries which are growing rapidly nationally, and other states may start with industries which are declining nationally. This influence on growth has been called the effect of demand acting through state differences in industrial composition. We have seen in Chapter 3 that this is an influence on state growth patterns. We have also seen that these influences were not the prime determinants of state growth patterns in the 1929–48 period.

The second reason for interstate variations in growth rates is the existence of differences in growth rates in the same industry. Under this argument the rapidly growing states contain industries which are growing more rapidly than their national counterparts, whereas the slowly growing states contain industries which are growing less rapidly than their national counterparts. The theories of growth developed in Chapter 4 were designed to explain how the second factor may generate interstate differences in growth rates.

A simple statistical measure was devised to summarize the relative importance of these two factors. The *actual* (A) growth rate in a given state can be viewed as the sum of a *hypothetical* (H) growth rate and an *internal* (I) growth rate.[1] The hypothetical growth rate is the rate that would have occurred if each industry in the state grew at the same rate as its national counterpart. The internal growth rate is defined as the difference between the actual and hypothetical growth rate. It measures the importance of local factors in producing a divergence between the actual state growth and that expected upon the basis of industrial composition. The theory developed in Chapter 4 adduced an explanation of differences in internal growth rates, not in hypothetical growth rates.

It will be recalled that in Chapter 3, we attempted to predict the actual growth rate of manufacturing employment on the basis of hypothetical rates. Predictions were carried out for three periods, 1919–29, 1929–47, and 1948–53. In only one period was there a significant relation between actual and hypothetical growth rates, namely, in 1948–53. In the other two periods, the correlation was not significantly different from zero. Since $A = H + I$, interstate differences in the actual rate of growth of manufacturing employment may be attributable to variations in internal growth rates among the states.

REALLOCATIVE EFFECTS OF GROWTH

In so far as there is no clear association between actual and hypothetical growth rates, a negative association must exist between hypothetical and internal growth rates: $A = H + I$. Consider the set of states with hypothetical growth rates above the mean. Since their actual growth rates are not above the mean, their internal growth rates must be below the mean. A similar argument applies to states with hypothetical growth rates below the mean. For the period 1929–47, a highly significant negative relationship existed between hypothetical and internal growth rates. This means that, on the average, states with favorable industrial compositions had unfavorable internal growth rates; and states with unfavorable compositions had favorable internal growth rates.

We propose an explanation for the observed negative relation between hypothetical and internal growth rates. States with high hypothetical growth rates produce products whose demands are growing rapidly in the nation. An expansion of the output of these products requires an increase in the inputs of productive services employed in these industries. The additional productive services may come from other industries in the manufacturing sector or from migration into the manufacturing sector of a state. In the first case, the other manufacturing industries in the state must be adversely affected. Their internal growth rates will be reduced, since they are losing resources to the more rapidly growing sectors. In so far as migration occurs into the manufacturing sector, either from other states or from the nonmanufacturing sector of a state, the decline in internal growth rates is mitigated or offset.

States with negative (or low) hypothetical growth rates produce products the demands for which are not growing nationally. These industries release resources which flow to the other manufacturing industries or out of the manufacturing sector entirely. In so far as the resources flow to the manufacturing industries which are not declining (nationally), their internal growth rates are raised. Emigration from the manufacturing sector, as a result of a negative hypothetical growth rate, tends to offset the stimulus to the internal growth rate.

It is possible for states with low hypothetical growth rates to have very high internal growth rates, as will occur when there has been a change in the resource-supply schedules facing the manufacturing industries of such states. An example of the type of resource shift that would result is the transfer of branches of the textile industry from the northeastern to the southeastern states. It would produce a high internal rate of growth in the southeastern states and a low internal rate in the northeastern states. Such a phenomenon could yield the observed negative relation over the population of states between hypothetical and internal growth rates.

The growth of population in underdeveloped states has in the past occurred at such a rate that employment opportunities could not keep pace with increases in the labor force. We should, therefore, expect to find that in these states a simultaneous and opposing movement of resources is going on. While labor is moving out to take advantage of higher wages elsewhere, capital is moving in to take advantage of lower wages. The result is likely to be an ambiguous relationship between migration and economic growth. We saw in Chapter 4 that immigration is positively associated in a partial regression with the rate of economic growth. Growing states attract workers; declining states export workers. Without denying the significance of this relation, however, it is important to recognize that below the surface of this pattern variations and contradictions appear which must be understood. Not only may growing states attract people, they may also export people. They may even export people and grow in terms of the size of the labor force if emigration is less than the increase in population due to natural causes. Far from regarding this type of behavior as contradictory to the earlier model, we see it is precisely the type of behavior that will tend to equalize wage rates and the returns to capital.

This theory will be elaborated and tested in subsequent sections. It is compatible with the data and hence is offered as an explanation of the negative relation between hypothetical and internal growth rates and of interstate differences in internal growth rates.[2] We shall first develop and then test our explanation for the observed relation between hypothetical and actual growth rates.

THEORETICAL FRAMEWORK

Let us first assume that the quantity of labor is fixed in a state and is fully employed in two industries, X and Y, whose products are sold in a national market. The state may be sufficiently large that its producers in either industry affect the price of their product in the national market.

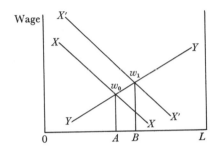

FIGURE 5.1

Whether they do or not is not relevant to this part of the analysis. Capital is assumed to be mobile, and each firm adjusts its stock of capital such that the marginal revenue product is equal to the nationally determined rent per dollar of capital. Labor is assumed to be mobile between these two industries within the state.

The long-run demand for labor, by the X industry, is given by the XX schedule in Figure 5.1. At each point on this schedule (1) the marginal revenue product of capital is equal to the exogenously determined rent per dollar of capital and (2) the marginal revenue product of labor is equal to the wage rate. The schedule is downward sloping because of either the existence of decreasing returns to scale for a fixed number of individual firms, or the rising supply prices of inputs other than labor and capital, or the ability of all the firms in the industry in the state acting together to affect the market price of the product. The quantity of capital employed varies to satisfy condition (2).

If the fixed quantity of labor available in the state is $0L$, then the demand for labor schedule in the Y industry is given by the Y schedule. The origin, which refers to this schedule, is at L and the quantity of labor employed increases as one moves from L to 0. The conditions (1) and (2) above apply to the Y industry as well as to the X industry.

Given the quantity of labor $0L$ in the state employed in manufacturing,

$0A$ labor will be employed in the X industry and LA will be employed in the Y industry. The wage is w_0 in each industry, since competition is assumed to prevail in the labor market. If the demand for X rises nationally, its price will rise, and the demand for labor schedule will shift to $X'X'$. The new wage is w_1. Let us initially assume that the residents of the region do not increase their demand for Y and that the national demand for Y is unchanged. Labor is released from the Y industry as the wage is increased and flows to the X industry. In the long-run equilibrium, employment has increased by AB in the X sector and has declined by the

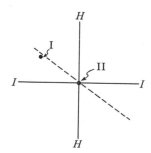

FIGURE 5.2

same amount in the Y sector. Growth in the X sector has occurred through the release of resources in the Y sector. The net result is that the actual growth of manufacturing employment in the state has been zero. The hypothetical growth rate has been positive as a consequence of the national growth of the X industry. Finally, the internal growth rate is negative as a consequence of the forced contraction of the Y industry.

The above case may be contrasted with another state with industries Z and Y, where it is assumed that the national demands for Z and Y are both stable. In the absence of change in the supply schedules of labor and capital in the state, no growth occurs in either industry in this state. If the H and I growth rates are plotted (see Figure 5.2), we begin to see how a negative relation between H and I may be generated. Up to this point, our negative relation reflects the fact that industries which are growing nationally expand in a state by inducing other industries in the state to release resources.

We shall now examine a case where the expansion of one industry, X, in a state leads the income earners to increase their demand for the products of a second industry, Y. Again it will be assumed that the quantity of labor is fixed.

When the U.S. demand for X increases, the price of X rises and there is an increase in the return to resources in the region producing X. The income of the region increases, and there is a corresponding increase in the demand for the product of the Y industry. The shift in the demand curve for labor in Y depends upon the local marginal propensity to consume the Y product. Under "normal" conditions, i.e., when the marginal propensity to consume product Y is less than unity, the resources still flow from Y to X (Figure 5.3). Initially, industry X employed $0A$ and industry Y employed LA workers, at a wage of AW_0. When the demand for X increased, raising the labor demand schedule to $X'X'$, the greater induced demand for Y raised the labor demand schedule to $Y'Y'$ and the state

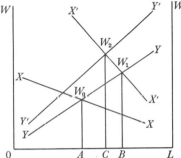

FIGURE 5.3. State I

wage to CW_2. Nevertheless, resources were transferred from the Y to the X sector. To be sure, only AC of labor was transferred, whereas AB workers would have been transferred had there been no induced demand for the products of the Y sector. A comparison of state I (Figure 5.3) with state II (Figure 5.2) still reveals the negative association between hypothetical and internal growth rates. State I still has a positive hypothetical and negative internal rate of growth.

THE CRUCIAL ROLE OF INTRASTATE AND INTERSTATE MIGRATION

The negative association between hypothetical and internal growth rates may be attenuated or reversed completely if there is sufficient migration into the manufacturing sectors (X and Y) in response to a growth in demand (Figure 5.4). The initial equilibrium wage is W_0, with $0M$ employed in the X industry and ML employed in the Y industry. Again, we shall assume an expansion in the U.S. demand for X and a resulting expansion in the region's demand for Y. Let us also assume that the national industry X is expanding by a rate which when multiplied by $0M$, the employment in X, happens to equal the increment MN. There is then a minimum amount of migration into the manufacturing sector required to permit this state to grow as fast as its hypothetical rate indicates.

This is the increment MN. Migration will then permit the wage to rise to W_3, but no higher. If the migration were less than MN, the wage would rise higher than W_3. On the other hand, if there were a movement of more than MN workers into the sector, employment in Y would grow. As a result, hypothetical and internal employment growth would be positively associated.

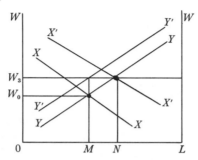

FIGURE 5.4. State II

EMPIRICAL ANALYSIS

The above framework will be subjected to empirical test for the period 1929–47. It should be noted that data on employment growth and the computed hypothetical and internal rates will refer to manufacturing employment. That is, the movement of labor into the manufacturing sector can occur either through intrastate shifts of employment from nonmanufacturing sectors or through migration from other states. We shall again use the manufacturing employment ratio as a proxy variable to measure the possibilities of the first type of movement.

The 48 states were classified into four categories in terms of their hypothetical and internal growth rates. A state could have a hypothetical growth rate above or below the median, and it could have a positive or a negative internal rate of growth. To be sure, states with above the median hypothetical growth rates tended to have negative internal growth rates, while states with below the median hypothetical growth rates tended to have positive internal growth rates. The consequence is that the cell frequencies are unlikely to be independent of the method of classification. Nevertheless, we may examine the average behavior of the observations in each cell.

In each cell, there were states which experienced net immigration of labor, and there were others which experienced net emigration of labor. In Table 5.1, the individual states are identified, together with the values of the average percentage of the labor force in manufacturing in 1940 and the rate of migration from 1930 to 1950 as a percent of the 1930 population.

TABLE 5.1. CLASSIFICATION OF STATES BY HYPOTHETICAL AND INTERNAL GROWTH RATES

	Positive internal growth rates			Negative internal growth rates	
State	Manufac-turing employ-ment ratio, percent, 1940	Migra-tion rate, percent, 1930–1950[a]	State	Manufac-turing employ-ment ratio, percent, 1940	Migra-tion rate, percent, 1930–1950[a]
		Above median hypothetical growth rates:			
Michigan	25.5	6.69	Connecticut	43.5	6.94
Indiana	30.0	2.38	Illinois	28.6	−0.09
Kansas	9.1	−14.65	Maryland	26.1	20.33
California	16.5	61.64	Delaware	28.9	14.62
Iowa	11.4	−11.69	Ohio	33.4	2.02
Oklahoma	7.7	−29.85	New York	27.3	2.75
Texas	9.9	0.96	Wisconsin	25.5	−4.22
Colorado	10.2	3.87	New Jersey	36.5	4.12
Virginia	20.1	6.15	Missouri	18.9	−5.86
Nebraska	6.9	−21.20	Pennsylvania	33.3	−7.77
Utah	11.0	−6.06	Wyoming	5.3	−1.06
			Massachusetts	36.8	−2.72
			Vermont	22.0	−12.81
		Below median hypothetical growth rates:			
North Dakota	2.5	−34.98	Maine	32.8	−6.42
West Virginia	17.6	−18.94	Arizona	8.4	31.70
Kentucky	11.9	−18.65	Florida	11.7	54.27
Nevada	4.5	52.53	New Hampshire	39.5	−1.18
Louisiana	12.9	−6.44	Rhode Island	45.8	0.35
South Dakota	4.5	−27.78	Washington	21.6	30.63
Georgia	18.5	−14.65	Idaho	7.9	−3.01
Tennessee	18.3	−5.55			
Alabama	17.4	−19.38			
Montana	7.4	−12.08			
Oregon	20.9	33.23			
Arkansas	9.9	−28.88			
New Mexico	6.4	8.35			
Mississippi	9.2	−26.45			
Minnesota	12.5	−6.24			
North Carolina	26.9	−11.24			
South Carolina	22.8	−19.51			

[a] Based on 1930 population.

This classification is further refined and summarized in Table 5.2. Here we have split apart in each cell the states that experienced immigration from those which experienced emigration during the period.

The data summarized in Table 5.2 are compatible with the theory that the greater the rate of migration into the manufacturing sector of a state, the greater will be the internal growth rate.

1. States with positive internal growth rates had higher rates of net immigration than states with negative internal growth rates, given the hypothetical growth rates. Consider the states with hypothetical growth rates above the median. Among the states with positive internal growth rates, the rate of net immigration was, on the average, 13.62 percent, whereas the rate of net immigration was only 8.46 percent among the states with negative internal growth rates. Similarly, consider the states with hypothetical growth rates below the median. The rate of net immigration was 31.37 percent among the states with positive internal growth

TABLE 5.2. VARIABLES ASSOCIATED WITH INTERNAL GROWTH RATES IN MANUFACTURING, 1929–47, AMONG 48 STATES

	Positive internal rates			Negative internal rates		
	a	*b*	*n*	*a*	*b*	*n*
Above median hypothetical rates:						
Net immigration	18.7	13.62	6	32.6	8.46	6
Net emigration	9.2	−7.69	5	24.3	−4.93	7
Below median hypothetical rates:						
Net immigration	10.6	31.37	3	21.9	29.24	4
Net emigration	13.7	−17.91	14	26.7	−3.54	3

a = percent of total employment in manufacturing in 1940
b = percent of net migration 1930–50 to 1930 population
n = number of states

rates and 29.24 percent among the states with negative internal growth rates.

2. There were, relatively and absolutely, more states which experienced net emigration of labor among the states with positive internal growth rates than among the states with negative internal growth rates. Of the 28 states with positive internal growth rates, 19 had net emigration of labor; but of the 20 states with negative internal growth rates, only 10 had net emigration of labor.

3. Among the states which experienced net emigration of labor, the rate of net emigration was greater among the states with positive internal growth rates than states with negative internal rates.

The data cited in (2) and (3) support the view that states with positive internal growth rates had greater excess supplies of labor than states with negative internal growth rates. Otherwise, why would there be a greater rate of net emigration from the first set of states?

4. States with positive internal growth rates in manufacturing had smaller fractions of the labor force in manufacturing than states with negative internal growth rates, given the hypothetical growth rate and the net migration position of the state. For example, among the states with hypothetical growth rates above the median which experienced net immigration of labor, the manufacturing ratio was 18.7 percent for positive internal rates and 32.6 percent for negative internal rates. This situation also prevailed whether the states had high or low hypothetical growth rates or whether states had net immigration or net emigration of labor.

According to the reasoning of Chapter 4, the manufacturing ratio reflects the potential labor supply available to the manufacturing sector, solely from an intrastate, intersector shift of resources. When the demands rise for the products of the state's industries, greater migration into the manufacturing sector is expected to occur in states with low manufacturing ratios than in states with high manufacturing ratios. Thereby, positive internal growth rates are expected to occur among the states with low ratios, as, in fact, occurs in the data found in Table 5.2.

We conclude that the rate of intrastate and interstate migration is greater among the states with positive internal rates of growth than among states with negative internal rates of growth. Among the states that export labor, i.e., have labor surplus, the rate of net emigration is greater among the states with positive internal growth rates than among the states with negative internal growth rates. This difference indicates that there is a greater labor surplus among the former set of states. The data are quite in accord with what our theory leads us to believe. Hence, we maintain that our theory is a reasonable explanation of the negative relation between hypothetical and internal growth rates.

The role of migration in interstate growth differences can best be appreciated when we synthesize the above data with the information on growth of capital, employment, and wages presented in Chapter 3. In Table 5.3, the 48 states are classified into four categories by their position with regard to the growth rates of nonagricultural capital and nonagricultural employment. Instead of data on wage levels and wage growth, however, we have entered the rate of migration and the manufacturing employment ratio from Table 5.1.

The results of this classification are tabulated in Table 5.4. Unlike the presentation in Table 5.2, Table 5.4 does not separate the experience of those states which experienced immigration from those states which have

TABLE 5.3. CLASSIFICATION OF 48 STATES BY GROWTH OF NONAGRICULTURAL CAPITAL AND GROWTH OF NONAGRICULTURAL EMPLOYMENT, 1929–1948

	Greater than average growth rate of capital			Less than average growth rate of capital	
	Manufacturing employment ratio, percent, 1940	*Migration rate, percent, 1930–1950*		*Manufacturing employment ratio, percent, 1940*	*Migration rate, percent, 1930–1950*
Greater than average growth rate of employment:					
North Carolina	26.9	−11.24	California	16.5	61.64
South Carolina	22.8	−19.51	Delaware	28.9	14.62
Florida	11.7	54.27	Ohio	33.4	2.02
New Mexico	6.4	8.35	Wisconsin	25.5	−4.22
Idaho	7.9	−3.01	West Virginia	17.6	−18.94
Wyoming	5.3	−1.06	Connecticut	43.5	6.94
Oregon	20.9	33.23	Michigan	25.5	6.69
Nevada	4.5	52.53			
Virginia	20.1	6.15			
Utah	11.0	−6.06			
Texas	9.9	0.96			
Arizona	8.4	31.70			
Washington	21.6	30.63			
Indiana	30.0	2.38			
Tennessee	18.3	−5.55			
Louisiana	12.9	−6.44			
Colorado	10.2	3.87			
Less than average growth rate of employment:					
Georgia	18.5	−14.65	Maine	32.8	−6.42
Alabama	17.4	−19.38	Minnesota	12.5	−6.24
Mississippi	9.2	−26.45	Missouri	18.9	−5.86
Montana	7.4	−12.08	Iowa	11.4	−11.69
North Dakota	2.5	−34.98	Nebraska	6.9	−21.20
South Dakota	4.5	−27.78	Kansas	9.1	−14.65
Arkansas	9.9.	−28.88	Kentucky	11.9	−18.65
			Oklahoma	7.7	−29.85
			Rhode Island	45.8	0.35
			New York	27.3	2.75
			Pennsylvania	33.3	−7.77
			Illinois	28.6	−0.09
			New Hampshire	39.5	−1.18
			Vermont	22.0	−12.81
			Massachusetts	36.8	−2.72
			New Jersey	36.5	4.12
			Maryland	26.1	20.33

experienced emigration. Table 5.4 shows the following variables for each state:

n = number of states experiencing immigration
m = number of states experiencing emigration
a = percentage of total employment in manufacturing
b = average migration ratio
y = average nonagricultural wage paid in 1929
y^* = percentage growth of y, 1929–48

These last two items were presented originally in Chapter 3. The average migration ratio is computed by subtracting the negative from the positive entries in the cell.

TABLE 5.4. CLASSIFICATION OF STATES BY EMPLOYMENT GROWTH AND CAPITAL GROWTH, 1929–48

Greater than average capital growth		*Less than average capital growth*	
Greater than average employment growth:			
$n = 10$	$y = \$1,187$	$n = 5$	$y = \$1,517$
$m = 7$	$y^* = 131.8\%$	$m = 2$	$y^* = 101.5\%$
$a = 14.6\%$		$a = 27.3\%$	
$b = 10.07\%$		$b = +9.82\%$	
Less than average employment growth:			
$n = 0$	$y = \$1,040$	$n = 4$	$y = \$1,335$
$m = 7$	$y^* = 130.1\%$	$m = 13$	$y^* = 107.3\%$
$a = 9.95\%$		$a = 23.5\%$	
$b = -23.46\%$		$b = -6.56\%$	

Table 5.4 suggests a number of very important conclusions concerning the way growth has occurred during this two-decade period:

1. Immigration coincided with greater than average growth of non-agricultural employment; emigration coincided with less than average growth of employment.

2. Immigration appeared to act as a deterrent on wage growth in the group of states with high employment growth and low capital growth. Note that the initial wage is higher for this group than for the other three, and this wage undoubtedly served as a stimulant to the migrants. Also, note that this group had a very high manufacturing employment ratio. This ratio confirms our previous notion that such states will expand primarily through the attraction of labor from other states rather than from other sectors of the region. It is noteworthy that there are only two states with a high manufacturing ratio which underwent expansion

despite emigration. These are North Carolina and South Carolina, where expansion was possible because of the high reproduction rate of population in rural areas.

3. We see here the group of states which retarded during the period. This group shows low capital growth and low employment growth. It also has a very high manufacturing employment ratio and an average wage which is higher than that possessed by the groups with high capital growth. The major difference between this retarded group and the group with high employment growth, high wages, and low capital growth appears to be the role of migration. Thus, we see that migration plays a strong role in the determination of regional growth patterns and in the effects of growth on the wage. In addition, the character of the region's labor-supply function is a determinant of the rate at which capital will grow in the state.

6. MODELS OF GROWTH AND ALLOCATION

We have examined the role of inter- and intraregional transfers of the labor supply. In this chapter we shall identify additional implications of intersectoral shifts on the returns to resources. Our concern is with the effects of such movements on the returns to labor and capital. We shall develop models which identify the interactions between growth, reallocation, and the payments to labor and capital. The interactions operate through changes in the proportions at which the resources are combined in different activities.

It is clear that a region contains a wide range of economic activities that use labor and capital in different proportions. These range from such heavy users of capital as railways and public utilities to such light users as beauty parlors and window washers. For some problems, the sectoral differences in capital-labor ratios and the changes in such ratios may be regarded as unimportant. For the class of problems examined in this chapter, however, the capital-labor ratios and their changes are of key importance.

In the models to be considered, it will be assumed that the capital-labor ratios determine the marginal productivities of capital and labor. In addition, we shall make sufficient assumptions to insure that there is a unique relation between the composition of output and the payments to capital and labor in the region. The meaning of such a relation may be illustrated through a simple numerical example:

Suppose there are two industries in the region, X and Y. We shall assume that Y is labor-intensive, producing one-unit of output under fixed proportions with 10 workers and one unit of capital. Further, assume that X is capital-intensive, producing one unit of output under fixed proportions with one worker and 10 units of capital. Also, assume the region contains 100 workers and 100 units of capital. The maximum amounts of X and Y which might be produced can then be described by a production possibility curve in the XY plane (Figure 6.1). There is only one combination of outputs which will fully employ both resources. Call this point *a* with coordinates *Xa*, *Ya*.[1] Movements along this surface between points *a* and *b* require the capital-intensive industry, *X*, to contract and the labor-intensive industry, *Y*, to expand. Under the assumptions we are using, namely, fixed proportions within each production function, this movement would result in the employment of fewer units of capital than are originally available. Therefore, the price of capital would fall to zero. The reason is that the contracting industry yields up resources in the proportion of 10 capital units to one labor unit, while the expanding industry hires resources in the proportion of 10 labor units to one capital unit.

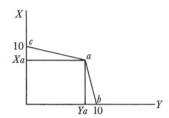

FIGURE 6.1

Similarly, a movement along the production possibility curve from *a* in the direction of *c* would result in the employment of fewer units of labor than are available. The price of labor would fall to zero.

The above example is hardly a literal description of the functioning of a market economy. Resource shifts do not have to result in the unemployment of factors in the long run. In practice, the proportions in which resources are combined can vary. Note, however, that the variation of resource prices is directly implied by any resource shift within a region where we hold constant the stock of resources. Thus, when the stock of resources is allowed to shift, movements will occur in response to relative employment opportunities in this and other regions. One of the chief influences on these opportunities is the output composition of the region.

The above example serves as a starting point for an analysis of regional growth in terms of (1) the composition of output between labor-intensive and capital-intensive sectors, (2) variations in the ratio of capital to labor employed in each industry, (3) the returns to labor and capital, and (4) the rates of migration of labor and capital. To connect these four phenomena, we shall expound a model of production relations which is more complex than the preceding specification of fixed proportion production functions. In order for our model to provide a continuous link between the composition of output and the return to labor and capital, we shall assume that production functions for output are homogeneous of the first degree. This assumption implies that the marginal productivities of labor and capital are both functions of the ratio of capital to labor employed. If it can be shown that the composition of output determines a unique ratio of capital to labor in each sector, then a direct link is provided between the composition of output among final products and the distribution of that output between labor and capital.[2] Once this link is provided, it may be used in analyzing the growth of the region through the returns to migration.

An example will make this theory clear. Suppose that a region produces only two commodities, both of which are sold in the national market. Suppose further that no other commodities are produced. The determination of the prices of these commodities is made in the national market. Specification of the prices of the two outputs will determine the composition of output, which in turn will determine the ratio of capital to labor in the two sectors. This ratio will determine the marginal physical products of capital and of labor. If there is perfect competition in resource markets within the region, the money wage will be the same in both industries, as will the rent on a dollar's worth of capital. Determination of the money wage and the money rent on capital then provides the signal to resources to move into the region or out of the region. If the resulting money rent on capital is higher than the rate paid in other regions, capital will flow in; if it is lower, capital will flow out.

Note that in the analysis which follows, we shall make less restrictive assumptions than those given in the above example. We shall generally assume that only one sector price is determined in the national market and one determined within the region.

The formal link between the composition of output and the returns to labor and capital is provided by the box diagram in Figure 6.2. This device has been used to demonstrate the convexity of the production possibility curve under the assumptions of two outputs, two inputs,[3] and a lack of reversibility of the factor proportions in each industrial sector.

Very briefly the argument runs as follows: Assume an economy with fixed quantities of two resources, called L and K. Assume that the economy can produce two commodities, X and Y. Assume that the production functions for X and Y are homogeneous of the first degree.

Now the production possibility curve in Figure 6.2 may have a number of shapes under the above assumptions. If the two production functions are identical, they will be mirror images of each other. The resulting production possibility curve is a straight-line function, $X'Y'$. Its corresponding contract curve in the box diagram is the straight line, XY. The consequence of such a production possibility curve is that the ratio of factor proportions would not change with a reallocation of resources.

Let us now, however, specify that the production functions differ from each other in the sense that Y is labor-intensive relative to X; that is, for any common ratio of factor prices, the ratio of capital to labor hired in Y will be lower than the ratio hired in X. This condition precludes the possibility of reversing factor proportions. The resulting contract curve is shown in the box diagram as the broken curve, XY.

An intuitive argument will indicate why the corresponding production possibility curve in the $X'Y'$ plane is concave to the origin. Consider point A in the box diagram. Originally, it was an efficient point in the sense that it was on the straight-line contract curve. Corresponding to A is

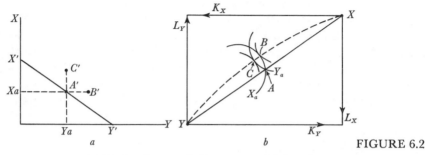

a   b   FIGURE 6.2

(a) Production possibility curve   (b) Box diagram

point A' on the down-the-line production possibility curve, showing the resulting amounts of X and Y that could be produced. Now let us examine point A under the assumption that factor proportions vary in the two production functions. A is no longer an efficient point, as the contract locus goes through X, B, C, and Y, where C and B are points of tangency between the production isoquants of X and Y. It is possible to produce more X than Xa and still get Ya, or it is possible to produce more Y than Ya and still get Xa. The possibilities are shown by points C and B on the contract curve of the box diagram and by the corresponding points C' and B' in the XY plane. Thus, the production possibility curve is a surface which is concave to the origin of the XY plane. By varying A continuously from X to Y in the box diagram, one could trace out the production possibility curve in the same manner.

The resulting concave and continuous production possibility curve establishes the link between the composition of output and the factor proportions, for the slope of the continuous production possibility curve is equal to the ratio of the long-run marginal costs of the two commodities. Establishment of the price ratio P_X/P_Y establishes a unique point in the XY plane, a unique point on the contract curve, unique ratios of capital to labor in each sector, and therefore unique values of the marginal products. It will be true that in both sectors labor will receive the same wage and capital the same rent, since these were the constraints under which the contract curve was defined. It is also true that the price ratio established must be consistent with the production of some of both commodities.

An important implication of this framework is the influence of allocation on the real wage. This relation is best known through the pathbreaking article of Samuelson and Stolper noted previously. If, because of a shift of relative prices, the labor-intensive sector were to expand at the expense of the other, an increase in the marginal product of labor and a fall in the marginal product of capital would occur. This result can be seen in our box diagram as the movement along the contract curve from point C to point B. The resulting shift of resources has caused the ratio of capital to labor to rise in both sectors. With the assumptions about homogeneity of the production functions, these changes in the ratio of capital to labor produce the indicated changes in the marginal products.

Another important implication of the framework arises from the specification of one of the sectors as a capital goods sector and the other as a consumer goods sector. Suppose Y, the labor-intensive sector, produces capital goods, while X, the capital-intensive sector, produces consumer goods. Then the marginal productivity of capital in the capital goods sector is a pure number which is formally identical with the interest rate. An expansion of capital goods production at the expense of consumer goods yields a rise of capital-labor ratios in each sector. The interest rate declines. On the other hand, if capital goods production is capital-intensive, its expansion yields an increase of the interest rate.[4]

ACCUMULATION AND THE REAL WAGE

The preceding framework is useful in so far as it enriches our understanding of the process of growth. Our conception of the impact of accumulation on the real wage will take on a considerable degree of sophistication. According to the aggregative model of growth developed in Chapter 3, the growth of the real wage is positively related to the growth of the total ratio of capital to labor in a state. If, however, we disaggregate and consider a region with several industries, then the growth in the real wage does not depend solely upon the growth in the regional capital-labor ratio. An increase in the ratio of capital to labor in the region may not lead to a rise in the ratio of capital to labor in each of the component industries. Instead of a rise in the real wage, a reallocation of the region's output may occur in favor of the commodity produced by the capital-intensive sector. While it might be objected that this is an unnecessary complication of a simple problem, the objection ignores the reallocation which very likely accompanies the growth process. We have already seen the theoretical and empirical grounds for believing that growth is essentially a reallocative process. In the United States a growing region undergoes a shift of resources from agricultural to nonagricultural sectors, from nonmanufacturing to manufacturing sectors, and into those sectors producing nontransportable items of capital such as roads, bridges, highways, sewers, office buildings, factories, and private dwellings. The mere duplication of existing facilities would require this last type of shift.

On the basis of the preceding framework, we shall show how the growth of the real wage is affected by the reallocation among sectors and by the over-all growth in the regional capital-labor ratio. The accumulation of capital relative to the quantity of labor may raise the marginal physical product of labor in each industry. In that event the real wage of labor will have risen in terms of every good produced in the state. For the uniform rise in the real wage to occur, accumulation must raise the ratio of capital to labor in all output sectors. We shall see that this process requires accumulation to be accompanied by an increase in the relative price of output in the sector which is labor-intensive. The reason is the same as that indicated previously in the static case, where we demonstrated the effect of reallocation on the real wage.

We have already specified the conditions under which the ratio of capital to labor employed in each industry depends upon the relative price of the outputs. The necessary assumptions are that (1) production functions for the two outputs are homogeneous of first degree and (2) with given resources there is a unique ratio of capital to labor for each production function which will yield a given marginal rate of substitution between the two products.

These conditions guarantee that factor proportions in the two sectors are unique functions of the relative prices of their output. A rise in the proportion of capital to labor in both sectors requires that there be an increase in the relative price of output in the labor-intensive sector. If during accumulation the relative prices of output remained unchanged, the factor proportions would not change. All that would happen would be a simultaneous reallocation of output in favor of the sector which is capital-intensive, with no change in marginal physical products.

The influence of accumulation on the marginal physical product of labor may be demonstrated graphically with the aid of the box diagram.[5]

In Figure 6.3, the quantity of labor employed is measured along the vertical axis, capital along the horizontal. Inputs for sector Y (labor-intensive) are measured from the lower left-hand origin, inputs for sector X are measured from the upper right-hand origin. The ray from each origin shows the ratio of labor to capital that would be employed at a given set of factor prices in the production of each commodity. At their intersection point, α, the isoquants (not shown) are tangent to one another; and their slope at this point gives the marginal rate of substitution between L and K employed in both sectors. This slope corresponds to the relative

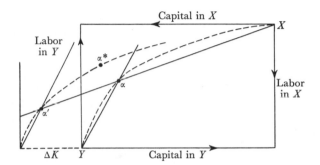

FIGURE 6.3

prices of the factors. The dashed line through α is the contract curve showing other maximum values of X that could be produced for other given values of Y. It is assumed that α is the only efficient point in the box with this value of the marginal rate of substitution. Under these assumptions every point on the contract curve will be represented by a corresponding point on a convex production possibility curve in X and Y. The combination of X and Y at α will be produced only for a unique value of P_x/P_y. Therefore, the capital-labor ratios in X and Y will be used only for that value of P_x/P_y. If the value of P_x/P_y changes, then production will shift to some other point on the contract curve,[6] and other values of the capital-labor ratios will be employed.

Now let us increase the amount of capital by ΔK. This shifts the horizontal dimension of the box as shown in Figure 6.3. At α', where the production of X has increased and Y decreased, the capital-labor ratio is unchanged in each sector, and the marginal rate of substitution between the products X and Y is unchanged. Therefore, the value of P_x/P_y at α' is the same as at α. If, however, output had shifted to α^* (on the new contract curve going through α'), the capital-labor ratios in both industries would have risen. This would occur when the price of Y had risen relative to the price of X.

Thus, we have reached the following conclusions:

1. Accumulation will lead to an increase in the marginal product of labor when it is accompanied by a rise in the ratio of capital to labor in each industry sector.

2. This increase will occur when the price of output of the labor-intensive sector rises relative to the price of output of the capital-intensive sector.

3. This situation means that the output of the capital-intensive sector has failed to expand by enough to leave the ratios of input combinations unchanged.

4. If accumulation leads to an increase in the marginal product of labor, it will also result in a decline in the marginal product of capital.

ACCUMULATION AND INEFFICIENCY

The previous conclusions are based on the assumption that the process of accumulation begins and ends with a position of allocative efficiency. The question of the effect of accumulation on the marginal products of labor and capital then resolves itself into a question of the location of the final equilibrium point on the new contract curve.

This analysis is too restrictive, however, to be completely applicable to the historical situations which we have observed among regions of the United States. Wage differentials have always existed between agricultural and nonagricultural employments. They have also existed within the nonagricultural sector between manufacturing and mining, on the one hand, and occupations which are typically lumped together under the heading of services, on the other hand. Some of the differences in money wages may be consistent with long-run equilibrium of the labor market for a variety of reasons such as the payment in kind practiced in agriculture and differences in skill composition of the sectors.

The magnitude and distribution of these differences, however, some of which will be examined below, suggest a serious degree of inefficiency in the labor market, especially in the period prior to World War II. In some states, for example, the manufacturing and mining wage appeared to be as much as twice as large as the services wage. In other states, the difference was as small as 20 percent in favor of manufacturing. The differences appeared large primarily in states characterized by low manufacturing ratios and suggest a high degree of overemployment of labor in the labor-intensive sectors of a number of states. Let us therefore analyze the effects of accumulation when the preaccumulation allocation is inefficient and when wage differentials exist between the X and Y industries.

The elimination of misallocation and therefore of the wage differentials can, but does not necessarily, mean that the average wage in a region will rise. While it is true that the marginal product of labor will rise in the low-wage sector as capital enters and labor leaves, it is also true that the marginal product will fall in the high-wage sector as capital leaves and labor enters. The net effect on the average wage must also take into account the repercussion on the prices of outputs of the two sectors as one expands and the other contracts, for under competition the money wage is the product of the output price and the marginal product

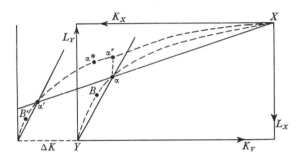

FIGURE 6.4

of labor. The final answer depends on whether the percentage rise in the low-wage sector is greater than the percentage fall in the high-wage sector. There is no a priori answer to this question, so that we must conclude that the elimination of misallocation may have no effect by itself on the money wage.

Nevertheless, we must take into account the existence of this misallocation in determining the influence of accumulation on the marginal product of labor. This analysis is carried out in Figure 6.4. Assume that efficient point α is consistent with the long-run equilibrium of demand and supply in industries X and Y. Further, assume that the preaccumulation allocation was inefficient and was located at α'' in Figure 6.4. This situation would involve an overemployment of labor in the labor-intensive sector Y and yield the wage differentials mentioned previously. At point α'', the marginal product of labor in Y and the wage per worker in Y all are lower than they would be at α, while the marginal product of labor and the wage per worker are higher in X than they would be at α. Furthermore, if the relative price of output in the two sectors is at all sensitive to the change in relative supplies, the price ratio P_x/P_y will be higher at α'' than at α. This difference will not occur, of course, if the two products are export goods whose prices are set in the national market.

In the context of this analysis and the problems to which it applies, it is extremely likely that the relative price P_x/P_y will be affected. The historical evidence indicates overemployment of labor in the service sector, and this consideration will be carried into our analysis.

Now let us examine the impact of accumulation. Suppose that α'' becomes an efficient point as a result of the accumulation ΔK; that is, it becomes a point on the new contract curve going through α' and α^*. Further, suppose that the price ratio in effect at α'' remains unchanged because of the nature of changes in demand conditions for the two sectors accompanying the accumulation. The result would be a change in allocation between the two sectors such that the marginal physical product of labor in the two sectors is either lower or unchanged from the situation when labor was misallocated.

This result can be seen in the following way. Initial demand conditions were such that α would be the efficient point with a value of the price ratio equal to P_x/P_y. At α'' the price ratio in effect was higher than P_x/P_y because more Y and less X was produced than at α. Let the price ratio at α'' be called P_x/P_y''. There is an efficient production point, B, corresponding to P_x/P_y'', which is to the lower left of α. Corresponding to B is an efficient point, B', on the new contract curve with the same price ratio. If, when α'' becomes efficient, the price ratio remains at P_x/P_y'', allocation will move B'. At B' the ratio of capital to labor in X is lower than at α'', while the ratio in Y is not perceptibly changed from what it was when α'' was inefficient. At B', the money wage in X is equal to that in Y because of a fall of the wage in X.

We see that the movement from α'' to B' is a depressant on the marginal physical product of labor outweighing any stimulus to the wage from the elimination of the misallocation. Thus, the elimination of misallocation will not necessarily raise wages in a region when accompanied by accumulation. A rise in wages depends on the final production point.

Note that if P_x/P_y had fallen below P_x/P_y'', there could have been an increase in wages. For example, if P_x/P_y had fallen sufficiently, allocation could have remained at α'' after it became efficient. All the additional capital (ΔK) would then have been used in Y to raise the marginal physical product of labor in that sector up to a level where the money wage in Y again equaled that in X.

Thus, the conclusions are the same as those yielded by our earlier analysis when we began with an efficient allocation. In order for the marginal product of labor to rise as a consequence of accumulation, there must be an increase in the relative price of labor-intensive goods.

APPLICATION OF THE FRAMEWORK

The period between 1929 and 1953 witnessed a marked reallocation of labor both among and within states. Within states there was a shifting between labor-intensive and capital-intensive sectors. We shall examine some of the effects of these shifts in the growth of wages and shall concentrate on the nonagricultural sector of the state. Within this sector, we identify two groups of activities that may roughly be regarded as labor-intensive and capital-intensive. We shall refer to the labor-intensive sector as the "services" sector. It includes industries which are commonly classified under the headings of wholesale and retail trade; finance, insurance, and real estate; personal and business services; and construction. The capital-intensive sector includes manufacturing and mining. We have deleted from this classification individuals engaged in transportation, public utilities, and government. In 1950, these excluded groups made up 23 percent of the nonagricultural labor force.

The classification of the activities in each state into a services and a manufacturing-mining sector allows us to examine the allocative effects operating when resources are shifted from a labor-intensive to a capital-intensive sector. Our capital-intensive group is further distinguishable from the labor-intensive group by another characteristic—namely, the production of transportable products. While this characteristic is partially shared by the services sector, there is far less activity in this sector which results in the sale of a product in a place different from where it was produced. The consequence is that the prices of products produced in the manufacturing-mining sector are influenced by developments in the national market. Conversely, the prices of products produced in the services sector are mainly, though of course not exclusively, affected by developments in the region's domestic market. As a consequence of these relationships, we shall be able to use this dichotomy later in a concluding synthesis of the growth process among regions.

Focusing attention on the two sectors of each state (see Table 6.1), we see that in 1929 the manufacturing wage was higher in every state than the service wage. The difference ranged from 146 percent higher in Oklahoma to 12 percent higher in Connecticut, Florida, and Maryland. If the states are grouped into regions, then the greatest discrepancy was 72 percent in favor of manufacturing in the Mountain-Pacific region, while the smallest was 34 percent in the New England–Middle Atlantic region. In the following 25-year period, there was a strong convergence pattern in evidence. In all states but Pennsylvania, Connecticut, and Massachusetts the wage in services rose more rapidly than the wage in manufacturing. By 1953, the differential in wages in the two sectors had appreciably narrowed or completely disappeared. The largest differential in 1953 was 71 percent in favor of manufacturing in Wyoming, while the smallest was 27 percent in favor of services in Maryland.

Undoubtedly, some of these patterns reflect a change in composition within state sectors. For example, the failure of the manufacturing wage to grow as rapidly as the service wage in Maryland may be attributable to the growth of employment related to activities of the Federal government. While government employment is not included in our services sector, the expansion of such employment would affect the going wage for many types of service labor in private employment.

This reversal of wage differentials in favor of services also occurred in North Carolina and Georgia. Very likely some changes in composition may have played a role in the reversal of the wage positions of the two sectors. In manufacturing, the relative growth of textiles and the decline of lumbering represent a shift from high-paying to low-paying industry, for in these two industries, the labor force has different sex and skill compositions. In addition, an important change in composition may have occurred within the services sector. As the income of these regions rose, the demand for certain types of professional services must have risen by the same or a greater proportion. The increased importance of this group (doctors, lawyers, engineers, teachers) within the services sector as well as the increased earnings they enjoyed must have played an important role in raising service wages and salaries in these states.

Nevertheless, the nationwide growth of service wages relative to manufacturing wages may be a phenomenon that requires a more general explanation than simply a change in composition of the work force. Clearly, changes in skill or sex composition within the two sectors played some role; but they do not provide a general explanation.

A more acceptable explanation for the narrowing or elimination of the differential is simply an increase in the efficiency of the labor market. In low-income states, the services sector generally reflects the employment opportunities open to less skilled members of the labor force: the Negro, the uneducated, the immigrant, and the casual female laborer. One would regard the wage in services as a barometer of employment opportunities in agriculture as well as in many part-time occupations in the nonagricultural sphere. It would be this wage which would indicate to potential unskilled migrants what they could earn if they stayed at home. In addition, the service wages would indicate to potential unskilled migrants from other states what their return would be if they entered the service sector after migrating.

The lower wage in services than in manufacturing is an indication that the labor market was not operating with complete efficiency. An efficient allocation of resources would require a shift of labor out of services into the manufacturing-mining sector, but these shifts require time to attract new capital. The major force producing the equalization during the 1929–53 period was undoubtedly World War II. The war produced a rapid expansion in the demand for labor in manufacturing at the same time that the armed services drew off about 25 percent of the prewar labor force. The result was a transfer of labor from the services sector and an increase in the service wage relative to the manufacturing wage.

Table 6.1 shows the behavior of this wage differential in 1929 and 1953 among the 48 states. The differential is expressed as the ratio of the average wage per employee in the manufacturing sector to the wage in the services sector. The states are grouped geographically into four major regions: (1) South Atlantic, East South Central, and South West; (2) Mountain and Pacific; (3) New England and Middle Atlantic; and (4) East North Central and West North Central.

This initial grouping is made on the basis of geographic proximity, plus some a priori reasons for believing that development patterns will be similar within each group. These reasons arise from the historical nature of development in each of the four regions. As it turns out, there is substantial heterogeneity in each group; and some of the averages are shown separately for subregions such as the South Atlantic and Pacific regions.

Table 6.1 shows well-defined regional patterns of wage differentials. In 1929 the smallest differentials occur in the East, both in the New England–Middle Atlantic group (34 percent in favor of manufacturing) and in the South Atlantic group (36 percent in favor of manufacturing). The largest differentials are in the combined East South Central and Southwest regions (69 percent in favor of manufacturing) and in the Mountain region (78 percent in favor of manufacturing). Such differentials conform closely to the relative importance of manufacturing in the region.

In Chapter 5 we used the manufacturing employment ratio to measure the possibility that manufacturing might attract labor from other sectors. It was mentioned that there was a strong negative correlation between the manufacturing employment ratio and the ratio of manufacturing wages and salaries per worker to state per capita income. The state per capita income includes both wages and the return to property in all sectors of the state's economy. Here in Table 6.1, we see this result in even stronger form, for the 1940 manufacturing employment ratio is negatively related to the wages differential within the nonagricultural sector. Where the differential was smallest, the manufacturing employment ratio is

TABLE 6.1. WAGE DIFFERENTIALS BETWEEN MANUFACTURING
AND SERVICE SECTORS—48 STATES, 1929 AND 1953

	Ratio of wages per employee in manufacturing-mining to wages per employee in services		Ratio of growth of wages in manufac-turing-mining to growth of wages in services,	Manufac-turing employ-ment ratio,	Residual from regression of wage growth on growth of capital-labor ratio
	1929	*1953*	*1929–53*	*1940*	
South Atlantic, East South Central, and Southwest:					
Delaware	1.848	1.438	0.778	28.9	+
Maryland	1.134	0.730	0.644	26.1	+
Virginia	1.256	1.043	0.830	20.1	+
West Virginia	1.620	1.491	0.920	17.6	−
North Carolina	1.379	0.980	0.711	26.9	+
South Carolina	1.312	1.043	0.795	22.8	+
Georgia	1.197	0.964	0.805	18.5	−
Florida	1.116	1.038	0.930	11.7	+
Kentucky	1.581	1.348	0.853	11.9	−
Tennessee	1.380	1.175	0.851	18.3	+
Alabama	1.479	1.115	0.754	17.4	−
Mississippi	1.790	1.001	0.559	9.2	−
Arkansas	1.511	1.138	0.753	9.9	−
Louisiana	1.596	1.253	0.785	12.9	+
Oklahoma	2.465	1.469	0.596	7.7	−
Texas	1.738	1.388	0.799	9.9	+
Group average	1.525	1.163	0.773	16.86	
South Atlantic average	1.358	1.091	0.802	21.57	
East South Central and Southwest average	1.693	1.236	0.744	12.15	
Mountain and Pacific:					
Montana	1.857	1.509	0.813	7.4	−
Idaho	1.779	1.419	0.798	7.9	−
Wyoming	2.114	1.709	0.808	5.3	−
Colorado	1.491	1.337	0.897	10.2	−
New Mexico	1.793	1.652	0.921	6.4	+
Arizona	1.947	1.272	0.653	8.4	+
Utah	1.829	1.520	0.831	11.0	+
Nevada	1.417	1.249	0.881	4.5	+
Washington	1.571	1.156	0.736	21.6	−
Oregon	1.684	1.293	0.768	20.9	−
California	1.502	1.195	0.796	16.5	+
Group average	1.726	1.392	0.809	10.92	
Pacific average	1.586	1.215	0.767	19.67	
Mountain average	1.778	1.458	0.825	7.64	

Table 6.1 (*continued*)

	Ratio of wages per employee in manufacturing-mining to wages per employee in services		Ratio of growth of wages in manufac-turing-mining to growth of wages in services,	Manufac-turing employ-ment ratio,	Residual from regression of wage growth on growth of capital-labor ratio
	1929	1953	1929–53	1940	
New England and Middle Atlantic:					
Maine	1.388	1.210	0.872	32.8	—
New Hampshire	1.482	1.176	0.793	39.5	—
Vermont	1.709	1.156	0.676	22.0	—
Massachusetts	1.181	1.227	1.039	36.8	—
Rhode Island	1.168	1.120	0.959	45.8	—
Connecticut	1.121	1.201	1.071	43.5	+
New York	1.291	1.099	0.851	27.3	—
New Jersey	1.581	1.120	0.708	36.5	—
Pennsylvania	1.189	1.299	1.093	33.3	—
Group average	1.346	1.179	0.896	35.8	
East and West North Central:					
Ohio	1.568	1.351	0.862	33.4	—
Indiana	1.793	1.389	0.775	30.0	—
Illinois	1.278	1.147	0.897	28.6	—
Michigan	1.608	1.478	0.919	25.5	+
Wisconsin	1.587	1.416	0.892	25.5	—
Minnesota	1.549	1.340	0.865	12.5	—
Iowa	1.582	1.420	0.898	11.4	—
Missouri	1.338	1.293	0.966	18.9	—
North Dakota	1.537	1.090	0.709	2.5	—
South Dakota	1.747	1.305	0.747	4.5	—
Nebraska	1.766	1.316	0.745	6.9	—
Kansas	1.760	1.524	0.866	9.1	+
Group average	1.593	1.339	0.845	17.40	

highest: 35 percent in New England and 21 percent in the South Atlantic region. Where the differential is greatest, the manufacturing ratio is lowest: 12 percent in the East South Central and Southwest, 7.6 percent in the Mountain states.

Table 6.1 reveals that by 1953 convergence of wages in the two sectors had changed the relative importance of the remaining differential among the states. Again the smallest differential exists in the New England–Middle Atlantic region (18 percent in favor of manufacturing) and in the

South Atlantic region (9 percent in favor of manufacturing). The largest differentials are now to be found in the Mountain states (46 percent in favor of manufacturing) and in the East and West North Central states (34 percent in favor of manufacturing).

This result indicates that over the period 1929–53, the wage payments per worker did not grow at a uniform rate in the two sectors of each state. In one group of states (namely, the East South Central–Southwest region) service wages have far outstripped manufacturing wages in growth; in fact, they grew 37 percent faster.

The third column in Table 6.1 shows the ratio of wage growth in manufacturing to wage growth in services for each state. Only in Massachusetts, Connecticut, and Pennsylvania did manufacturing wages per employee grow more rapidly than service wages; in all other states, service wages grew faster. The fastest relative growth of service wages occurred in the East South Central–Southwest region (the index had an average value of 0.744) and in the Pacific-Mountain region (the index had an average value of 0.767). The slowest relative growth of service wages occurred in the New England–Middle Atlantic region (the index had an average value of 0.896) and in the East and West North Central region (the index had an average value of 0.845).

The importance of these differentials will be seen when they are used in conjunction with the box diagram to illustrate movements of resources between the two sectors. We may treat each state as a closed economy with a fixed supply of the resources, labor and capital, producing two types of goods in a labor-intensive and a capital-intensive sector. Some states will have an efficient allocation of resources in the sense that production will be found on a point on the contract curve in the box diagram and on the boundary of the production possibility curve. Other states will have an inefficient allocation, and production will be found off the contract curve of the box diagram and below the boundary of the production possibility curve. In addition, each state will experience a certain accumulation of capital over time and a certain addition to the labor force. We shall ignore changes in the over-all size of the labor force throughout the remainder of the argument, since they will not affect its substance.

As the accumulation goes on, there are changes in output composition and resource combinations in response to changes in the relative prices of outputs and to changes in the efficiency of utilization of the labor force. As we have seen previously, it is conceivable that accumulation could be accompanied by a change in the composition of such output that there would be no increase in the ratio of capital to labor in each sector. As a consequence, the money wage per worker would reflect only price level changes within the region's economy, and the total return to capital would reflect only price level changes and changes in the number of units of capital. If, however, the capital-labor ratio rises in both sectors of the region's economy, the money wage per worker will receive an additional impetus from the increase in the marginal product of labor, while the total money return to capital will receive a negative impulse from the decline in the marginal product of capital. Note that the only circumstance under which the capital-labor ratio might rise in one sector and fall in the other occurs when we start from a position of misallocation off the contract curve. All movements along the contract curve imply that the capital-labor ratio changes in the same direction in both sectors.

In applying the framework to the 48 states in the 1929–53 period, we shall attempt to identify the states in which the marginal product of labor rose. We shall carry out this identification by making use of the statistical regression between changes in the money wage payments per worker and changes in the money payments to capital relative to the number of workers.

For the period 1929–53, let

W^* = percentage change in nonagricultural money wage payments
R^* = percentage change in total payments to nonagricultural capital[7]
L^* = percentage change in total nonagricultural employment
$X = R^* - L^*$
$Y = W^* - L^*$

The regression between Y and X was formed to yield[8]

$$Y = 0.892X + 146.00 \qquad r = 0.63$$
$$(0.160) \qquad (85.00)$$

where the standard errors of the regression coefficients are shown in parentheses. The positive constant in the equation tells us that the distribution of factor payments tended to turn in favor of labor in states where $R^* - L^*$ was below a given value X' and in favor of capital where $R^* - L^*$ is above X' (Figure 6.5).[9] In fact, X' is so large that Y exceeds X for almost every element in the sample.

The coefficient of X indicates that for every 10 percent that the increase in the return to capital exceeded the increase in the number employed, there would be a 9 percent rise in the wage per worker. We may expect this coefficient to reflect primarily the differential effect on regional wages of changes in the prices of goods produced in the region. The fact that the coefficient falls short of unity suggests that there are errors in the measurement of X or influences on the return to capital which are not reflected in wages. The chief of these latter influences would be the reallocation of resources within the state.

One method of identifying the states which are responsible for the failure of the coefficient of X to equal unity is to choose those observations where X is above the sample mean and Y below, and conversely. There are, however, only 10 such states.[10] A more sensitive method of identification is to examine the positive and negative residuals from the regression. The states with positive residuals would show a greater degree of growth

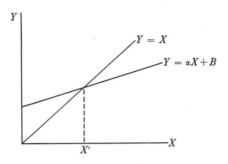

FIGURE 6.5

in wages than that predicted by the growth of capital when combined with the regression line. Similarly, states with negative residuals would show a growth of wages smaller than predicted.

The positive and negative residuals demonstrate strong regional effects. These are shown as plus and minus signs in column 5 of Table 6.1 and are summarized in Table 6.2.

TABLE 6.2

South Atlantic, East and West South Central, Mountain, and Pacific	New England and Middle Atlantic	East and West North Central
Wage growth greater than predicted by regression:		
15	1	2
Wage growth less than predicted by regression:		
13	8	10
—	—	—
Total 28	9	12

Treating Table 6.2 as a contingency table, we find that the residuals are significantly associated with the regional classification.[11] Table 6.2 indicates that the strongest wage increases beyond that predicted in the regression occurred in the South Atlantic, East and West South Central, Mountain, and Pacific. The other two major regional groupings show a predominance of weaker increases over that predicted by the regression.

In analyzing these residuals, we may now inquire as to the influence of changes in the marginal product of labor and changes in the composition of state output. It will be recalled that an increase in ratio of capital to labor in both sectors is necessary to raise the marginal product of labor and that a necessary condition for this to occur is an increase in the relative price of output in the labor-intensive sector. If the states with positive residuals did experience increases in the relative price of the labor-intensive sector, then we would attribute these residuals to changes in the marginal product of labor.

It is, of course, not possible to observe directly the change in the relative prices in the two sectors of each state. We may, however, infer the direction of this change from our earlier index of the change in the wage differential. This index, shown in Table 6.1, is termed the "index of relative growth of service wages." An increased wage in services relative to manufacturing wages is ordinarily an indication of an increase in the relative price of services output to manufacturing output. This change in relative prices occurs in response to two possible sets of forces acting simultaneously. One is the increased efficiency of the labor market and the closing of the differential in wage payments. This is a movement from a point off the contract curve to a point on the contract curve. The second is a change in allocation and in the stock of capital such that services have a growth in price relative to the products of manufactures. This is an aspect of growth that we shall discuss in the next chapter.

There is one exception to the above relations. The movement from a point off the contract curve to a point on the contract curve does not necessarily imply an increase in total wage payments. It was pointed out earlier, in the section, "Accumulation and Inefficiency," that the elimination of misallocation does not necessarily raise wages, even when accompanied by accumulation. An increase in wages depends on the final production point. An example was presented where the manufacturing wage fell relative to the service wage as a result of a decline of the marginal product of labor in manufacturing, through an expansion of the manufacturing sector. At the same time, there was no decline in the relative price of the manufacturing sector's output. This case indicates that the use of the index of change in the wage differential is not a statistical identity for changes in the relative prices of the two sectors. We have then the following logical possibilities:

1. Relative output prices remain unchanged. The labor market becomes efficient, and manufacturing expands relative to services. The payments to labor decline.

2. Relative output prices move in favor of the domestic sector. The payments to labor rise.

Our use of the index of change in wage differentials is then predicated on the assumption (which is refutable because of a counter possibility) that the second set of relations has been in operation: namely, that the prices of services have risen relative to manufactures and that this rise has provided a positive stimulant to the marginal product of labor.

TABLE 6.3. CLASSIFICATION OF RESIDUALS FROM REGRESSION BETWEEN WAGE GROWTH AND GROWTH OF THE CAPITAL-LABOR RATIO, 48 STATES, 1929–53

	Large negative residuals	Middle group	Large positive residuals
Increase in wages in services sector relative to increase in wages in manufacturing sector:			
Greater than median	4	10	9
Less than median	12	5	6

A test of this hypothesis is provided by analyzing the residuals from the regression in terms of the index of changes in the wage differential. A hint of this relation is evident in Table 6.1, for the greatest number of positive residuals occurs in the regions (South Atlantic, for example) where the service wage has experienced the greatest rise relative to the manufacturing wage. Carrying out the classification in detail for all 48 states yields Table 6.3.

The states were divided into three groups according to the size of the

TABLE 6.4

	South Atlantic, East and West South Central Mountain, and Pacific	New England and Middle Atlantic	East and West North Central
Concordance	11	5	5
Nonconcordance	14	4	7

residuals. A significance test on the contingency table yields a value χ^2 of 6.267, with two degrees of freedom. It is statistically significant at the 5 percent level.

It should be noted that the above relationship does not predominate in any particular region to the exclusion of others. While the residuals from the regression do have an identifiable regional distribution in terms of sign, the concordant elements in Table 6.3 do not.

Let us define a concordance as the occurrence of either of the following pairs of events: a large positive (large negative) residual from the regression accompanied by a greater (less) than median growth of service wages relative to manufacturing wages. Concordances consist of the events in the upper right and lower left boxes of Table 6.3, 21 observations in all. Call the remaining observations nonconcordances. We then have the regional distribution in Table 6.4. Treating Table 6.4 as a contingency table, we are unable to reject the hypothesis that the distribution of concordances is independent of regional classification. We obtain a value of χ^2 of 1.23, which with two degrees of freedom, is not significantly different from zero.

THE INTERACTION AMONG GROWTH, REALLOCATION, AND THE WAGE

The final evidence in support of the analysis presented in the preceding section will be examined here. In order to carry this out, it is first necessary to restate the growth process as it apparently operates among regions of the United States.

At any moment of time there appear to be two major sets of economic forces in operation that influence the growth process in different regions. Each of these forces operates through the relative profitability of investment in different regions. Nevertheless, they have been identified and separately analyzed in the preceding chapters.

The first set of forces arises from the differential impact of changes in demand for the export products of different regions. This differential impact arises solely because each region is in the short run producing a given bundle of goods for export. The shifts of resources from other employments necessary to respond to export opportunities may take a considerable period of time. It is this force which is partially responsible for the failure of wages to converge among states in a number of the periods analyzed in earlier chapters.

The second set of forces operates through the impact of wage levels upon the profitability of investment. We have seen that a complicated process operates here because of the ambiguous influence of low wages. On the one hand, low wages attract capital. On the other hand, high wages attract migrants and are responsible for shifting the labor-supply functions of high-wage areas in a manner conducive to the continuation of the growth process.

Whichever of the above two forces are dominant, they both make themselves felt through an expansion of investment in the region. This expansion sets into motion the familiar investment-income multiplier and an increase of regional spending on all commodities. The services sector will be a strong beneficiary of this spending. Construction, also included in our definition of the services sector, receives an impetus in the form of demands for new plants, housing, and public utilities. How far this spending on services shifts the relative price of the services sector upward depends on the initial impetus to growth. If this impetus is an increase in the demand for the region's exports, then the respending of income on services will very likely shift the relative prices of services to manufactures higher than existed prior to the initiation of the growth process. In the next chapter, we specify a model where this must occur.

Superficially, it would appear that an increase in service prices could offset any initial increase in the export price and wipe out the higher marginal efficiency of investment generated by the export boom. If the growth process is to continue in a static framework of unchanged technology, there can be no rise in the marginal product of labor, as this rise would imply a fall in the marginal product of capital. Under this view, if the marginal product of labor does rise, it will impede the growth process by leading to a lower marginal efficiency of investment.

The above view, however, ignores the possibility that capital goods are exclusively imported, for then we could have a rise in the prices of both export and domestic sectors relative to the prices of capital goods, a rise in the relative price of the labor-intensive services sector, a rise in the marginal efficiency of investment, a rise in the marginal physical product of labor, and a fall in the marginal physical product of capital. Such a framework is developed in the next chapter.

If we reexamine the data on wage growth, capital growth, and employment growth used in the regression equation, we see a confirmation of these processes. We may look again at the 21 states in which the residuals from the regression accorded with our theory of reallocation. In 9 of these states, positive residuals were associated with a greater than average growth of service wages relative to manufacturing wages. In 12 states, negative residuals were associated with less than average growth of service wages relative to manufacturing wages. If our theory of the growth process is correct, then the 9 states with the positive residuals should be growing in capital relative to employment compared with the 12 states with negative residuals.

This process in fact occurs. If we examine the 9 states, we find an average growth of capital relative to employment of 182.70 percent. In the 12 states with negative residuals, the average growth of capital relative to employment is 153.30 percent.[12] This is not an obvious result in view of the independence of the residuals in the regression from the independent variable X used in the regression. There is no statistical reason that one group should have a higher value of the independent variable than the other. Thus, we can confirm our view of the growth process. The re-allocation in favor of the labor-intensive services sector occurred in the group of states undergoing the greatest growth. This yielded the increased marginal product of labor which we observed.

7. ECONOMIC GROWTH, DISTRIBUTION OF INCOME, AND MOVEMENT OF CAPITAL

In the preceding chapter we investigated changes in the allocation of resources and their effects on factor prices. It was shown how these changes accompany the growth of U.S. regions. In this chapter we shall present a model of regional economic growth which generates the observed behavior. The purpose of constructing a model is to narrow, on a priori grounds, the range of possible behavior. Without a model one does not know all of the relationships that may exist or which possible relationships to rule out.

With the aid of the model we hope to show that certain apparently unrelated events can be generated by a common body of economic relationships. In particular we shall show that the relationships which explain the events described in Chapter 6 also provide an explanation for growth differentials and movements of capital between regions. Thus, the model synthesizes three sets of events: growth, capital movements, and changes in the distribution of factor payments.

The analysis is presented in terms of regions of the United States. It does not in fact matter whether the regions of the model are parts of the same country or individual countries sharing a common currency and engaged in free trade with free resource movements. For this reason, the model is useful in the analysis of international as well as regional growth phenomena.

First, we shall describe the functions and variables of the model and its equilibrium characteristics. Second, we shall focus on two independent disturbances which yield changes in the allocation of resources and in factor payments. These disturbances are a change in export prices and a change in the inter-sectoral wage differential. We shall derive an equation for the growth of wage payments and the payments to capital: the explanatory power of this equation is subjected to statistical test. Third, we shall show how these disturbances alter the growth path of the region and bring about a movement of capital between regions. The fourth and last part of the chapter is a mathematical appendix which contains the derivations of the expressions presented in the earlier parts.

A MODEL OF ECONOMIC GROWTH[1]

A growth model should serve a number of purposes. First, it should show the equilibrium time paths of accumulation and resource allocation. Second, it should demonstrate the interactions among resource allocation, the payments to resources, and the determinants of growth. *Nation* Third, it should show the reactions of the economic system to changes in the data. Fourth, it should indicate the instrumental variables in the system which are amenable to influence by government policy.

In constructing a growth model for regions of the United States, an even narrower group of specifications must be satisfied. First, the model must show the influence of changes in export demands (prices) on the *Region* equilibrium growth paths of the region. Second, it must show the reallocative processes which occur—for example, the movement of resources between domestic and export sectors, the changes in wage differentials, the influences on the rate of return on investment, and the changes in the supply of labor. Third, it must generate the patterns of interregional resource shifts which have been observed, for example, the movements of labor and capital from declining to growing regions. These goals may be accomplished with the aid of the following model:

It is assumed that the region's economy produces two goods: X, a capital-intensive export good, and Y, a labor-intensive domestic good. The domestic good is consumed at home. The economy uses two types of productive services: the services of labor, L, and of capital, K. It is assumed that capital is indestructible. Both resources are, under certain circumstances, freely movable between the two industries. The economy consumes three types of goods: X, Y, and a third class of goods, M, which are imported and not produced at home. C_x will denote the domestic consumption of X. Corresponding to the three consumed goods are their prices P_x, P_y, and P_m. Corresponding to the productive services are w, the price per unit of labor, and P_k, the initial purchase price of a unit of capital. It will be assumed that savings S are a fixed fraction of the region's produced income Z. Each item of consumption is also assumed to be a fixed fraction of income. It is assumed that all capital goods are imported, at a fixed price P_k, and that business firms may borrow in the national capital market at a rate of return, r, which is fixed. It is also assumed that the labor force is growing over time at a fixed percentage rate, L^*.

In order to examine the economy's adjustments to disturbances, it will be necessary to describe its characteristics at a position of equilibrium. The following assumptions lead to a set of behavior and identity relations.

Export and import prices and the rate of return on investment are fixed:

$$P_x = \bar{P}_x \tag{1}$$

$$P_m = \bar{P}_m \tag{2}$$

$$P_k = \bar{P}_k \tag{3}$$

$$r = \bar{r} \tag{4}$$

The production of X and Y both make use of capital and labor. Both production functions are homogeneous of the first degree in their respective inputs. Export production is capital-intensive relative to domestic goods production:

$$X = f(L_x, K_x) \tag{5}$$

$$Y = h(L_y, K_y) \tag{6}$$

The money wage in exports equals the value of the marginal product of labor in that industry. The same holds true in the domestic sector:

$$w_x = P_x f_L \tag{7}$$

where f_L is the marginal physical productivity of labor in exports.

$$w_y = P_y h_L \tag{8}$$

where h_L is the marginal physical productivity of labor in the domestic sector.

The money wage in the export sector is higher than the money wage in the domestic sector. The differential is an exogenously determined constant. The purpose of this assumption is to provide an explicit variable for later analysis of changes in the differential:

$$w_x = \gamma w_y \tag{9}$$

$$\gamma = \bar{\gamma} > 1 \tag{10}$$

There is full employment of both resources:

$$L_x + L_y = \bar{L} \tag{11}$$

$$K_x + K_y = \bar{K} \tag{12}$$

The rate of return on capital in both productive sectors equals the borrowing rate set in the national market:

$$\bar{r}\bar{P}_k = \bar{P}_x f_k \tag{13}$$

where f_k is the marginal physical productivity of capital in exports.

$$\bar{r}\bar{P}_k = P_y h_k \tag{14}$$

where h_k is the marginal physical productivity of capital in Y.

The social product of the region equals the money value of the final goods and services produced:

$$Z \equiv XP_x + YP_y \tag{15}$$

The expenditure of the social product is divided between savings and the consumption of the three types of goods, each drawing a fixed percentage of income. We are assuming the absence of net income payments to foreign owners of capital. That is, we assume the absence of any past net foreign lending or borrowing:[2]

$$Z = S + C_x P_x + MP_m + YP_y \tag{16}$$

$$C_x P_x = cZ \tag{17}$$

$$YP_y = dZ \tag{18}$$

$$S = sZ \tag{19}$$

Note that the relation $MP_M = (1 - c - d - s)Z$ is implied by the preceding four equations.

The growth rate of the labor force is a demographically determined constant:

$$\frac{dL}{dt}\frac{1}{L} \equiv L^* = \lambda \tag{20}$$

The growth rate of the capital stock during a given period is defined equal to the ratio of investment to the initial stock of capital:

$$\frac{dK}{dt}\frac{1}{K} \equiv K^* \equiv \frac{I}{K} \tag{21}$$

$$\varepsilon \equiv \frac{L_x}{L} \tag{22}$$

This last equation is a definition of the share of the labor force in the export sector. It will play a key role in the changes to be analyzed.

There is an accounting identity that the money value of income Z is the sum of the wages bill W and the payments to capital R:

$$Z \equiv W + R \tag{23}$$

$$W \equiv w_x L_x + w_y L_y \tag{24}$$

$$R \equiv r P_k (K_x + K_y) \tag{25}$$

We now have 25 equations in 24 unknowns. One equation is redundant. For example, we do not need Equation (12), which states that the supply and the demand for capital are equal. The reason, simply stated, is that the satisfaction of the marginal conditions [Equations (7), (8), (13), and (14)] at the equilibrium prices and the equality of aggregate demand and supply [Equation (16)] imply that the actual capital stock K equals the desired stock $(K_x + K_y)$.

These variables may take on different values through time, and they should be thought of as having time subscripts. There are, however, no lagged relations, so that the subscripts will be omitted. Only the stock of capital has a time dimension different from that of the other variables. The stock of capital will have one value at the beginning of a period and another at the end, owing to a positive rate of investment.

The economy depicted in the above system is growing through time at an equilibrium rate determined by the rate of growth of the labor supply. (See Proof a at the end of this chapter.) This follows from the assumptions that all externally determined prices are held constant and that technological change is absent. The equilibrium growth path is balanced in the sense that the two sectors maintain constant shares of the labor force, and their output values maintain constant shares of regional product. In addition, the shares of output paid to labor and capital bear a constant proportion to each other.

In this model the allocation of resources between the two sectors is determined by the external prices, P_k, P_x, and r, as may be seen by reproducing the box diagram of Chapter 6 (Figure 7.1). The contract curve is defined as the set of points for which it is impossible to raise the output of X for a given level of Y. This definition implies that the value of the marginal product of labor is equal in the two sectors ($w_x = w_y$, or $\gamma = 1$) and that the value of the marginal product of capital is equal in the two sectors ($P_x f_k = P_y h_k$). We wish, however, to consider cases where $\gamma \neq 1$, where the wage in X exceeds the wage in Y. For each given value of γ greater than unity, we shall get a contract curve above the given curve for which $\gamma = 1$. The ratio of labor to capital in Y will be greater than the ratio that would prevail if $\gamma = 1$. Hence, the "inefficient contract curve" $YDFX$ is above the contract curve $YMEX$.

We can now demonstrate that with given stocks of labor and capital the allocation of resources is determined by the external prices P_k, P_x, and r. If we look at Equation (13), $\bar{r}\bar{P}_k = \bar{P}_x f_K$, we see that these external prices determine the value of f_K, the marginal physical product of capital in exports. Under the assumption that the production function is homogeneous of first degree, the value of f_K determines the ratio of labor to capital in the export sector. This is shown in Figure 7.1 as the ray out of the X origin which intersects points E and D. A given, assumed, value of γ tells us which contract curve we are on. Suppose we are on the contract

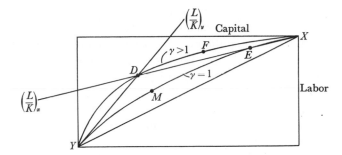

FIGURE 7.1

curve with point D. Then we have determined the ratio of labor to capital in the Y sector and the physical amounts of X and Y produced. In addition, we can determine the price of Y, the money wage in each sector, the return to capital, and the value of Z, regional income. Note that this process leads to the determination of YP_y, the value of domestic sector output, and Z, the value of regional income.

The system depicted does not require the balance of payments on current account $(XP_x - C_xP_x - MP_m - IP_K)$ to be equal to zero, as may be seen by rewriting Equation (15) in terms of the usual national income accounting definitions:

$$Z \equiv \text{consumption} + \text{investment} + \text{exports} - \text{imports}$$

$$\quad\ \ \text{C} \quad + \quad IP_K \quad + \quad \text{E} \quad - \quad \text{N} \qquad (15.1)$$

When Equation (15.1) is subtracted from Equation (16), we have

$$IP_K - S = N - E$$

We see that the region may in equilibrium be an importer or an exporter of capital in the sense that it runs a current account deficit or surplus.

Another feature of this model is the intersectoral wage differential (γ) described in Equations (9) and (10). One may well inquire: Why introduce a wage differential where none is needed to explain the equilibrium of the region's economy? The answer is that wage differentials have been observed, and they have declined over time as the economy has become more efficient. The differential has been generated by labor market immobilities and by lagged adjustment of labor supply to new job opportunities. The lags are due perhaps to tastes, ignorance, and the lack of training. Such differentials are observable not only in American regions but between the rural and urban sectors of other developed economies. We have seen earlier that the narrowing of the wage differential and the accompanying labor-supply shifts play an important role in raising the output level of low-income regions. Output gains are achieved as labor shifts from low- to high-productivity sectors.

A question remains whether we have chosen the most useful way to analyze γ, the intersectoral wage differential. We have a choice between regarding γ as exogenous and allowing the model to determine $\varepsilon = L_x/\bar{L}$, and the contrary case. In the contrary case, the model would determine the value of γ, once we specify an exogenous level of ε, due perhaps to labor market immobilities or preferences for employment in the low-wage sector. As a matter of convenience we have chosen γ rather than ε to be exogenous. It should be borne in mind that when we analyze disturbances in γ, they imply changes in the distribution of the labor force.

A second question is whether changes in γ are independent of changes in the other exogenous variables. If they are not independent, then it is, of course, necessary to introduce an additional relation determining the value of γ as a function of the other independent variables. The evidence on the dependence of γ is mixed. On the one hand, the statistical analysis of preceding chapters would suggest that γ and changes in γ are independent of changes in the other exogenous variables. For example, changes in γ would appear to be independent of changes in export prices. This conclusion follows from the evidence that the states which grew and enjoyed a labor-force shift from low- to high-income sectors did not necessarily receive any differential stimulus in the form of a more rapid rise of export prices. In these states, the stimulus to growth appeared to be the labor-force shift and the more elastic supply of labor rather than the increased demand for exports.

On the other hand, there is historical evidence to suggest that the magnitude of intersectoral labor-force shifts and the elimination of the intersectoral wage differential are related to the level of aggregate demand in the U.S. economy as a whole. The magnitude of these shifts and the elimination of the differential were far more important phenomena in the 1920s, 1940s, and 1950s, during periods of relatively full employment, than they were during the depression of the 1930s. For this reason, it is not possible to divorce γ and changes in γ from the conditions of demand for a region's exports.

What we have done, therefore, is to recognize that the intersectoral labor-force shift may be induced by rising export prices. It may also be an autonomous factor. Nevertheless, we continue to treat the wage differential γ and its changes as exogenous. Thus, we avoid the need to construct an arbitrary explanation for the value of γ. We shall assume that γ is a number greater than unity; further, that when γ changes, it approaches unity.

Still another feature of the model is the factor-intensity assumption made in the production functions, Equations (5) and (6). We have assumed that the export sector is capital-intensive relative to the domestic sector. As we shall explain in the Mathematical Appendix, our specific assumption is that the share of output paid to labor is greater in the domestic than in the export sector. This assumption implies that ratio of factor proportions L/K is greater in the domestic than in the export sector. (See Proof *b* at the end of this chapter.) It will be seen that this assumption is necessary in order to obtain certain results with regard to the movement of capital. It is also necessary to insure that a rise in export prices leads to an increase in the quantity of export goods produced because the price of Y is a dependent variable. A question arises: Why make these particular assumptions about capital intensity? Why not assume the contrary, namely, that exports are a handicraft, with the bulk of the capital used in the domestic sector?

First, it should be clear that some capital-intensity assumption must be made in order to have a convex transformation function. If factor intensities were identical, the transformation function would be a straight line. Reallocation of resources would occur with no changes in relative prices and no changes in factor returns.

The particular factor-intensity assumption is based upon observation of the characteristics of the sectors which are regarded as producing export goods and domestic goods. This issue was treated in Chapter 6. We remarked that the manufacturing-mining sector appears to be more capital-intensive than the other nonagricultural activities classified under the heading of wholesale and retail trade; finance, insurance, and real estate; personal and business services; and construction. In addition, the manufacturing-mining group appears to produce transportable products to a greater degree than does the second group, although exceptions undoubtedly exist. The only domestic sector to violate the above assumptions is transportation and communication, but these industries provide inputs to the export sector. They will enjoy a rise in demand if there is a rise in export prices and output. Consequently, they are in a somewhat different position from other domestic goods, which have been treated solely as final consumer goods. For these reasons, we feel that the factor-intensity assumptions are reasonable.

CHANGES IN THE ALLOCATION OF RESOURCES AND IN THE DISTRIBUTION OF FACTOR PAYMENTS

In the absence of exogenous disturbances, the regional economy will grow in a stable, balanced fashion, determined by the rate of growth of the labor supply. If we conceive of a nation made up of regional economies of the above type, then each will grow at a rate determined by its respective L^*. These growth rates may be altered through migration with consequent variation of L^*, but migration alone cannot alter the equilibrium allocation of resources or the distribution of payments to labor and capital. These can be changed only by altering one of the exogenous determinants of resource allocation: P_x, P_k, r, or γ.

In this section we shall analyze the consequences of two types of disturbances: a rise of export prices, $P_x^* > 0$, and a narrowing of the inter-sectoral wage differential, $-\gamma^* > 0$. It is felt that these two disturbances plus differences in L^* are the three most important influences on regional growth differentials. Because these are treated as independent disturbances, it will be possible to derive separate expressions for the effect of each disturbance on the equilibrium values of the system. We shall be concerned with the effects of such disturbances on the allocation of resources and on the distribution of factor payments.

We shall first examine the effects of a rise of export prices, other exogenous factors held unchanged at existing levels. We may discern the immediate impact of a rise of export prices by referring back to Figure 7.1 and to Equation (13). Recall that the equation states the equilibrium condition for the use of capital in the export sector:

$$\bar{r}\bar{P}_k = \bar{P}_x f_k \tag{13}$$

Using starred superscripts to denote percentage changes, we have

$$0 = P_x^* + f_k^* \tag{13.1}$$

If the export prices rise, the marginal physical product of capital must fall; that is, the ratio of labor to capital in the export sector must fall. In the box diagram the total quantities of labor and capital are given. When the equilibrium *ratio* of labor to capital in X declines, the allocation of the given quantities of labor and capital will change the equilibrium position from D to F. The ratio of labor to capital will also fall in the domestic sector. Wages will rise in both sectors. Because of the greater labor-intensity of domestic goods, the domestic sector price will rise relative to the export sector price. The rise in the ratio of the output of Y to the output of X and the rise in the relative price of Y is a substitution effect *within* a given box. There is also an expansion effect, which will change the dimensions of the box and affect the final equilibrium. The complete adjustments to the rise in export prices require an increase in the over-all stock of capital relative to the number of workers in the economy. The reason stems from the rise in domestic and export prices relative to the price of imported capital goods, which imposes an extra demand for capital over and above the demand needed to keep pace with the growth of the labor supply, as may be seen if we refer again to Equation (13). Write $f_k^* = uQ_x^*$, where $Q = L_x/K_x$ and u is the (positive) elasticity of the marginal productivity of capital in the export sector. Since $Q^* \equiv L^* - K^*$, we may derive the expression $K_x^* = P_x^*/u + L_x^*$. Since $\varepsilon \equiv L_x/L$, the expression may also be written

$$K_x^* = \frac{P_x^*}{u_x} + L^* + \varepsilon^* \qquad (26)$$

It is proved in the Appendix that K_x^* is positive. (See Proof *d* at the end of this chapter.) The growth in the capital stock of the export sector has a secular element, L^*, plus a disturbed element, $(P_x^*/u) + \varepsilon^*$, resulting from the rise in the price of exports. Note that ε^* may be positive or negative. It represents the equilibrium shift in the share of the labor force in exports resulting from the rise in export prices. A similar expression for the growth of capital in the domestic sector is

$$K_y^* = \frac{P_y^*}{u_y} + L^* - \frac{\varepsilon^* L_x}{L_y} \qquad (27)$$

While K_y^* may be positive or negative, it is shown in the Appendix (Proof *e*) that the over-all rate of accumulation for the economy rises as a consequence of the rise in export prices. That is, K^*, the weighted sum of K_x^* and K_y^*, is positive. (See Proof *e* in the Appendix.)

The complete adjustment to the rise of export prices produces a shift of labor between the two sectors. This shift is shown as ε^*, the percentage change in $\varepsilon = L_x/L$. It is shown in the Appendix (Proof *c*) that, when export prices rise,

$$\varepsilon^* = \frac{P_x^*}{\alpha_x} (1 - \sigma)(\alpha_y - \alpha_x)(1 - \varepsilon) \qquad (28)$$

where ε^* may be positive or negative and

$P_x^* =$ rise in export prices
$\alpha_x =$ share of export output paid to labor
$\alpha_y =$ share of domestic output paid to labor
$\sigma =$ elasticity of substitution between capital and labor

σ is assumed the same in the two sectors; $1 - \varepsilon$ is the initial share of the labor force employed in the domestic sector. Within the framework of our assumption that domestic goods are labor-intensive, the sign of ε^* depends upon the value of σ. If $\sigma = 1$, as in the case of Cobb-Douglas production functions, then $\varepsilon^* = 0$. There is no relative shift of labor between sectors. Initially, the output of X tends to contract relative to the output of Y as a result of the rise in the relative price of Y; but capital is accumulated, and the box expands in the manner described previously in Figure 6.4. The final quantity of labor in the X sector (out of a given labor force) may be higher, the same, or lower than it was prior to the capital accumulation. The labor employed at point α' compared with point α (Figure 6.4) represents an increase in the fraction of the labor force employed in the X sector. If $\sigma = 1$, then the vertical height of α' would be the same as the vertical height at α. There would be no change in the industrial composition of the labor force. To conclude, in order that a rise of export prices produce such a shift, it is necessary that $\sigma \neq 1$.

In addition to a possible shift of labor between sectors, the rise of export prices may also alter the distribution of factor payments between labor and capital. We have already seen that the rise of export prices leads to a fall in the ratio of labor to capital in the two producing sectors to keep the rate of return constant. The effect on the distribution of income within each sector depends upon the elasticity of substitution. If the elasticity is less than unity, the distribution will turn in favor of the factor which has decreased in relative quantity, in this case, labor. If the elasticity exceeds unity, the distribution will turn in favor of the factor which has increased in relative quantity, in this case, capital.

Besides the altered distribution of factor payments within each sector, there is an effect on the over-all distribution arising from a shift of relative importance between sectors. If resources shift to the capital-intensive sector, there is an influence tending to move the entire distribution of income in favor of capital. We have seen, however, from the solution for ε^* that this second type of shift also depends on the value of the elasticity of substitution. We may therefore derive an equation for the effects of rising export prices on the distribution of income which depends primarily on σ. The derivation is presented in the Appendix (Proof f).

We have

$$W^* - R^* = \frac{P_x^*}{\alpha_x}(1 - \sigma)[(\alpha_y - \alpha_x)(H - J) + 1] \tag{29}$$

where W^* = rise of total wage payments

R^* = rise of total payments to capital

$J = R_x/R$ = share of total payments to capital going to capital in the export sector

$H = W_x/W$ = share of total payments to labor going to wages in the export sector

The terms P_x^*, α_x, α_y, and σ have been defined.

The expression in brackets in Equation (29) is positive because α_x, α_y, J, and H are all positive terms less than unity. Consequently, the value of $W^* - R^*$ in Equation (29) depends solely upon σ. If σ is less than unity, the rise of export prices leads to an allocation of resources which turns the distribution of factor payments in favor of labor. Note that this expression has already incorporated in it the solution for ε^*. Therefore, it already takes into account the result that $\varepsilon^* > 0$ when $\sigma < 1$. By itself this is a factor turning the distribution in favor of capital. Within the context of the model, this effect is not strong enough to change the above result. We see, therefore, that when export prices rise, the distribution of factor payments will turn in favor of labor if $\sigma < 1$.

Finally, let us note that the complete adjustment to the rise of export prices will yield a rise in the output of export goods. This rise is not shown in Figure 7.1 because that diagram does not show the expansion of the capital stock. It is proved in the Appendix (Proof g), however, that export output rises as a result of the rise in export prices. We obtain the following equation for the rise of export goods output:

$$X^* = L^* + \frac{P_x^*}{\alpha_x}[(1 - \sigma)(\alpha_y - \alpha_x)(1 - \varepsilon) + \sigma(1 - \alpha_x)] \tag{30}$$

The first term is the secular rise in export goods production, and the second term shows the rise in response to the higher price. Note that the expression in brackets is positive for all positive values of σ so long as our factor-intensity assumption is maintained ($\alpha_y > \alpha_x$).

Let us now turn our attention to the effects of the narrowing of the intersectoral wage differential, $-\gamma^*$. We may visualize the initial effects of the narrowing of the wage differential by looking once more at the box diagram of Figure 7.1. When γ declines exogenously from a number exceeding unity to equal unity, we move from one contract curve to another. The ratio of labor to capital in exports is fixed by the external conditions $\bar{r}$, $\bar{P}_k$, $\bar{P}_x$. Therefore, when γ moves to unity, we move along the ray L_x/K_x from point D to point E. This movement represents the use of a lower labor-capital ratio in the domestic goods sector, and it has the following repercussions.

Wages are now higher in the domestic sector and unchanged in the export sector. The price of domestic sector output will rise, and the level of regional income will rise. The price of domestic sector output is now higher relative to the price of imported capital goods. Consequently, the rate of capital accumulation in the domestic sector may increase. Given the total quantities of labor and capital (i.e., the dimensions of the box), the movement from D to E implies that the fraction of the labor force employed in the domestic goods sector will rise and that its output will expand. This is a substitution effect. However, the narrowing of the wage differential will be accompanied by an increase in the total stock of capital available. The dimensions of the box will be greater. In the final equilibrium, the fraction of the labor force employed in the domestic sector will decline, so that the rate of output in the export sector will increase.

The demand facing the products of the export sector is perfectly elastic at price P_x, and the supply of the capital good input is also perfectly elastic. When capital is substituted for labor in the domestic goods industry, the liberated labor is available for employment in the export industry. Since the demand for exports is perfectly elastic, its final equilibrium rate of output increases. Recall that there is no change in the money wage paid in this industry. All that has happened is that the wage in the domestic sector has risen to equal this wage. Since the equilibrium capital-labor ratio is given, capital and employment both rise proportionately. We shall present here the effects of the wage narrowing $(-\gamma^*)$ on the share of labor in the export sector and upon the distribution of factor payments.

The fraction of the labor force in the export sector ε increases as a result of the narrowing of the wage differential. We have (see Proof c in the Appendix)

$$\varepsilon^* = -\gamma^*[\alpha_y + (1 - \alpha_y)\sigma](1 - \varepsilon) \qquad (28.1)$$

Note that $-\gamma^*$ is positive by assumption. The term in brackets is positive. Therefore, the export sector gains in its share of the labor force as a result of the narrowing of the wage differential. For this reason there is a rise of export goods output and an increase in the rate of capital accumulation in the export sector. In the Appendix (Proof h) it is shown that there may be a decline in the rate of capital accumulation in the domestic sector.

Nevertheless, the over-all rate of capital accumulation rises for the economy as a whole.

The narrowing of the wage differential also has a possible effect on the distribution of income. We have already seen that the labor-capital ratio will fall in the domestic sector. This fall will alter the distribution of factor payments within that sector, provided that $\sigma \neq 1$. In addition, there is a movement of labor to the export sector, with the possibility that this capital-intensive sector will become relatively more important in the economy. We may derive (see Proof i in the Appendix) an expression which shows the effects of the narrowing wage differential upon the distribution of factor payments:

$$W^* - R^* = -\gamma^*(1 - \sigma)[\alpha_y(1 - J) + (1 - \alpha_y)(1 - H)] \quad (31)$$

The sign of the large term in brackets is positive. Consequently, the sign of $W^* - R^*$ depends upon σ, the elasticity of substitution. When $\sigma = 1$, $W^* - R^*$ is zero. When $\sigma < 1$, the expression is positive; and when $\sigma > 1$, the expression is negative. The major effect of the narrowing of the wage differential is through the distribution of factor payments within the domestic sector. Even though labor shifts to the export sector, this effect is outweighed in importance by the changes that occur in the domestic sector. The intersectoral effects on the distribution of factor payments appear to be small.

We have now completed the examination of the effects of the two disturbances on the allocation of resources and the distribution of factor payments. We wish to use these theoretical relationships to throw additional light on the events described in Chapter 6. We shall show that the wage behavior described earlier is consistent with the predictions of the model.

Two alternative procedures suggest themselves, but only one leads to meaningful statistical results. We could combine Equations (29) and (31) into one equation of the form

$$W^* - R^* = \beta_1 w_x^* - \beta_2 \gamma^* \quad (32)$$

because $w_x^* = P_x^*/\alpha_x$, as proved in the Appendix. In this formulation, the coefficients β_1 and β_2 have the values

$$\beta_1 = (1 - \sigma)[(\alpha_y - \alpha_x)(H - J) + 1]$$

$$\beta_2 = (1 - \sigma)[\alpha_y(1 - J) + (1 - \alpha_y)(1 - H)]$$

In both expressions the terms within the brackets are known and measurable. The only unknown is the value of σ. If we were to estimate the coefficients β_1 and β_2 through statistical techniques, this would constitute a test of the hypothesis that σ is constant among the observations of the sample. Estimation of β_1 and β_2 would provide an estimate of σ. If σ were not constant among the observations, our technique would be of little value. If, in fact, σ were greater than unity in some observations and less than unity in others, our estimates of β_1 and β_2 would be very close to zero. Some variation of σ is likely to exist in view of the fact that our observations consist of a cross-section sample of states.

There is a second procedure which is more meaningful than the first. It is possible to estimate σ from the expression (see Proof j in the Appendix)

$$1 - \sigma = \frac{W_x{}^* - R_x{}^*}{w_x{}^*} \tag{33}$$

where $W_x{}^*$ = increase in wage payments in the export sector
$R_x{}^*$ = increase in payments to capital within the same sector
$w_x{}^*$ = increase in the wage per worker in that sector

We may use this estimate of σ to complete the construction of the coefficients β_1 and β_2. A description of the method used to construct the terms α_x, α_y, H, and J is found in Proof k of the Appendix. The terms β_1 and β_2 vary from one observation to the next. We may now regard the right side of Equation (32) as the expected change in $W^* - R^*$ under our theory. We may test the validity of the theory by comparing actual and expected values and interpreting whatever errors may arise.

The terms in Equations (32) and (33) were measured in the following manner:

W^* = percentage growth of nonagricultural wages and salaries between 1929 and 1953
$W_x{}^*$ = percentage growth of manufacturing and mining wages and salaries in the same period
$w_x{}^*$ = percentage growth of manufacturing and mining wages and salaries per worker in the same period
R^* = percentage growth of nonagricultural income produced by capital
$R_x{}^*$ = percentage growth of income produced by capital in manufacturing and mining
$-\gamma^*$ = $w_y{}^* - w_x{}^*$ = difference between percentage growth of wages and salaries per worker in the domestic sector and the same for the manufacturing-mining sector

All these variables were computed for the 48 states.[3] If we compute the right-hand side of Equation (32), we find that the expected changes are

correlated with the actual changes. The coefficient of correlation is
+0.617, which is statistically significant at the 1 percent level. We also
find that the fitted regression line has a positive intercept at the Y axis;
in other words, errors of prediction (actual minus expected) are negatively correlated with the level of the predicted change (Figure 7.2). The
line through the origin shows the prediction that actual values equal
expected values where the expected values are computed from Equation
(32). The equation with the positive intercept is the fitted regression
relation between actual and expected values.[4] It can be seen that the

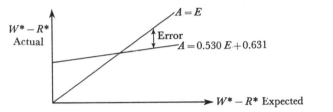

FIGURE 7.2

errors of prediction tend to become negative with increasing magnitudes
of the variables. Associated with this is the fact that the variance of the
expected change exceeds the variance of the actual change.

The regression relation is unusual. Ordinarily, a constructed hypothetical measure of change has smaller variance than the actual magnitude
being predicted. The consequence is that the errors are positively correlated with the actual measured change. In the case being examined,
an error has been introduced into the expected measure of change which
has increased its variance. An examination of the data reveals that the
variation in the estimate of σ is responsible. This is shown in a contingency table of possible occurrences (Table 7.1). The two events
classified by Table 7.1 are the sign of the error, $A - E$, actual change
minus expected change; and the sign of the deviation, that is, expected
change minus mean expected change. Two numbers are shown in each
box: the first is n, the number of occurrences; the second is the mean
estimate of σ, the elasticity of substitution.

TABLE 7.1	*Negative error*[a]		*Positive error*[a]	
	n	$\bar{\sigma}$	n	$\bar{\sigma}$
Positive deviation[b]	16	0.243	7	0.263
Negative deviation[b]	3	0.634	22	0.847

[a] Actual change minus expected change.
[b] Expected change minus mean expected change.

The pattern of occurrences reveals the negative correlation between the two classified variates. The means of the estimate of σ also reveal a pattern. The larger estimates of σ are associated with positive errors of prediction and smaller expected changes in $W^* - R^*$, while the smaller estimates of σ are associated with negative errors of prediction and larger expected changes in $W^* - R^*$. We would expect on theoretical grounds that these errors in σ have produced the errors in $W^* - R^*$, for Equation (32) tells us that, as σ gets larger, $W^* - R^*$ gets smaller. This pattern suggests an error in the estimates of σ, namely, that the variance of σ is too large. There are two possible reasons for this error, and both may have some validity. First, we have used Equation (33) to estimate σ. This method of estimation is correct only if the other independent variables are unchanged. Therefore, there may be error[5] in the estimate of σ_x. Second, we have used the assumption $\sigma_x = \sigma_y$ to derive Equation (32), and we use the assumption in order that the estimate of σ_x will serve as the estimate of σ. Therefore, error may arise if, in fact, σ_x is unequal to σ_y. Examination of the data suggests that σ_x is more variable than σ_y and confirms the suspicion voiced above.

To provide a check on this source of error, the following procedure was employed. Equation (33) was replaced by the following empirical rule: where the estimate of σ fell between zero and 0.6, the value of 0.5 was used; where the estimate of σ exceeded 0.6, a value of 0.75 was used. These two values of σ were then employed to compute a β_1 and β_2 for each state. Twenty-four observations had a σ equal to 0.5, and 24 a σ equal to 0.75. An expected change $W^* - R^*$ was computed and compared with the actual change. As anticipated, these expected changes had a smaller variance than the actual. The correlation between the two, which was still significant at 1 percent, was $r = +0.487$. In addition, the regression equation had a slope not significantly different from unity and an intercept not significantly different from zero.[6]

To recapitulate, we have estimated changes in the distribution of factor payments from our theory of regional growth. Approximately 38 percent of the variance of such changes may be explained by our theory. The unexplained variation is due to other disturbances to the system, which we have failed to include. It is also due to errors of measurement in the construction of the expected terms, particularly errors in the measurement of σ.

We have shown how the distribution of factor payments alters in consequence of disturbances to a balanced growth process. Equation (32) shows the expected changes derived from the disturbances $P_x^* > 0$ and $-\gamma^* > 0$. These expectations are partially confirmed by the data.

THE MOVEMENT OF CAPITAL BETWEEN GROWING
AND DECLINING REGIONS

In this section we shall investigate the influence of three disturbances on the growth of a region's output and upon the movement of capital between regions. These disturbances are a rise of export prices $P_x^* > 0$, a narrowing of the wage differential between export and domestic sectors $-\gamma^* > 0$, and a change in the rate of growth of the labor supply $dL^* > 0$. We saw in the previous section that the first two disturbances could have an influence on the allocation of resources and distribution of factor payments. The third disturbance could not.

We shall parallel the method of analysis followed previously. It will be assumed that the region under investigation is growing in a balanced fashion consistent with the model cited at the beginning. It will also be assumed for convenience that this region is neither importing nor exporting capital; that is, its balance of payments on current account is zero. The purpose of this assumption is to permit identification of the capital movement due to the above disturbances. We saw in Chapter 1 that capital movements are consistent with balanced growth equilibrium paths if there are divergences between regions in their savings patterns, production functions, or rates of population growth and technological change. We shall, however, ignore these possibilities, turning instead to the capital movements that accompany the displacement of the economy from one balanced growth path to another.

We saw earlier that the region was growing at a rate determined by L^*, the growth of the labor force. If we assume therefore that savings equal investment at time t, they will both be equal at time $t + 1$, since they grow at the same rate. Let us perturb this growth path by the introduction of the disturbances and see whether there is a movement of capital. We shall show that the disturbances produce two effects. First, they lead to a higher growth rate of output. Second, they lead to an import of capital from other regions. The reason is that the increased capital demanded by the region's producers cannot be supplied out of the region's savings. The investment rate rises more rapidly than savings. At the end of the chapter we shall investigate the degree of permanence of the adjustments. We shall see the conditions under which the capital import is permanent and the conditions under which the higher rate of output growth is permanent.

Under what conditions will a disturbance to the growth path lead to an import of capital? Assume that in an initial period prior to the disturbance investment equals savings, so that no capital import occurs. Recall that investment is the growth of the capital stock and savings a given fraction of income.[7] We then have $I_0 = S_0$, where $S_0 = sZ_0$ and $I_0 \equiv K_0 K^* = K_0 L^*$. Note that I_0, S_0, and Z_0 refer to flows during the zero period, while K_0 refers to the stock of capital at the beginning of the zero period. Therefore, $K_1 = K_0(1 + L^*)$.

Assume that in the next period there is a disturbance which raises the amount of capital demanded at the same time that it leads to a higher rate of output. Call D the disturbed increment to the growth of the capital stock, and E the disturbed increment to the growth of regional income. During the disturbed period, $K^* = L^* + D$. Therefore,

$$I_1 \equiv K_1 K^* = K_1(L^* + D) = K_0(1 + L^*)(L^* + D)$$

and $S_1 = sZ_1 = sZ_0(1 + L^* + E)$. We may therefore investigate the conditions under which capital import will occur during period 1 as a consequence of the disturbances. We have

$$I_1 - S_1 = I_0\left[D\left(\frac{1 + L^*}{L^*}\right) - E\right] = I_0\left[(D - E) + \frac{D}{L^*}\right] \qquad (34)$$

Capital imports occur when investment exceeds savings, or in terms of Equation (34), if the bracketed expression is positive. What about the long run? Suppose capital imports occur in period 1 as a result of the above disturbances. Does this mean they will occur in later periods as well? Not necessarily. For example, we may investigate the possibility that capital imports occur in period 2, when the economy is again growing at L^*.

If $I_2 \equiv K_2 K^*$, where $K^* = L^*$, then $K_2 = K_1(1 + L^* + D)$ and $K_1 = K_0(1 + L^*)$. Therefore,

$$I_2 = L^* K_0(1 + L^*)(1 + L^* + D)$$

and

$$S_2 = sZ_2 = sZ_1(1 + L^*) = sZ_0(1 + L^*)(1 + L^* + E)$$

so that

$$I_2 - S_2 = I_0(1 + L^*)(D - E) \qquad (35)$$

Thus, in later periods the prospects for continued capital import are different and, in fact, weaker than the possibility of capital import in period 1. Even if capital imports occur in period 1, if $D = E$, they will not occur in later periods.

A numerical example can be used to show how this process works itself out through time (Table 7.2). In the example we shall assume that the disturbance leads to capital import in period 1 but to no further capital movement in later periods, since we assume $D = E$. It will be assumed that $s = 10$ percent, that $L^* = 1$ percent, and that $D = E = 4$ percent.

It can be seen that the disturbance, which raises the desired capital stock and income by 4 percent, leads to a greater rise in investment than in savings, for savings rise by 10 percent of the disturbed rise in income, while investment rises by the amount of the disturbed rise in the capital stock. Note that the validity of the example does not depend upon the units in which K and Z are measured, for a change in units will require a change in s to maintain the initial equality $I_0 = S_0$.

TABLE 7.2

Period	K	Z	I	S	K*, percent
0	1,000	100	10	10	1
1	1,010	105	50.5	10.5	5
2	1,060.5	106.05	10.605	10.605	1

The disturbance leads to a rise in investment which exceeds the rise in savings. Capital imports occur. In later periods we have assumed that no further capital movement occurs. Therefore, the initial capital movement is not reversed in subsequent periods.

Let us now investigate more deeply the expressions D and E in terms of the disturbances. The discussion will focus first on the two disturbances P_x^* and γ^*, which were analyzed in the previous section. Later in this section we shall show the effects of dL^*, a rise in the growth rate of the labor force.

Both expressions, D and E, may be regarded as functions of the disturbances $P_x^* > 0$ and $-\gamma^* > 0$. We shall for analytic convenience deal with w_x^* instead of P_x^*. In Proof l of the Appendix it is proved that $w_x^* = P_x^*/\alpha_x$:

$$D = aw_x^* - b\gamma^*$$

$$E = kw_x^* - m\gamma^*$$

The coefficients stand for the following terms (all the variables were previously defined):

$$a = \sigma + (J - \varepsilon)(1 - \sigma)(\alpha_y - \alpha_x)$$

$$b = \sigma(1 - J) + (J - \varepsilon)[\alpha_y + (1 - \alpha_y)\sigma]$$

$$k = Ac + (1 - A)a$$

$$m = Ad + (1 - A)b$$

In the expressions for k and m, A refers to the ratio W/Z, the ratio of total wage payments to regional product, and $1 - A = R/Z$. In addition,

$$c = 1 + (H - \varepsilon)(1 - \sigma)(\alpha_y - \alpha_x)$$

$$d = (1 - H) + (H - \varepsilon)[\alpha_y + (1 - \alpha_y)\sigma]$$

Expressions a, b, k, and m are positive. Therefore, the disturbances yield a rise in the growth of the stock of capital and a rise in the rate of output.

The analysis on these expressions is carried out in Proof m of the Appendix. We show that capital imports will generally occur in period 1 in response to the disturbances $P_x{}^* > 0$, $-\gamma^* > 0$. That is, $I_1 - S_1$ is positive. In addition, we show that capital imports in subsequent periods depend upon the value of the elasticity of substitution. If $\sigma \geq 1$, the capital import will be permanent, for the stock of capital will in period 1 rise by the same or a greater proportion than the level of output; but, if $\sigma < 1$, the capital import will not be permanent, and in later periods capital will be exported. The reason is that the stock of capital has, in period 1, risen by less than the level of income. Therefore, in later periods, when the economy again grows at L^*, savings will tend to exceed investment.

The above two disturbances are temporary in nature. That is, we assumed a once-and-for-all rise in export prices and the same for the closing of the wage differential. We might also consider a disturbance which is itself permanent, namely, a rise in L^*. We shall analyze dL^* in isolation from the other disturbances. We need not explain why L^* rises. It might rise because of induced migration or because of a change in other demographic characteristics. In the same manner as previously, we would write our expressions D and E as functions of dL^*, the rise in L^*. These are quite simple, however. (See Proof n in the Appendix.)

We prove that $D = dL^* = E$; that is, the disturbed rise in population growth raises the growth of the capital stock and the growth of output in the same amount, so that $I_1 - S_1$ is positive. Capital imports occur in period 1. Moreover, in later periods, the capital movement continues, for $I_2 - S_2$ may be written (see Proof o)

$$I_2 - S_2 = I_0(1 + L^* + D)\frac{D}{L^*} \tag{36}$$

Note that this expression differs from expression (35), where $I_2 - S_2 = I_0(1 + L^*)(D - E)$. The reason for the difference is not hard to find. When L^* rises by dL^*, the disturbance is permanent. The growth rate of the capital stock is permanently accelerated. In the earlier example, when we derived expression 2, the growth rate of the capital stock was perturbed for one period and then resumed its secular level of L^*.

These differences may be seen intuitively in terms of the arithmetic example presented earlier. Suppose that the K^* had remained at 5 percent in subsequent periods after period 1. Then the example would have shown the figures in Table 7.3.

TABLE 7.3

Period	K	Z	I	S	K*, percent
0	1,000	100	10	10	1
1	1,010	105	50.5	10.5	5
2	1,060.5	110.25	53.025	11.02	5
3	1,113.525	115.762	55.67	11.57	5

There would be a permanent import of capital period after period. The reason is that we can no longer satisfy the condition for zero import of capital through time, namely, $K_t L^* = s Z_t$. This brings us back to a point made at the beginning of this chapter. We noted that capital movements between regions are consistent with the condition that they all grow along balanced but different growth paths. We see above one condition making for such capital movements, namely, a change in L^*, or differences in L^* between two otherwise similar regions.

To recapitulate, the model presented provides a picture of an open economy moving along a balanced growth path determined by the rate of growth of the labor supply. We have disturbed the equilibrium by changing the values of three exogenous variables, P_x, γ, and L^*. We have shown that the disturbances alter the distribution of factor payments and the rate of growth. In addition, they produce a movement of capital. We have seen that the hypothesized changes in the distribution of factor payments and in the growth rate accord with the empirical evidence described in the previous chapter. It is more difficult to evaluate the results on capital movements. Data on capital movements between U.S. regions are the subject of current research. Findings by J. T. Romans indicate that capital moves among U.S. regions in accordance with our theory;[8] that is, capital moves from regions of low growth to regions of high growth. This is what we would expect.

The model we have presented is a vehicle for understanding the most important aspects of the growth process. The three disturbances are, in our view, the key to the growth differentials among U.S. regions. In the absence of such disturbances and assuming they all shared the same value of L^*, all regions would grow at the same rate. In drawing such a conclusion, it is assumed that regions do not differ in the rate of techno-logical change or that such differences are dependent upon the three disturbances.

MATHEMATICAL APPENDIX

In the following proofs we shall define only those terms which have not been defined in the text.

Balanced Growth under Equilibrium Conditions

a. To prove that the economy grows at an equilibrium rate de-termined by the rate of growth of the labor force, so that

$$L^* = K^* = I^* = S^* = Z^*$$

We may write total regional product as the sum of factor payments to labor and capital, where W denotes total wages and R total payments to capital:

$$Z \equiv W + R \tag{1}$$

so that the growth of income is

$$Z^* \equiv AW^* + (1 - A)R^*$$

where $A \equiv W/Z$, $1 - A \equiv R/Z$. Note the use of starred superscripts to indicate percentage changes. This notation will be used throughout.

Further write the growth of payments to labor and capital:

$$W^* \equiv HW_x^* + (1 - H)W_y^* \tag{3}$$

where $H = W_a/W$

$$R^* \equiv JR_x^* + (1 - J)R_y^* \tag{4}$$

where $J = R_x/R$

Let us examine the growth of payments to labor and capital in the two production sectors. First look at the total wage payments in the export industry:

$$W_x \equiv w_x L_x$$
$$W_x^* \equiv w_x^* + L_x^* \tag{5}$$

However, $L_x \equiv L\varepsilon$, so that we may write

$$W_x^* \equiv w_x^* + L^* + \varepsilon^* \tag{5.1}$$

It will be proved that $w_x^* = 0$. Therefore, Equation (5.1) is

$$W_x^* = L^* + \varepsilon^*$$

In similar fashion we may write the growth of wage payments in the domestic goods industry:

$$W_y \equiv w_y{}^* + L_y{}^* \tag{6}$$

It will be proved below that $w_y{}^* = 0$. In addition, note that

$$L_y \equiv L(1 - \varepsilon)$$

so that

$$L_y{}^* \equiv L^* - \varepsilon^* \frac{L_x}{L_y}$$

Therefore,

$$W_y{}^* = L^* - \varepsilon^* \frac{L_x}{L_y} \tag{6.1}$$

Finally, examining the payments to capital in the export sector, we have

$$R_x = K_x \bar{r} \bar{P}_k \tag{7}$$

Therefore,

$$R_x{}^* = K_x{}^*$$

It will be proved below that $K_x{}^* = L_x{}^* = L^* + \varepsilon^*$, so that

$$R_x{}^* = L^* + \varepsilon^* \tag{7.1}$$

In similar fashion we may write

$$R_y{}^* = K_y{}^* \tag{8}$$

It will be proved below that $K_y{}^* = L_y{}^* = L^* - \varepsilon^* L_x/L_y$, so that

$$R_y{}^* = L^* - \varepsilon^* \frac{L_x}{L_y} \tag{8.1}$$

Let us now rewrite Equation (2) in terms of the components shown in expressions (5.1), (6.1), (7.1), and (8.1):

$$Z^* = L^* + \varepsilon^* \left\{ A\left[H - (1 - H)\frac{L_x}{L_y} \right] + (1 - A)\left[J - (1 - J)\frac{L_x}{L_y} \right] \right\} \tag{9}$$

We may derive a second expression for Z^* by rewriting the demand condition for domestic sector goods:

$$YP_y = dZ \tag{10}$$

so that

$$Y^* + P_y{}^* = Z^* \tag{11}$$

We shall prove below that $P_y{}^* = 0$. Therefore,

$$Y^* = Z^* \tag{11.1}$$

Let us write Y in terms of its homogeneous production function:

$$Y = h(K_y, L_y) = K_y \cdot j(Q_y)$$

where $Q_y \equiv L_y/K_y$. Therefore, $Y^* = K_y^* + j^*$. However, we shall prove below that $Q_y^* = 0$, so that $j^* = 0$. Therefore, $Y^* = K_y^* = L^* - \varepsilon^* L_x/L_y$. We may rewrite (11.1):

$$Z^* = L^* - \varepsilon^* \frac{L_x}{L_y} \tag{11.2}$$

Let us combine expressions (9) and (11.2) to eliminate Z^* and L^*:

$$0 = \varepsilon^* \left(1 + \frac{L_x}{L_y}\right)[AH + (1-A)J] = \varepsilon^* \left(1 + \frac{L_x}{L_y}\right)\frac{XP_x}{Z}$$

Consequently, $0 = \varepsilon^*$. From this it follows that

$$Z^* = L^* = K_x^* = K_y^* = W_x^* = W_y^* = R_x^* = R_y^*$$

It also follows that

$$K^* = L^* \qquad W^* = L^* \qquad R^* = L^*$$

It remains to show that $I^* = S^* = L^*$. Recall the definition

$$I \equiv K^*K = L^*K$$

$$\Delta I \equiv K^*I = L^*I$$

Therefore,

$$I^* \equiv \frac{\Delta I}{I} = L^*$$

In addition, we have the savings function $S = sZ$, so that

$$S^* = Z^* = L^*$$

Finally let us prove the points passed over earlier. To prove that

$$w_x^* = 0 \tag{12}$$

recall the condition for equilibrium of the capital market: $\bar{r}\bar{P}_k = \bar{P}_x f_k$. In view of the fact that the first three terms are unchanged, we have $0 = f_K^*$. By assumption of homogeneity, it follows that $0 = f_L^*$. Now write the definition of the wage in the export sector:

$$w_x = P_x f_L$$

From this we may write

$$w_x^* = P_x^* + f_L^*$$

Both of the right-hand terms equal zero. Consequently, $w_x^* = 0$.

To prove that

$$w_y{}^* = 0 \tag{13}$$

recall the definition of the wage differential:

$$w_x = \gamma w_y$$

$$\gamma = \bar{\gamma}$$

From these we may write

$$w_x{}^* = \gamma^* + w_y{}^*$$

$$\gamma^* = 0$$

In addition, $w_x{}^* = 0$. Consequently, $w_y{}^* = 0$.

To prove that

$$K_x{}^* = L_x{}^* \tag{14}$$

write the capital market equilibrium condition, $\bar{r}\bar{P}_k = \bar{P}_x f_k$. Recall that $f_k{}^* = 0$. We may write $f_k{}^* = u_x Q_x{}^*$, where $Q_x \equiv L_x/K_x$, and u is the elasticity of the marginal productivity of capital. Since $Q_x{}^* = 0$, $L_x{}^* - K_x{}^* = 0$.

To prove that

$$K_y{}^* = L_y{}^* \qquad P_y{}^* = 0 \qquad Q_y{}^* = 0 \tag{15}$$

write the labor and capital equilibrium conditions for the domestic sector:

$$\bar{r}\bar{P}_k = P_y h_k$$

$$w_y = P_y h_L$$

Introducing percentage changes, we have

$$0 = P_y{}^* + h_k{}^* = P_y{}^* + u_y Q_y{}^*$$

where u_y is the elasticity of the marginal productivity of domestic sector capital. In addition,

$$0 = P_y{}^* + h_L{}^* = P_y{}^* + v_y Q_y{}^*$$

where v_y is the elasticity of the marginal productivity of domestic sector labor. In view of the fact that $u_y \neq v_y$, only zero values of $P_y{}^*$ and $Q_y{}^*$ will satisfy the above equations. Since $Q_y{}^* = 0$, $K_y{}^* = L_y{}^*$.

b. On the labor-intensity assumptions, we assume that the share of output paid to labor in the domestic sector exceeds the share of output paid to labor in the export sector. This assumption implies that the ratio of factor proportions, $L/K = Q$, is greater in the domestic than the export sector.

Write α_y as the share paid to labor in the domestic sector and α_x as the share paid to labor in the export sector, where

$$\alpha_y \equiv \frac{w_y L_y}{Y \cdot P_y} \qquad \text{and} \qquad \alpha_x \equiv \frac{w_x L_x}{X \cdot P_x}$$

To prove that, when $\alpha_y > \alpha_x$, $Q_y > Q_x$:

$$\alpha_y > \alpha_x \tag{1}$$

$$\alpha_y - \alpha_y \alpha_x > \alpha_x - \alpha_y \alpha_x \tag{2}$$

since both α are positive.

$$\gamma(\alpha_y - \alpha_y \alpha_x) > \alpha_x - \alpha_y \alpha_x \tag{3}$$

where γ is defined as before and $\gamma \geq 1$:

$$\gamma \frac{\alpha_y}{1 - \alpha_y} > \frac{\alpha_x}{1 - \alpha_x} \tag{4}$$

$$\frac{\gamma w_y L_y}{r P_k K_y} > \frac{w_x L_x}{r P_k K_x} \tag{5}$$

However, $\gamma w_y = w_x$. Therefore,

$$\frac{L_y}{K_y} > \frac{L_x}{K_x} \tag{6}$$

Changes in the Allocation of Resources and in the Distribution of Factor Payments

c. To prove that

$$\varepsilon^* = (1 - \varepsilon)\left\{\frac{P_x^*}{\alpha_x}(1 - \sigma)(\alpha_y - \alpha_x) - \gamma^*[\alpha_y + (1 - \alpha_y)\sigma]\right\} \tag{1}$$

By giving either disturbance a zero value, one may derive Equations (28) and (28.1) shown in the text of this chapter. Write the definition of the region's product:

$$Z \equiv W_x + W_y + R_x + R_y \tag{2}$$

Define $\alpha_x \equiv L_x f_L / X$, $\alpha_y \equiv L_y h_L / Y$, $V \equiv X P_x / Z$, etc. Write the percentage change in product:

$$Z^* \equiv \alpha_x V W_x^* + \alpha_y(1 - V)W_y^* + (1 - \alpha_x)V R_x^* \\ + (1 - \alpha_y)(1 - V)R_y^* \tag{3}$$

The four terms may be decomposed as follows:

$$W_x{}^* \equiv w_x{}^* + L^* + \varepsilon^* = w_y{}^* + \gamma^* + L^* + \varepsilon^*$$

$$W_y{}^* \equiv w_y{}^* + L^* - \varepsilon^* \frac{L_x}{L_y}$$

$$R_x{}^* = K_x{}^* \equiv L_x{}^* - Q_x{}^*$$

$$R_y{}^* = K_y{}^* \equiv L_y{}^* - Q_y{}^*$$

We shall prove below that $-Q_x{}^* = \sigma_x w_x{}^*$ and that $-Q_y{}^* = \sigma_y w_y{}^*$. Assume that $\sigma_x = \sigma_y$, and substitute above. We have

$$R_x{}^* = L^* + \varepsilon^* + \sigma w_x{}^* = L^* + \varepsilon^* + \sigma w_y{}^* + \sigma \gamma^*$$

$$R_y{}^* = L^* - \varepsilon^* \frac{L_x}{L_y} + \sigma w_y{}^*$$

When these four terms are substituted into the above expression for Z^*, we obtain

$$Z^* = L^* + w_y{}^* [V \cdot D + (1 - V)B]$$

$$+ \varepsilon^* \left[V - (1 - V)\frac{L_x}{L_y} \right] + \gamma^* V \cdot D \quad (4)$$

where $D \equiv \alpha_x + (1 - \alpha_x)\sigma$

$$B \equiv \alpha_y + (1 - \alpha_y)\sigma$$

We may obtain a second relationship in Z^* by investigating the demand for domestic sector products. We have $Y \cdot P_y = dZ$, so that $Y^* + P_y{}^* = Z^*$. We shall prove below that

$$P_y{}^* = \alpha_y w_y{}^*$$

and that

$$Y^* = L^* - \varepsilon^* \frac{L_x}{L_y} + w_y{}^*(1 - \alpha_y)\sigma$$

so that

$$Z^* = L^* - \varepsilon^* \frac{L_x}{L_y} + w_y{}^*[\alpha_y + (1 - \alpha_y)\sigma] \quad (5)$$

When Equation (5) is subtracted from Equation (4), we solve for ε^*:

$$\varepsilon^* = \frac{w_y{}^*[B - D] - \gamma^* D}{1 + L_x/L_y} \quad (6)$$

However, note that

$$w_y{}^* = w_x{}^* - \gamma^*$$

$$B - D = (1 - \sigma)(\alpha_y - \alpha_x)$$

$$1 + \frac{L_x}{L_y} = \frac{1}{1 - \varepsilon}$$

In addition, we shall prove that $w_x{}^* = P_x{}^*/\alpha_x$. When these expressions are substituted into Equation (6), we obtain Equation (1), the solution for ε^*.

To prove that

$$-Q_x{}^* = \sigma w_x{}^* \tag{1}$$

and

$$-Q_y{}^* = \sigma w_y{}^* \tag{2}$$

recall Equation (13) of the text, $\bar{r}\bar{P}_k = \bar{P}_x f_k$. Introduce the rise of export prices:

$$0 = P_x{}^* + f_k{}^* = P_x{}^* + u_x Q_x{}^* \tag{3}$$

Therefore,

$$-Q^* = \frac{P_x{}^*}{u_x} \tag{4}$$

We shall prove below that $\alpha_x w_x{}^* = P_x{}^*$ and that $\alpha_x/u_x = \sigma$. When these equations are substituted into Equation (4), we obtain Equation (1). A similar procedure may be used to derive Equation (2).

To prove that

$$P_x{}^* = \alpha_x w_x{}^* \tag{1}$$

and

$$P_y{}^* = \alpha_y w_y{}^* \tag{2}$$

recall Equations (13) and (7) of the text, $\bar{r}\bar{P}_k = \bar{P}_x f_k$, $w_x = \bar{P}_x f_L$. Introducing the rise in export prices, we have

$$0 = P_x{}^* + u_x Q_x{}^* \tag{3}$$

$$w_x{}^* = P_x{}^* + v_x Q_x{}^* = P_x{}^* \left(\frac{u - v}{u}\right) \tag{4}$$

We shall prove below that $(u - v)/u = 1/\alpha$. The same procedure applies to Equation (2).

To prove that

$$Y^* = L^* - \varepsilon^* \frac{L_x}{L_y} + w_y{}^*(1 - \alpha_y)\sigma \tag{1}$$

write Y in terms of its homogeneous production function:

$$Y = K_y j(Q_y)$$

$$Y^* = K_y^* + j^*$$

However, $j^* = \alpha_y Q_y^*$, by definition. Therefore,

$$Y^* = K_y^* + \alpha_y Q_y^* = L_y^* - (1 - \alpha) Q_y^*$$

$$= L^* - \varepsilon^* \frac{L_x}{L_y} - (1 - \alpha_y) Q_y^* \qquad (2)$$

However, $-Q_y^* = \sigma w_y^*$. Therefore, substituting in Equation (2), we obtain Equation (1).

To prove that $(u - v)/u = 1/\alpha$, write the homeogeneous production function $X = f(L, K) = K \cdot g(Q)$. Write the following first and second derivatives:

$$f_L = g' \qquad f_k = g - Qg'$$

$$f_{LQ} = g'' \qquad f_{KQ} = -Qg''$$

The elasticity of the marginal productivity of labor is defined as $v \equiv f_L^*/Q^* = Qf_{LQ}/f_L = Qg''/g$. Similarly, for the elasticity of the marginal productivity of capital, we have $u \equiv Qf_{KQ}/f_K = -QQg''/(g - Qg')$. It follows from these definitions that

$$u - v = \frac{-Qg''g}{g'(g - Qg')} = \frac{uX}{Lf_L}$$

Therefore,

$$\frac{u - v}{u} = \frac{X}{Lf_L} = \frac{1}{\alpha}$$

To prove that $\alpha/u = \sigma$, the elasticity of substitution σ is defined as minus the ratio of the percentage change in factor proportions to the percentage change in marginal productivities:

$$\sigma \equiv \frac{-(L/K)^*}{(f_L/f_K)^*} = \frac{-Q^*}{f_L^* - f_K^*} = \frac{-Q^*}{vQ^* - uQ^*} = \frac{1}{u - v}$$

In addition, $\alpha = u/(u - v)$. Therefore, $\sigma = \alpha/u$.

d. To prove that the growth rate of capital in the export sector is increased when there is a rise of export prices, the wage differential remaining constant, we have

$$K_x^* = \frac{P_x^*}{u_x} + \varepsilon^* + L^* \qquad (1)$$

This results from the disturbance $P_x^* > 0$ to Equation (13) in the text. Recall that $1/u_x = \sigma/\alpha_x$. Substitute the solution for ε^* to obtain

$$K_x^* = L^* + \frac{P_x^*}{\alpha_x} [\sigma + (1 - \sigma)(\alpha_y - \alpha_x)(1 - \varepsilon)] \qquad (2)$$

The expression in brackets is positive for all nonnegative values of σ, as long as the factor-intensity assumption $\alpha_y > \alpha_x$ is maintained.

  e. By a similar argument it can be shown that the rise of export prices has no definite effect on K_y^*, the growth of capital in the domestic sector:

$$K_y^* = \frac{P_y^*}{u_y} + L^* - \varepsilon^* \frac{L_x}{L_y} \qquad (1)$$

Note that

$$\frac{P_y^*}{u_y} = \frac{P_x^*}{u_x} \qquad (2)$$

This follows from the equalities

$$w_x^* = w_y^* \qquad P_x^* = \alpha_x w_x^* \qquad P_y^* = \alpha_y w_y^* \qquad \frac{1}{u} = \frac{\sigma}{\alpha} \qquad \sigma_x = \sigma_y$$

Substitute the value of ε^* and note that

$$\frac{L_x}{L} = \frac{\varepsilon}{1 - \varepsilon} \qquad (3)$$

We obtain

$$K_y^* = L^* + \frac{P_x^*}{\alpha_x} [\sigma - (1 - \sigma)(\alpha_y - \alpha_x)\varepsilon] \qquad (4)$$

The expression in brackets is not positive for all values of σ when $\alpha_y > \alpha_x$.
  To prove that the over-all rate of capital accumulation is increased when export prices rise, that is,

$$K^* \equiv J(K_x^*) + (1 - J)(K_y^*) \qquad (5)$$

where $J \equiv R_x/R = K_x/K$, substitute the previously derived expressions for K_x^* and K_y^*:

$$K^* = L^* + \frac{P_x^*}{\alpha_x} \cdot \sigma + \frac{P_x^*}{\alpha_x} (J - \varepsilon)(1 - \sigma)(\alpha_y - \alpha_x)$$

$$= L^* + \frac{P_x^*}{\alpha_x} \{\sigma [1 - (J - \varepsilon)(\alpha_y - \alpha_x)] + (J - \varepsilon)(\alpha_y - \alpha_x)\} \qquad (6)$$

All terms in the equation are positive; $\alpha_y - \alpha_x$ is positive and less than unity by assumption. We shall show below that $J - \varepsilon$, which is less than unity, is positive when $\alpha_y - \alpha_x$ is positive.

To prove that $J - \varepsilon$ is positive when $\alpha_y - \alpha_x$ is positive, we shall prove (1) that $H > \varepsilon$ and (2) that $J > H$:

$$H \equiv \frac{W_x}{W} = \frac{W_x}{W_x + W_y}$$

$$\varepsilon \equiv \frac{L_x}{L} = \frac{w_x L_x}{w_x L_x + w_y L_y \gamma} = \frac{W_x}{W_x + W_y \gamma}$$

Therefore, $H \geq \varepsilon$, since $\gamma \geq 1$. We have $J \equiv R_x/R$. Introduce $V \equiv XP_x/Z$, $1 - A = R/Z$, $1 - \alpha_x = R_x/(X \cdot P_x)$. Therefore,

$$J = \frac{(1 - \alpha_x)V}{1 - A} \quad \text{and} \quad H = \frac{\alpha_x V}{A}$$

Consequently,

$$J - H = \frac{V(1 - V)}{A(1 - A)}(\alpha_y - \alpha_x)$$

f. To prove that, when export prices rise, the wage differential remaining unchanged,

$$W^* - R^* = \frac{P_x{}^*}{\alpha_x}(1 - \sigma)[(\alpha_y - \alpha_x)(H - J) + 1] \qquad (1)$$

we shall derive the equation in parts, treating W^* and R^* separately:

$$W^* = H \cdot W_x{}^* + (1 - H)W_y{}^* \qquad (2)$$

where $H = W_x/W$. By assumption $w_x{}^* = w_y{}^*$, since γ is assumed to be unchanged. Therefore,

$$W_x{}^* = L^* + \varepsilon^* + w_x{}^* \qquad (3)$$

$$W_y{}^* = L^* - \varepsilon^* \frac{L_x}{L_y} + w_x{}^* \qquad (4)$$

Therefore,

$$W^* = L^* + \frac{P_x{}^*}{\alpha_x} + \varepsilon^*\left[H - (1 - H)\frac{L_x}{L_y}\right] \qquad (5)$$

Note that by definition

$$H - (1 - H)\frac{L_x}{L_y} = \frac{H - \varepsilon}{1 - \varepsilon}$$

Substitute the value of ε^* to obtain

$$W^* = L^* + \frac{P_x{}^*}{\alpha_x}[1 + (1 - \sigma)(\alpha_y - \alpha_x)(H - \varepsilon)] \qquad (6)$$

Let us now examine R^*, the increase in payments to capital. In view of the definition $R \equiv \bar{r}\bar{P}_k K$, $R^* = K^*$. Consequently, we may use the earlier expression for K^*:

$$R^* = L^* + \frac{P_x{}^*}{\alpha_x} [\sigma + (1 - \sigma)(\alpha_y - \alpha_x)(J - \varepsilon)] \tag{7}$$

Subtract Equation (7) from Equation (6) to obtain Equation (1).

g. To prove that when export prices rise, export output rises according to the expression

$$X^* = L^* + \frac{P_x{}^*}{\alpha_x} [(1 - \sigma)(\alpha_y - \alpha_x)(1 - \varepsilon) + \sigma(1 - \alpha_x)] \tag{1}$$

write the output of the export sector in terms of its homogeneous production function:

$$X = K_x g(Q_x) \tag{2}$$

so that $\qquad\qquad X^* = K_x{}^* + g^* = K_x{}^* + \alpha Q_x{}^* \tag{3}$

However, $-Q^* = (\sigma/\alpha)P_x{}^*$, so that $X^* = K_x{}^* - \sigma P_x{}^*$. Substitute the solution for $K_x{}^*$, and obtain Equation (1).

h. To prove that when the wage differential narrows, export prices unchanged, $K_x{}^* > 0$, $K_y{}^*$ may be positive or negative, and $K^* > 0$:

$$K_x{}^* \equiv L_x{}^* - Q_x{}^* = L^* + \varepsilon^* - Q_x{}^* \tag{1}$$

However, by assumption $Q_x{}^* = 0$, since $P_x{}^* = 0$. Substitute the solution for ε^*:

$$K_x{}^* = L^* - \gamma^*[\alpha_y + (1 - \alpha_y)\sigma](1 - \varepsilon) \tag{2}$$

All terms are positive.

Now turn to $K_y{}^*$:

$$K_y{}^* \equiv L_y{}^* - Q_y{}^* = L^* - \varepsilon^* \frac{L_x}{L_y} - Q_y{}^* \tag{3}$$

Note that $-Q_y{}^* = \sigma w_y{}^*$ and that by assumption $-\gamma^* = w_y{}^*$. Therefore, $-Q_y{}^* = -\sigma\gamma^*$. Substitute this term and the solution for ε^*:

$$K_y{}^* = L^* - \gamma^* \{\sigma - \varepsilon[\alpha_y + (1 - \alpha_y)\sigma]\} \tag{4}$$

$K_y{}^*$ may be positive or negative. For as σ approaches zero, the term in brackets approaches $-\varepsilon\alpha_y$. Nevertheless, the over-all rate of capital accumulation K^* is increased by the narrowing of the wage differential:

$$K^* \equiv K_x{}^*(J) + (1 - J)K_y{}^* \tag{5}$$

Substitute the solutions for $K_x{}^*$ and $K_y{}^*$ from Equations (2) and (4).

Denote $B = \alpha_y + (1 - \alpha_y)\sigma$. We obtain

$$K^* = L^* - \gamma^*[(J - \varepsilon)B + \sigma(1 - J)] \tag{6}$$

All the terms in the equation are positive.

i. To prove that when the wage differential narrows, export prices being unchanged, the distribution of factor payments changes in the following manner:

$$W^* - R^* = -\gamma^*(1 - \sigma)[\alpha_y(1 - J) + (1 - \alpha_y)(1 - H)] \tag{1}$$

let us first define W^*:

$$W^* = W_x^*(H) + W_y^*(1 - H) \tag{2}$$

By assumption, $w_x^* = 0$ and $w_y^* = -\gamma^*$. Therefore,

$$W_x^* = L^* + \varepsilon^* \tag{3}$$

$$W_y^* = L^* - \varepsilon^* \frac{L_x}{L_y} - \gamma^* \tag{4}$$

Therefore, substituting the solution for ε^*, we obtain

$$W^* = L^* - \gamma^* [B(H - \varepsilon) + (1 - H)] \tag{5}$$

Since $R^* = K^*$, we may use Equation (5) and subtract to obtain

$$W^* - R^* = -\gamma^*[B(H - J) + (1 - H) - \sigma(1 - J)] \tag{6}$$

which simplifies to Equation (1) when we substitute the definition of $B = \alpha_y + (1 - \alpha_y)\sigma$.

j. To prove that

$$1 - \sigma = \frac{W_x^* - R_x^*}{w_x^*}$$

write the definitions of W_x^* and R_x^*:

$$W_x^* = w_x^* + L_x^* \quad \text{and} \quad R^* = \frac{P_x^*}{u} + L_x^* \tag{1}$$

However,

$$\frac{P_x^*}{u} = -Q_x^* = \sigma w_x^* \tag{2}$$

Therefore,

$$W_x^* - R_x^* = (1 - \sigma)w_x^* \tag{3}$$

k. Methods of constructing statistical estimates of H and J are as follows: H was estimated directly for each state from its definition, $H \equiv W_x/W$. We may write

$$H = \frac{1}{1 + \alpha_y(1 - V)/\alpha_x V} \tag{1}$$

We therefore know the value of $\alpha_y(1 - V)/\alpha_x V$. We then estimated the U.S. average value of α_y from Department of Commerce data on national income originating by industrial sector. It was assumed that α_y was the same in each state, but $\alpha_x = W_x/(W_x + R_x)$ was constructed for each state. With the knowledge of α_y, α_x, and H, we computed $(1 - V)/V$. We then constructed the estimate of J, where

$$J = \frac{1}{1 + (1 - \alpha_y)(1 - V)/(1 - \alpha_x)V} \tag{2}$$

Capital Movements

l. To prove that $D = aw_x{}^* - b\gamma^*$, where D is the disturbed rise in K^*, we recall that K^* has already been derived in Proof e, Equation (6). When export prices rise, we have

$$K^* = L^* + \frac{P_x{}^*}{\alpha_x} [\sigma + (1 - \sigma)(\alpha_y - \alpha_x)(J - \varepsilon)] \tag{1}$$

Recall that $w_x{}^* = P_x{}^*/\alpha_x$. In addition, recall Proof h, Equation (6). When the wage differential narrows, we have

$$K^* = L^* - \gamma^*[(J - \varepsilon)B + \sigma(1 - J)] \tag{2}$$

Adding the two disturbances to the secular term L^*, we have

$$K^* = w_x{}^*[\sigma + (1 - \sigma)(\alpha_y - \alpha_x)(J - \varepsilon)] \\ - \gamma^*[(J - \varepsilon)B + \sigma(1 - J)] + L^* \tag{3}$$

where the bracketed terms are the a and b we seek.

To prove that

$$E = kw_x{}^* - m\gamma^* \tag{4}$$

where E is the disturbed rise in Z, we shall first show that

$$W^* = cw_x{}^* - d\gamma^* + L^* \tag{5}$$

Recall Equation (6), Proof f. When export prices rise, we have

$$W^* = L^* + \frac{P_x{}^*}{\alpha_x} [1 + (1 - \sigma)(\alpha_y - \alpha_x)(H - \varepsilon)] \tag{6}$$

Recall Equation (5), Proof i. When the wage differential narrows, we have

$$W^* = L^* - \gamma^*[B(H - \varepsilon) + (1 - H)] \tag{7}$$

When Equations (6) and (7) are combined by addition of the disturbances to the secular term L^*, we have

$$W^* = L^* + w_x{}^*[1 + (1 - \sigma)(\alpha_y - \alpha_x)(H - \varepsilon)] \\ - \gamma^*[B(H - \varepsilon) + (1 - H)] \tag{8}$$

The bracketed terms are the c and d we seek.

Now let us turn to $Z^* = AW^* + (1 - A)R^*$, where $A = W/Z$. Recall that $R^* = K^*$, from the identity $R \equiv \bar{r}\bar{P}_kK$. Substitute Equations (3) and (8):

$$Z^* = L^* + w_x^*[Ac + (1 - A)a] - \gamma^*[Ad + (1 - A)b]$$

Ignore L^*, since it is the secular term. Therefore, the bracketed terms are the k and m we seek.

m. To prove that $I_1 - S_1$ is positive when $\sigma \geq 1$, we may write

$$I_1 - S_1 = I_0\left(D - E + \frac{D}{L^*}\right)$$

Since D is positive, it will be sufficient to show that $D - E \geq 0$ when $\sigma \geq 1$. Write

$$D - E = w^*(a - k) - \gamma^*(b - m) \tag{1}$$

We shall therefore determine when the two brackets are positive:

$$a - k = A(a - c) \tag{2}$$

This expression is positive if $a - c > 0$. Substituting

$$a - c = (\sigma - 1)[1 - (J - H)(\alpha_y - \alpha_x)] \tag{3}$$

we see that expression (3) is not negative if $\sigma \geq 1$. Let us now turn to the coefficient of $-\gamma^*$:

$$b - m = A(b - d) \tag{4}$$

which is positive if $b - d > 0$;

$$b - d - \sigma(1 - J) - (1 - H) + B(J - H) \tag{5}$$

where $B = \alpha_y + (1 - \alpha_y)\sigma$. This expression is not negative if $\sigma \geq 1$. Thus, we see that $(D - E) \geq 0$ when $\sigma \geq 1$.

To show that, when $\sigma < 1$, other empirical restrictions on a, k, b, and m are sufficient to make $I_1 - S_1 > 0$, write

$$I_1 - S_1 = I_0\left(D - E + \frac{D}{L^*}\right) \tag{1}$$

Substitute for D and E:

$$I_1 - S_1 = I_0L^* [w_x^*(a + aL^* - kL^*) - \gamma^*(b + bL^* - mL^*)] \tag{2}$$

Since w_x^* and $-\gamma^*$ are positive, it will suffice to show that their coefficients are positive. The term $a + aL^* - kL^* > 0$ when

$$\frac{a - k}{a} > -\frac{1}{L^*}$$

Substitute for k:

$$\frac{a - k}{a} = \frac{A(a - c)}{a}$$

Therefore, we must determine when

$$\frac{a - c}{a} > -\frac{1}{AL^*} \qquad (3)$$

where

$$\frac{a - c}{a} = \frac{(\sigma - 1)[1 - (J - H)(\alpha_y - \alpha_x)]}{\sigma + (1 - \sigma)(\alpha_y - \alpha_x)(J - \varepsilon)} \qquad (4)$$

The following empirical restrictions have been imposed to find the range of values of σ sufficient to satisfy inequality (3). These values are consistent with the data used to generate the estimates of $W^* - R^*$ in the text. Assume $L^* = 0.03$, $\alpha_x = 0.6$, $\alpha_y = 0.9$, $V = 0.5$, and $\gamma = 1.25$. Then we derive from the definitions the following values: $A = 0.75$, $J = 0.8$, $H = 0.4$, and $\varepsilon = 0.35$. When these numbers are substituted into expression (4), we find that σ need only be greater than -0.14 to satisfy the inequality. Thus, the above empirical restrictions plus the defined nonnegative value of σ combine to satisfy the inequality.

Let us turn to the coefficient of $-\gamma^*$ in Equation (2). The term $b + bL^* - mL^* > 0$ when

$$\frac{b - m}{b} = A\frac{(b - d)}{b} > -\frac{1}{L^*}$$

Substitute for m:

$$\frac{b - m}{b} = A\frac{(b - d)}{b}$$

Therefore, we must determine when

$$\frac{b - d}{b} > -\frac{1}{AL^*} \qquad (5)$$

where

$$\frac{b - d}{b} = \frac{B(J - H) + \sigma(1 - J) - (1 - H)}{B(J - \varepsilon) + \sigma(1 - J)}$$

$$B = \alpha_y + (1 - \alpha_y)\sigma \qquad (6)$$

If we employ the same empirical values as before for A, L^*, α_y, H, J, and ε, we find that inequality (5) is satisfied when $\sigma > -1.5$. Thus, the above empirical restrictions plus the nonnegative value of σ combine to satisfy the inequality.

n. Finally we shall consider the disturbance $dL^* > 0$. We shall examine this disturbance by itself, assuming no other disturbance.

To prove that $D = E = dL^*$, look back at expression (2) for R^*. Note that D is the disturbed rise in R^*, where, by assumption, $w_x^* = 0$ and $\gamma^* = 0$. Therefore, the only change in R^* is the change in L^*. Consequently, $D = dL^*$. By a similar argument the disturbed rise in wage payments is dL^*. Consequently,

$$E = A \cdot dL^* + (1 - A)dL^* = dL^*$$

o. To prove that when $D = dL^*$,

$$I_2 - S_2 = I_0(1 + L^* + D)\frac{D}{L^*}$$

we have $I_2 \equiv K_2 K_2^*$, where $K_2^* = L^* + D$ and $K_2 = K_1(1 + L^* + D)$, where $K_1 = K_0(1 + L^*)$. This means that capital was growing at the rate L^* during period 0 and at the rate $L^* + D$ in periods 1 and 2. Therefore,

$$I_2 = K_0(1 + L^*)(1 + L^* + D)(L^* + D)$$

In similar fashion we may write $S_2 = sZ_2$, where $Z_2 = Z_1(1 + L^* + D)$, $Z_1 = Z_0(1 + L^* + D)$, so that

$$S_2 = sZ_0(1 + L^* + D)^2$$

Therefore,

$$I_2 - S_2 = K_0 L^*(1 + L^* + D)\left[\frac{(1 + L^*)(L^* + D)}{L^*} - (1 + L^* + D)\right]$$

$$= I_0(1 + L^* + D)\frac{D}{L^*}$$

8. INTERTEMPORAL EFFICIENCY AND ACTUAL GROWTH PATTERNS[1]

Efficiency is a situation that cannot be improved upon without some cost. There may be efficiency during each period of time such that the production of good A cannot be increased without sacrificing some of good B. Graphically, this means that the economy is on the boundary of a negatively sloped production possibility curve. Nevertheless, the entire pattern[2] of growth over time could be inefficient. An alternative program may exist such that the economy could have the same physical consumption in period t as before and also have more of some, and no less of other, goods at period $t + 1$. If the growth program is inefficient, then the adoption of an alternative program could make some people better off without making anyone worse off than before. Social welfare *could* be increased by substituting an efficient pattern for an inefficient pattern and by redistributing the gains thereby resulting. A necessary condition for maximizing social welfare is an intertemporally efficient growth program.

First, we analyze the concept of an efficient growth program. It is shown that in a competitive economy with perfect foresight there will be an efficient program of capital accumulation. Second, we turn to the performance of the American economy and evaluate the regional and industrial aspects of its efficiency.

EFFICIENT PROGRAMS OF CAPITAL ACCUMULATION[3]

The production possibility curve indicates the maximum output of good A that can be obtained when the economy produces a given (feasible) output of good B. In a competitive economy, where the firms hire inputs at such a rate that the values of their marginal products are equal to the prices of the inputs, production will occur along the production possibility curve. Suppose that the vector of physical consumption[4] desired by the economy in period t is fixed. Then the output of period t less the physical consumption gives the net increase in stocks available as inputs in period $t + 1$. These inputs and the condition that the value of the marginal product of each input equal its price determine a production possibility curve in $t + 1$. To each *point* on the production possibility curve in period t corresponds an entire *production possibility curve in period* $t + 1$.   Figure 8.1 describes the production possibility curve in period t, where the initial stocks of goods less the given consumption is taken as the origin. Any point on the production possibility curve in Figure 1 therefore represents the stocks of goods A and B available as inputs in period $t + 1$.

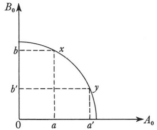

FIGURE 8.1

Production possibility curve in $t = 0$

When point x is chosen in period $t = 0$, then (a, b) are the quantities of A and B available as inputs in period $t = 1$. With these inputs the economy has production possibility curve X in period $t = 1$. The origin in Figure 8.2 is the given physical consumption of A and B in period $t = 1$. Similarly, if point y is chosen in period $t = 0$, the economy will have production possibility curve Y in period $t = 1$.

With the aid of these diagrams, we can explain the concept of an efficient program of capital accumulation. Suppose that the desired vector of physical consumption in both periods is given and the desired ratio of B to A in period $t = 1$ is given.   That is, the community desires to have stocks of B and A in a ratio given by ray $0R$ at the end of period $t = 1$. During the period $t = 0$, point y is efficient in so far as more A cannot be obtained without sacrificing some B. Nevertheless, it is inefficient in terms of the production possibilities existing in period $t = 1$. Point M', reached by producing at y in period $t = 0$, is inferior to point M, reached by producing at point x in the initial period. The economy would be able to consume the same vector of physical consumption and would have more of both final stocks A and B in period $t = 1$, with ratio given by ray $0R$, if it had produced at point x rather than at point y in $t = 0.$[5] If, however, the desired ratio of stocks in period

$t = 1$ were given by ray $0R'$, then the economy should choose point y rather than point x.

Although both x and y are efficient at $t = 0$, both are not efficient in terms of the final stocks desired by the economy at the end of period $t = 1$.

An efficient program of capital accumulation is one that will select a production *point* in period $t = 0$ (i.e., a point on the production possibility curve in Figure 8.1) which will maximize the amount of B for a given quantity of A available at the end of period $t = 1$. It involves choosing the points in Figure 8.1 which will give society the greatest range of choice in the subsequent period.

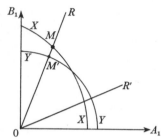

Production possibility curve in $t = 1$

FIGURE 8.2

A simple example of the difference between efficiency at a point in time and intertemporal efficiency can be given. Suppose that an economy can produce seed or fertilizer in a manner described by a concave production possibility curve. Then any point on the production possibility curve is efficient at $t = 0$. Suppose, however, that the economy produces a negligible amount of seed and a large amount of fertilizer in $t = 0$. Then the production possibility set in period $t = 1$ will be very limited. Since the economy produced very little seed in $t = 0$, it cannot produce much output in $t = 1$. Society would have been "better off" if the economy had increased the ratio of seed to fertilizer in the initial period.

Intertemporal Efficiency Conditions. Suppose we fixed the available stock of A at the end of period $t = 1$; call this quantity A_1. Then we want to determine the conditions for a maximum quantity of B_1, the available stock of B at the end of the period.[6]

There are two ways of producing B_1, as described in the following diagram, for a given A_1:

We could use more B_0 (in $t = 0$) to produce more B_1 (in $t = 1$), as described by the arrow from B_0 to B_1. Alternatively, we could sacrifice some B_0 to produce more A_0 in the initial period. This situation would correspond to a movement from x to y in Figure 8.1 and is described by the arrow from B_0 to A_0. With increased stocks of input A at the *beginning* of the second period, we could increase the production of B as described by the arrow from A_0 to B_1. To maximize B_1, given A_1, the increment to B_1 obtained by either route, B_0 to B_1 or B_0 to A_0 to B_1, must be the same. That is,

$$\frac{\Delta B_1}{\Delta B_0} = \left(\frac{\Delta B_1}{\Delta A_0}\right)\left(\frac{-\Delta A_0}{\Delta B_0}\right) \tag{1}$$

where the left-hand term is the left-hand route, B_0 to B_1. It represents the own rate of return on the use of B to produce more B. The right-hand term is the counterclockwise route, B_0 to A_0 to B_1. Some B_0 is given up to produce more A_0 in the ratio given by $(-\Delta A_0/\Delta B_0)$. This represents a movement along a production possibility curve.[7] With the increment of A_0, more B_1 is produced, and $(\Delta B_1/\Delta A_0)$ represents the marginal product of A in producing B. Equation (1) is the Dorfman-Samuelson-Solow condition for an efficient program of capital accumulation. When Equation (1) is satisfied, then society has maximized the final quantity of stock B for a given quantity of stock A available at the end of the final period.

Competitive Equilibrium and Intertemporal Efficiency. Dorfman, Samuelson, and Solow proved that in a competitive market with perfect foresight Equation (1) will be satisfied. An alternative proof of this important proposition is developed in this section in a way that will be amenable to our subsequent empirical work. Whereas they worked with own rates of return and rates of change of price, we shall work with marginal efficiencies of investment. We now prove that if firms invest in such a manner that the marginal efficiency of investment in all directions is equal, then an efficient program of capital accumulation has occurred. That is, if the marginal efficiency of investment in good A is equal to the marginal efficiency of investment in good B, for all A and B, then Equation (1) above is satisfied.

Suppose that there were a common interest rate i, and each firm invested in such a manner to equate the marginal efficiency of investment to the common interest rate. Then a firm which purchases an amount of B in period $t = 0$ at a price[8] $p_B(0)$, to produce more B in period $t = 1$, will have a marginal cost of $p_B(0)\,\Delta B_0(1 + i)$. It will have to recover its initial capital $p_B(0)\,\Delta B_0$ plus interest. The marginal revenue product of B in producing more B will be $p_B(1)\,\Delta B_1$, the value of the additional stocks at the end of period $t = 1$. If there is omniscient perfect competition, then

$$p_B(1)\,\Delta B_1 = p_B(0)\,\Delta B_0(1 + i) \qquad (2)$$

or
$$\frac{p_B(1)}{p_B(0)}\left(\frac{\Delta B_1}{\Delta B_0}\right) = 1 + i \qquad (2.1)^9$$

Similarly, consider a firm which purchases an additional unit of A in the initial period and uses it to produce B in the subsequent period. The marginal cost is $p_A(0)\,\Delta A_0(1 + i)$, and the marginal revenue product is $p_B(1)\,\Delta B_1$. If there is omniscient perfect competition, then

$$p_B(1)\,\Delta B_1 = p_A(0)\,\Delta A_0(1 + i) \qquad (3)$$

or

$$\frac{p_B(1)}{p_A(0)}\left(\frac{\Delta B_1}{\Delta A_0}\right) = 1 + i \qquad (3.1)$$

Now we prove that omniscient perfect competition produces an efficient program of capital accumulation, i.e., satisfies Equation (1) above. Suppose that (2) and (3) are true but that (1) is false. A contradiction will result. If (1) is false,

$$\frac{\Delta B_1}{\Delta B_0} \neq \left(\frac{\Delta B_1}{\Delta A_0}\right)\left(\frac{-\Delta A_0}{\Delta B_0}\right) \qquad (1.1)$$

but $\Delta B_1/\Delta B_0$ is given by Equation (2.1) and $\Delta B_1/\Delta A_0$ is given by Equation (3.1). Substituting into Equation (1.1), we get

$$(1 + i)\frac{p_B(0)}{p_B(1)} \neq (1 + i)\frac{p_A(0)}{p_B(1)}\left(\frac{-\Delta A_0}{\Delta B_0}\right) \qquad (2.2)$$

Under atomistic competition the slope of the production possibility curve is equal to the price ratio for each period of time:

$$-\frac{\Delta B_0}{\Delta A_0} = \frac{p_A(0)}{p_B(0)} \qquad (4)$$

Substitute (4) into (2.2), and we obtain

$$(1 + i)\frac{p_B(0)}{p_B(1)} \neq (1 + i)\frac{p_B(0)}{p_B(1)} \qquad (3.2)$$

or $1 \neq 1$—a contradiction!

Thus, we have proved that it is impossible to have omniscient perfect competition and an inefficient program of capital accumulation. To state it positively, we have shown that if firms maximize their profits and invest in such a way as to equalize marginal efficiencies of investment among goods produced, then the growth program will be efficient.

INTERTEMPORAL EFFICIENCY AND UNBALANCED GROWTH

Balanced growth means that each activity grows at the same rate. If there are m industries operating in n regions, there are mn activities. The von Neumann expansion gives the composition of output that will maximize the rate of growth of the slowest growing sector. In this growth

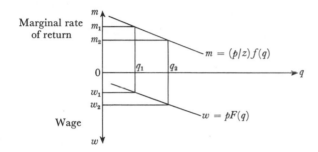

FIGURE 8.3

program, all goods grow at the same rate. Any good that grows at a faster rate will become a free good, and no goods are produced that cannot cover their costs.[10] Not only is this balanced growth program efficient, but it is an optimum way of growing under certain conditions.[11]

We now show how the intertemporal efficiency condition, Equation (1), can be satisfied although regions grow at different rates. Specifically, a given industry may grow at different rates in different regions and yet satisfy the conditions for intertemporal efficiency.[12]

Consider a given manufacturing industry i, which has firms located in n regions. Manufacturing technology, in the sense of a knowledge of production possibilities, is widely diffused within the United States. We can assume that each firm has the same production function regardless of its regional location. Assume that constant returns to scale prevail, but that there is some external limit to the size of firm sufficient to preserve competition. Finally, assume that each firm sells in a national market at the same f.o.b. price and purchases its inputs of machinery and loanable funds at the same price regardless of regional location.

Figure 8.3 describes the value of the marginal product of labor $pF(q)$ and the marginal rate of return on investment $m = (p/Z)f(q)$ for each firm in the industry. The term p/Z is the ratio of the price of output to the price of the capital good input. The ratio of capital to labor is q. Functions F and f are the marginal physical products of labor and capital, respectively.

If the common interest rate were m_1 and competition equalized the rates of return on capital, then all firms would have a rate of return on capital equal to m_1. In the given industry, $p/Z, f$, and F are the same for all firms. Hence, each firm must have the same q ratio of capital to labor. Since the equilibrium values of q and p are the same for all firms in the industry, wage equalization must also prevail in the long-run equilibrium. When the interest rate is m_1, then the long-run equilibrium wage is w_1 for all

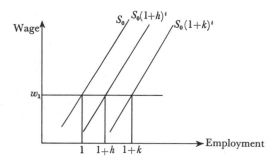

FIGURE 8.4

firms in this industry. We now show that a competitive equilibrium may require unbalanced growth.

When the wage is w_1 and the marginal rate of return is m_1 in all regions (in a given industry), the conditions for a competitive equilibrium are satisfied. No reallocation of labor and capital among the firms in this industry can increase output.

Let the supply of labor grow at h percent in region 1 and at $k > h$ percent in region 2 (see Figure 8.4).

Since at a wage of w_1 employment will grow at h percent per year in region 1 and at k percent per year in region 2, capital must grow at the same rate as employment to keep m_1 constant and equal to the common interest rate. Since the production function is subject to constant returns to scale, output, capital, and employment all grow at k percent in region 2 and at h percent in region 1. Unequal rates of growth among regions then are consistent with, and necessary for, competitive equilibrium under these conditions.

The reason for this failure of regions to grow at the same rates is that labor is not the output of an economic activity. If labor were slaves, then the own rate of return on slaves would be h percent in region 1 and k percent in region 2. The market would shift the production of slaves from region 1 to region 2 as long as the own rates of return differed. Then the economy would exhibit balanced growth. In a nonslave economy there is no reason for all activities to grow at the same rate.

One should note that our situation of unequal rates of growth among regions does not necessarily lead to migration from one region to another. The returns to labor are w_1 everywhere, and employment always grows as rapidly as the supply of labor. Hence, there are no economic incentives for mobility of labor.

DO FIRMS TEND TO APPROACH A COMPETITIVE EQUILIBRIUM?

Uncertainty arising from inexorable change is inherent in the processes of growth, maturity, and decline. Consumer tastes and incomes are constantly changing, and the development of new products and the discontinuance of the production of older products alter the production functions. When prices and production functions are changing, no firm can expect to predict marginal efficiencies of investment with perfect foresight. At best, the firm can hope to be moving in the "right direction." By "right direction" we mean that the higher the marginal efficiency of investment in a given industry, the greater will be its rate of growth. In the world of uncertainty, it is too much to expect that the *ex post* marginal efficiencies will be equalized.

Our analysis of the efficiency of the U.S. growth program is transformed into an analysis of the investment and growth behavior of firms. Several questions are raised concerning their behavior to see if, *ex post*, they have been tending towards an intertemporal competitive equilibrium.

First, are the most rapidly growing sectors those which have correctly forecasted the greatest marginal efficiencies of investment and conversely? If the answer is in the affirmative, then we conclude that firms have the ability to forecast the future with some degree of accuracy and that they gear their growth rates to profit opportunities.

Second, can we develop a method of predicting growth rates based upon the assumptions that firms can forecast the future with some success and seize upon expected profitable opportunities? The subsectors of the machinery industry, an industry not noted for its competitive behavior, were chosen for testing this theory. If a satisfactory predictive method can be developed, then our confidence in the view that firms are tending towards competitive equilibrium is further strengthened.

The Use of Ad Hoc Methods versus the Use of Economic Theory to Predict Growth Rates. The theory of the competitive firm and industry is a logical development of the assumption that, given a set of alternative points on the production function, the firm will select the points which it expects to be most profitable. Many dispute this theory on the grounds that firms are not able to forecast the future, so that decision-making is quite irrational in terms of profit maximization over the long run. If this contention is true, then we would not expect the growth program to be efficient, because marginal rates of return on investment are not equalized.

We must demonstrate that firms can forecast the future with some accuracy and that they do mold their behavior on the basis of these predictions. We demonstrate that a method of prediction based upon the assumption of profit-maximizing behavior is useful and, moreover, is at least as good a predictor of growth as a variety of ad hoc methods which have no rationale. Even if an ad hoc method predicted accurately, and as accurately as a method based upon maximizing behavior, it suffers from three deficiencies. First, there is clearly no reason to expect the same set of ad hoc methods to work for a subsequent period. Second, there is no understanding of why these ad hoc methods were chosen out of an infinity of methods. Third, an ad hoc method can hardly serve as a guide to public policy. It cannot suggest the factors which were responsible for the high or low growth rates. It cannot suggest what policies will or will not be efficacious in raising the region's rate of growth.

Ad Hoc Methods of Projection.—In the past, investigators have predicted regional growth patterns through a variety of methods. Most of these involve a weighting and projection of current or past rates of change. While these procedures are justifiable as exploratory devices, they have failed to provide accurate forecasts; and they offer no answers to questions of causation. Two procedures have experienced frequent employment and richly deserve retirement.

A frequently used method of projection is the application of past trends to predict current or future changes among regions or among the industries of a given region. When public officials ask, "Which industries will grow most rapidly in this locality?" the answer this technique provides is, "The industries which have already grown most rapidly in this locality or in neighboring localities." We shall see in a later section the errors such a method can yield.

Another method which is used is the weighting of growth trends. This assumes that the growth rate of a region is determined by the composition of industries which it contains. If these industries grow at a particular rate nationally, it is assumed that they will grow at the same rate in the region under examination. In order to know how fast a region is to grow, one first predicts the national growth rate of the region's industrial components. The predicted growth rates are then weighted by the proportion in which the components are presently combined in the region; this yields the projected growth rate for the region.

As a test of the usefulness of this second method, we have constructed projected growth rates of manufacturing employment for the 48 states. The projections were built up under highly favorable assumptions. Rather than attempt to predict the growth of the national industrial sectors, we used their actual growth rate over the period for which the projection was made. Thus, in projecting state growth between cycle peaks, we used the actual growth rates of 20 national industry groups. As predictors we used the hypothetical growth rates that were described in Chapters 3 and 5.

The results of these comparisons indicate the weakness of using weighted extrapolation of national growth patterns to predict the growth rate of a particular region. It is clear from the weak correlations that the growth rate of a region does not depend upon the national pattern of demand facing its industries. Differential growth rates are produced because a given industry grows at different rates in different regions.

Prediction Based on Economic Theory.—We derive and apply a method of predicting regional and industrial growth which is based on the theory of the competitive industry. We also show the extent to which these methods are limited in their scope by the available data on income and wealth categories for different regions.

An estimate of the relative marginal rate of return on investment between two regions is used to predict which region will have the greater growth of employment. The economic logic of this view is that business men strive to select the alternative which is expected to be most profitable. They will invest in and thus expand those industries where the marginal return on additional capital invested is expected to be the greatest. If firms act to maximize expected profits, as we assume, then an above-average rate of expansion will take place in the areas where the marginal rate of return on investment is expected to be higher than the average. In so far as capital and labor are complementary in production, the expansion will be reflected in a growth of employment.

Although little is known concerning the formation of expectations, some sensible statements can be made on the subject:

It would be foolish, in forming our expectations, to attach great weight to matters which are very uncertain. It is reasonable, therefore, to be guided to a considerable degree by the facts about which we feel somewhat confident, even though they may be less decisively relevant to the issue than other facts about which our knowledge is vague and scanty. For this reason, the facts of the existing situation enter, in a sense disproportionately, into the formation of our long-term expectations; our usual practice being to take the existing situation and to project into the future, modified only to the extent that we have more or less definite reasons for expecting a change.[13]

The businessman desires to make an investment in a given industry by, say, establishing a new plant. His choice of location of the investment depends upon past experience and future expectations. Future expectations are largely based upon past experience. Consequently, major factors which influence the location of this investment are the marginal rates of return which have occurred in the various possible geographical areas in which investments have been made. His choice will be that area with the highest marginal rate of return in the recent past. Experience will indicate whether the businessman was correct in his expectation of future marginal rates of return. If, *ex post*, the marginal rate of return on investment is lower in area X than in area Y, expectations will be revised in the light of this information. Future investment will be directed towards area Y rather than towards area X. Expectations are constantly revised on the basis of experience, but investment in any given period will be guided by the marginal rates of return that materialized in the previous period.

The actual rate of growth of employment in period t, $L(t)$, is affected by the expected rate of return in period t, $Em(t)$. We assume that the expected rate of return is strongly influenced by the actual rate of return in the previous period, $m(t-1)$. Moreover, the actual rate of return is partly determined by the actual rate of growth of employment. Schematically, the chain of causation postulated is as follows:

$$Em(t-1) \rightarrow L(t-1) \rightarrow m(t-1) \rightarrow Em(t) \rightarrow L(t)$$

In this manner one can see why there tends to be a relation between current and past rates of growth of employment $L(t-1)$ and $L(t)$. Our object is to test this hypothesis concerning the causal relationships in the growth process. Specifically, we focus upon the relation between $m(t-1)$ and $L(t)$.

The theoretical basis of our predictive method is as follows. Let us separate a given industry into two sectors which are distinguished only by their geographic location: one sector is New England, and one is the rest of the country. Let us assume that neither sector is in long-run equilibrium, where the marginal rate of return on capital (stock) is equal to the interest rate. For each sector we observe a point (A or B) on its marginal efficiency of investment schedule. The coordinates of the point are the observed marginal efficiency and rate of growth of capital. In

Figure 8.5 the marginal efficiency of an investment curve is denoted by "mei," and the sectors are denoted by "NE" (New England) and "US" (rest of the country), respectively. The dotted lines are the average rates of return schedules in the two sectors.

If we could truly observe the profit results of incremental investment within each sector, then the computed values of the marginal efficiency would equal the same interest rate ($0r$), and the schedules would differ only by their respective rates of investment. Actually, we can observe the

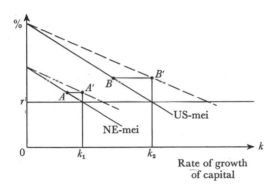

Rate of growth
of capital   FIGURE 8.5

entire investment experience of the firms in the sector only over a given period of time. What we compute as the rate of return is the average rate of return on the investment that has actually occurred. On a rate of growth of capital of $0k_1$, the average rate of return is the ordinate of point A equal to k_1A'; and on a rate of growth of capital of $0k_2$, the average rate of return is the ordinate of point B equal to k_2B'. The computed rate of return on investment will be greater in the sector which is undergoing the greater expansion. This behavior is consistent with an expansion in the number of firms or the growth in the scale of existing firms. In either case there is a greater rise in the demand for labor in the sector undergoing the more rapid expansion of capital.

Ideally, we seek to calculate the marginal rate of return on new investment by comparing the increment of a flow of proprietary income to the purchase price of additional assets. The marginal efficiency of investment is then the discount rate, r, which equates the discounted stream of returns with the purchase price of the additional assets, P. The appreciation in the price of the asset can be viewed as the return at the time the asset is sold. Hence, the yield on alternative investments discussed above is a special case of the concept employed here. The return, R, is total revenue minus total operating costs and taxes. In the continuous case,

$$P = \int_{t=0}^{n} R(t)e^{-rt}\, dt = \bar{R} \int_{t=0}^{n} e^{-rt}\, dt \qquad (5)$$

where n is the life of the asset. The first equality is the standard definition of the marginal rate of return r. The second equality states that there exists a total annual return $\bar{R}$ which can be considered a constant over time.[14]

If we treat all investments as perpetual, i.e., if we assume that replacement is always equal to the current period depreciation,

$$\int_{0}^{\infty} e^{-rt}\, dt = \frac{1}{r}$$

and $\bar{R}$ is now net of depreciation expense. Hence,

$$P = \bar{R}\frac{1}{r} \qquad (6)$$

the well-known capitalization formula. We should like to measure $\bar{R}/P = r$ for each industry and region, but numerous compromises with the theory must be made in view of the available data.[15]

1. The variable P consists of an increment of assets regardless of whether it is in fixed or working capital. There are no data on working capital by industry and region. We are therefore forced to use the marginal rate of return on additions to plant and equipment alone. Symbolically, it means that we can observe only some fraction of P. We should like to calculate $\bar{R}/P$, but we end up calculating $\bar{R}/I$, where I is investment in plant and equipment. $P - I$ consists of investment in working capital.

In so far as the two regions compared have the same ratio of I to P, no difficulty arises in comparing their marginal rates of return. We would expect that for a given industry interregional variations in I/P are small and hence our compromise with the data is not significant. Our independent variable is always the *relative* marginal rates of return, in a given industry, among regions. For this reason, the omission of data on working capital does not seem to be serious.

2. It is impossible to know in advance the future income stream of an investment. Furthermore, the limitations of the data are such that we can measure the value of income to property for only a discrete number of periods. Consequently, we measure the flow of new proprietary income

arising from investment as the difference between the level of proprietary income in two years. The particular years chosen are dictated by the availability of data. Because of our concern with manufactures, we have used the U.S. Department of Commerce Census of Manufactures for three years—1939, 1947, and 1954.

Over the n intercensus years, proprietary income rises by $R_1'n$ in region 1 and by $R_2'n$ in region 2. On the average, annual proprietary income rises by R_1' and R_2' in the two regions.

Our *measure* of the marginal efficiency of investment m_1 is R_1'/I_1 and of m_2 is R_2'/I_2. The *true* r_1 is equal to $\bar{R}_1/P_1$, and the true r_2 is $\bar{R}_2/P_2$.

If $R_1'/\bar{R}_1$ and $R_2'/\bar{R}_2$ are not very different,[16] then m_1/m_2 is approximately equal to r_1/r_2. That is, no significant bias is introduced into our relative rates of return by choosing these intercensus years as our sources of data on changes in proprietary income.

3. When computing the marginal efficiency of investment for a four-digit industry as identified in the Census of Manufactures, we employ the following definition:

Gross proprietary income = total value of shipments — cost of materials, containers, fuels, purchased electrical energy, and contract work
— wages and salaries
= value added — wages and salaries

Gross proprietary income includes depreciation, inventory decumulation, profits, interest, taxes, rents, insurance premiums, legal fees, and other business services purchased. Ideally, to be applicable to regional analysis, the figure should be reduced to net profits before the deduction of Federal income taxes, interest, and rents. Thus, it would be independent of the type of financing used and of the past decisions to own or rent plant and equipment.

4. The marginal return on net investment in plant and equipment cannot be calculated for industries identified in the Census of Manufactures. Net investment is not reported in the Census. What is reported is expenditures for plant and equipment, which is essentially a gross investment concept. What we have computed for these categories is the marginal rate of return on gross investment. This measure is then

$$m = \frac{\text{change in gross proprietary income}}{\text{expenditures for plant and equipment}}$$

In our other studies the marginal rate of return on gross investment has been adjusted so that it may reflect the return on net investment. This adjustment is frequently necessary in an analysis of the regional aspects of growth. Gross investment may include two categories which are not properly part of net investment. One is the replacement of obsolete equipment; the other is the purchase of old plant and equipment which is temporarily undervalued because of a secular decline in the industries using the equipment. In either case, a high rate of return on gross investment may not be indicative of long-run growth potential in a particular industry or area. This problem arose in other studies where the authors attempted to specify the particular New England industries in the chemical and metal-working field which had high marginal rates of return on net investment.[17]

The marginal rate of return on gross investment (m), rather than on net investment, is used as the independent variable in this study. Numerous compromises with the theory have been made in order to develop a predictive tool. The residuals between the actual and predicted growth rates are the sole indicators of how significant are the compromises made. If the predictive accuracy of our theory is high, then the assumptions made (concerning I/P, $R'/\bar{R}$) are not serious oversimplifications of reality. The crucial question is: How good a predictor do we have in view of the data limitations?

Predictions.[18] We are interested in predicting the growth of employment in specific industries from a knowledge of the rate of return on investment in those industries. We calculate this rate of return for both prior and concurrent periods relying mainly on the former as our predictor. The industries are the four-digit members of Census Group No. 35, Non-Electric Machinery. We predict the growth for the New England region; but this method could be used for any region in the country or for any industry for which data are available.

Define $\mu_i = m_{\mathrm{NE}} - m_{\mathrm{US}}$ as the difference between the return on gross investment in the ith industry in New England and the return for that industry in the United States. Also define L_{ij} as the rate of growth of employment in the ith industry and jth region between two periods and $\lambda_i = L_{i\mathrm{NE}} - L_{i\mathrm{US}}$ as the algebraic difference between the rate of growth of employment in the ith industry in New England and the rate for the same industry in the United States.

The values of m_i, L_i, μ_i, and λ_i are shown in the Tables 8.1 and 8.2 for the intervals 1939–47 and 1947–54. These periods were chosen because of the availability of data from the Census of Manufactures. The industry groups are those four-digit members of Group 35 which are represented in New England for the three dates.[19]

TABLE 8.1. VALUES OF MARGINAL EFFICIENCY OF GROSS INVESTMENT, m, GROWTH OF EMPLOYMENT, L, FOR NEW ENGLAND AND THE UNITED STATES, 1939-47, BY FOUR-DIGIT INDUSTRY IN THE MACHINERY GROUP

Industry No.	Title	m_{NE}	m_{US}	μ	L_{NE}	L_{US}	λ
3541	Machine tools	0.0686	0.8601	−0.7915	133.89	148.37	−14.48
42	Metalworking machinery	1.4239	2.1053	−0.6814	191.62	240.40	−48.78
43	Cutting tools, jigs, fixtures	1.3184	1.4548	−0.1364	249.28	288.46	−39.18
51	Food products machinery.	−0.9724	1.2085	−2.1809	92.70	203.65	−110.95
52	Textile machinery	1.1694	1.4633	−0.2939	206.80	201.03	+5.77
53	Woodworking machinery	5.4631	2.1779	+3.2852	363.29	345.93	+17.36
54	Paper industries machinery	0.9595	1.0165	−0.0570	235.33	240.54	−5.21
55	Printing trades machinery	2.0665	1.7159	+0.3506	276.67	204.77	+71.90
59	Special industry machinery	1.0743	1.4325	−0.3582	218.80	247.46	−28.66
61	Pumps and compressors	3.0791	1.5397	+1.5394	279.09	201.16	+77.93
62+63	Elevators, escalators, conveyers	4.1044	3.1842	+0.9202	188.74	263.82	−75.08
66	Power transmission equipment	0.8993	1.1793	−0.2800	156.25	241.58	−85.33
69	General industry machinery	2.0889	1.6074	+0.4815	310.94	205.83	+105.11
72	Typewriters	1.3513	0.9290	+0.4223	125.25	147.19	−21.94
83	Sewing machines	0.6503	0.8782	−0.2279	165.69	161.31	+4.38
85	Refrigeration machinery	0.7221	1.0228	−0.3007	212.32	274.68	−62.36
91	Valves and fittings	0.3497	1.3062	−0.9565	136.21	204.78	−68.57
93	Ball and roller bearings	1.0098	0.7193	+0.2905	205.91	235.21	−29.30
99	Machine shops	2.2195	1.2710	+0.9485	287.67	199.88	+87.79

Source: *Census of Manufactures, 1947 and 1939*, U.S. Department of Commerce, Washington, D.C.

TABLE 8.2. VALUES OF THE MARGINAL EFFICIENCY OF GROSS INVESTMENT, m, THE GROWTH OF EMPLOYMENT, L, FOR NEW ENGLAND AND THE UNITED STATES, 1947–54

Industry No.	m_{NE}	m_{US}	μ	L_{NE}	L_{US}	λ
3541	1.5875	1.3683	+0.2192	117.08	115.65	+1.43
42	0.5115	0.8661	−0.3546	87.14	108.15	−21.01
43	0.4639	0.5602	−0.0963	105.28	137.57	−32.29
51	2.1815	0.0370	+2.1445	318.43	89.92	+229.51
52	−0.4581	−0.3302	−0.1279	54.66	68.30	−13.64
53	3.4703	0.2469	+3.2234	115.92	73.76	+42.16
54	0.2758	0.3948	−0.1190	89.18	87.80	+1.38
55	0.2364	0.2227	+0.0137	77.69	88.26	−10.57
59	0.8690	0.2366	+0.6324	89.69	98.25	−8.56
61	1.6217	0.9328	+0.6889	79.37	107.45	−28.08
62+63	1.4070	1.0772	+0.3298	133.67	122.47	+11.20
66	0.6665	0.5100	+0.1565	122.08	91.82	+30.26
69	−0.0003	0.0756	−0.0759	51.59	80.14	−38.55
72	0.0674	0.3411	−0.2737	68.13	69.29	−1.16
83	0.0963	−0.0052	+0.1015	93.39	81.11	+12.28
85	0.8811	0.4267	+0.4544	121.70	99.69	+22.01
91	0.7649	0.7285	+0.0364	103.57	94.11	+9.46
93	−0.0784	0.0879	−0.1663	80.15	95.30	−15.15
99	1.0698	0.9487	+0.1211	167.19	166.23	+0.96

Source: With the exception of groups 3572 and (3562 + 3563), the entries of this table are derived from Jerome L. Stein and Mark B. Schupack, *The New England Machinery Industry in 1970* (Federal Reserve Bank of Boston, 1960).

Correlations between λ and μ are significant at the 5 percent level. For the period 1939–47, the following regression relation was obtained:

$$\lambda = 30.1752\mu - 14.6925 \qquad r = 0.5496$$
$$(11.1254) \qquad\qquad \text{(significant at the 5 percent level)}$$

For the 1947–54 period, the following regression was obtained:

$$\lambda = 48.94\mu - 6.68 \qquad r = 0.7892$$
$$(17.69) \qquad\qquad \text{(significant at the 1 percent level)}$$

There is a good reason that the regression coefficient and the correlation coefficient of the regression for the 1939–47 period are lower than they are in the regression for the 1947–54 period. This results from the greater errors of measuring gross investment in the earlier period.[20]

Since no data on gross investment for 1939 were available for New England four-digit industries, investment was estimated by multiplying the ratio of gross investment to value added in 1947 by the 1939 value added. In the 1939–47 period the denominator of m is an average of the gross investment *estimate* in 1939 and the *reported* gross investment figure in 1947, but in the 1947–54 period the denominator of m is an average of two *reported* gross investment figures.

There is evidence that the ratio of gross investment to value added differed between 1939 and 1947. Consequently, the errors of measurement of the m variable were probably greater in the earlier period. It can easily be shown that errors of measurement in the independent variable reduce the regression and correlation coefficients.[21] A comparison of the two regression equations above supports this hypothesis. If this interpretation is correct, then the *relation* between μ and λ may have been more stable than is indicated by the equations above.

Tests of Predictive Power. What emerges so far is that the relative rate of growth was positively and significantly correlated with the realized relative rate of return. Sectors which had, in fact, the highest profitabilities for expansion did, in fact, expand most rapidly. The "invisible hand" led the regional firms in the direction of competitive equilibrium. The result is the more remarkable inasmuch as it occurred in the machinery industry, where atomistic competition is not universal.

Our claim that firms act to maximize profits, i.e., move towards a competitive equilibrium, will be tested in the following manner. Three statistical hypotheses are implied by our theory.

The growth position of an industry is determined by its relative rate of return in the prior period. The predicted *relation* between λ_t and μ_{t-1} is given by the regression line for the prior period.

Comparisons were made between the results of this method and the results of a number of ad hoc projection techniques which had no rationale but were devised for this specific situation. Our motivation was: name any conceivable technique, and its accuracy will be compared with ours. The ad hoc techniques took the following forms:

1. Assume $\lambda_{i47} = \lambda_{i39}$ for each industry. This simply projects the λ_i forward from its 1939–47 value to an identical value for 1947–54.

2. Assume $\lambda_{i47} = \bar{\lambda}_{39}$ for each industry. This means that the λ_i for each industry for the 1947–54 period was simply the mean of the λ_i for the prior period. In a sense this implies that the growth rates in the region are a fixed differential of the U.S. growth rate, which does not differ by industry. This technique assumes only a regional effect on growth. This hypothesis will be discussed in more detail.

3. Assume $\lambda_{i47} = 0$ for each industry; that is, the λ_i for each industry

for the 1947–54 period is 0. There is no difference between the U.S. and the New England growth rates in each industry, and there is no influence on current growth behavior from events of the past.

4. Assume $\lambda_{i47} = \lambda_{i39} + \frac{1}{2}(\lambda_i - \bar{\lambda})_{39}$; that is, in the subsequent period λ_i regress back to their 1939 mean value by one-half the difference between their mean and actual values. This is a variant of (2) above.

It should be pointed out that there are no a priori grounds to judge which ad hoc model should be used as a null hypothesis against our theoretical structure. We started with the first in mind and then developed the others when detailed examination of the data revealed a

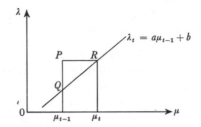

FIGURE 8.6

substantial degree of regression back to the mean among the λ_i between one period and the next. There are no a priori reasons for expecting the λ_i to regress to a common value in a subsequent period. We suspect that it occurred between the two periods under examination because of the economic events going on at the time. The first period encompasses the rapid return to full employment and the expansion of wartime activities. The consequence is that the first period represented a reutilization of capacity for wartime purposes that would have not been renewed in the long run. The second period represents mainly a return to prewar secular tendencies in a number of significant New England machinery sectors.

Two other statistical hypotheses are implied by our theory:

Where an industry's growth was overestimated or underestimated in the prior period, we claim that its subsequent growth position will conform more closely to the regression.

If the estimating equation, $\lambda_t = a\mu_{t-1} + b$, fails to predict the industry's growth rate for the later period, this failure is due to a change in the marginal rate of return.

Graphically, the three hypotheses can be described by Figure 8.6. The regression coefficients a and b are based upon the actual μ's and λ's for 19 subsectors of the machinery industry in period $t - 1$, 1939–47. If P is the rate of growth for a particular industry in 1939–47, then the second hypothesis claims that it will fall to Q during the period 1947–54. If it does not fall, then the third hypothesis claims that μ rose from μ_{t-1} to μ_1: the movement has been from P to R.

As we shall see, this theory, as embodied in the three statistical hypotheses, is consistent with the facts in the case of the machinery industry in New England and the United States.

Tables 8.3 and 8.4 summarize the errors of prediction using the regression techniques and then the alternative techniques. In Table 8.3, we see the values of λ_i which the different techniques specify. These values of λ_i were then combined with the U.S. growth rates to produce projections of employment for each of the 19 New England machinery industries for 1954. The projections were subtracted from actual New England employment in these industries in 1954, and an absolute percentage error was computed. The absolute percentage errors and their unweighted means are shown in Table 8.4.

A comparison of the regression technique with the ad hoc projections shows the former in a very favorable light. In Table 8.4 we see that the average absolute percentage error is 29 percent for the regression technique. This compares with 60 percent for simple extrapolation, with 21 percent for extrapolation of $\bar{\lambda}_{39}$, with 21 percent when we assume no differences between regional growth rates, and with 39 percent when we assume the λ_i regress halfway to their mean. A comparison of performance by individual industries for each technique is shown in Table 8.5.

It can be seen that regression is clearly superior to simple extrapolation; it fares better than the latter in 14 out of 19 cases. It fares slightly better (10 out of 19) than prediction 4. It fares slightly worse than prediction 3 and quite badly relative to prediction 2. The success of the regression method is explained below, where it is shown to be consistent with the theory of growth developed in this book. In fact, it may even be considered a further test of our theory.

Consistency of Data with Our Statistical Hypotheses. How consistent are the data with our predicting theory? The salient conclusions of our theory are as follows:

1. The relative growth (λ) of a New England industry is determined by the relative return on investment (μ).

2. Where an industry's growth is underestimated (overestimated) in period 1, this growth will increase (decrease) in period 2.

3. Failure to predict λ in period 2 from the regression in period 1 would be due to changes in μ from one period to the next.

We have seen the first hypothesis confirmed by the good regression results between μ and λ for the two time periods under examination and

Table 8.3. VALUES OF λ_i FROM VARIOUS PREDICTIVE TECHNIQUES AND ERRORS OF PREDICTION, 19 MACHINERY INDUSTRIES IN NEW ENGLAND

Industry No.	λ from regression	Actual λ, 1939-47	Actual λ,[a] 1947-54	λ_{47} regress halfway to mean[b]	$\lambda - \lambda_{47}$[c]	$\lambda_{39} - \lambda_{47}$[d]	$\bar{\lambda}_{39} - \lambda_{47}$[e]	...[f]
3541	−38.57	−14.48	+1.43	−13.02	−40.00	−15.91	−12.99	−14.45
42	−35.25	−48.78	−21.01	−30.17	−14.24	−27.77	+9.45	−9.16
43	−18.81	−39.18	−32.19	−25.37	+13.48	−6.89	+20.73	+6.92
51	−80.50	−110.95	+229.51	−61.25	−310.01	−340.46	−241.07	−290.76
52	−23.56	+5.77	−13.64	−2.90	−9.92	+19.41	+2.08	+10.74
53	+84.44	+17.36	+42.16	+2.90	+42.28	−24.80	−53.72	−39.26
54	−16.41	−5.21	+1.38	−8.39	−17.79	−6.59	−12.94	−9.77
55	−4.11	+71.90	−10.57	+30.17	+6.46	+82.47	−0.99	+40.74
59	−25.50	−28.66	−8.56	−20.11	−16.94	−20.10	−3.00	−11.55
61	+31.76	+77.93	−28.08	+33.18	+59.84	+106.01	+16.52	+61.26
62 + 63	+13.08	−75.08	+11.20	−43.32	+1.88	−86.28	−22.76	−54.52
66	−23.14	−85.33	+30.26	−48.44	−53.40	−115.59	−41.82	−78.70
69	−0.16	+105.11	−38.55	+46.77	+38.39	+143.66	+26.99	+85.32
72	−1.95	−21.94	−1.16	−16.75	−0.79	−20.78	−10.40	−15.59
83	−21.57	+4.38	+12.28	−3.59	−33.85	−7.90	−23.84	−15.87
85	−23.76	−62.36	+22.01	−36.96	−45.77	−84.37	−33.57	−58.97
91	−17.58	−68.57	+9.46	−40.06	−27.04	−78.03	−21.02	−49.52
93	−5.92	−29.30	−15.15	−20.43	+9.23	−14.15	+3.59	−5.28
99	+13.93	+87.79	+0.96	+38.11	+12.97	+86.83	−12.52	+37.15

a Error from ad hoc hypothesis 3.
b This is the prediction $\lambda_{47} = \lambda_{39} + \frac{1}{2}(\lambda - \bar{\lambda}_{l39})$.
c Error from regression.
d Error from ad hoc hypothesis 1.
e $\bar{\lambda}_{39} = -11.56$, error from ad hoc hypothesis 2.
f Error from ad hoc hypothesis 4.

TABLE 8.4. ABSOLUTE PERCENTAGE ERRORS OF PREDICTION OF 1954 NEW ENGLAND EMPLOYMENT IN MACHINERY FROM VARIOUS TECHNIQUES

Industry No.	From regression	$\lambda_{i47} = \lambda_{i39}$	$\lambda_{i47} = \bar{\lambda}_{39}$	$\lambda_{i47} = 0$	$\lambda_{i47} = \lambda_{i39} + \frac{1}{2}(\lambda_i - \bar{\lambda})_{39}$
3541	34.16	13.59	11.09	1.22	12.34
42	16.34	31.87	10.82	24.11	10.52
43	12.81	6.54	19.69	30.68	6.58
51	97.05	100.00	75.39	71.77	91.00
52	18.15	35.51	3.80	24.95	19.65
53	36.44	21.40	46.31	36.39	33.89
54	19.95	7.38	14.51	1.55	10.96
55	8.32	106.11	1.30	13.59	52.43
59	10.59	14.47	6.55	20.75	3.97
61	75.38	133.57	20.81	35.37	77.17
62+63	1.37	64.59	17.08	8.35	40.77
66	43.74	94.69	34.25	24.79	64.47
69	55.04	259.05	32.93	55.31	145.99
72	1.16	30.50	15.26	1.70	22.89
83	36.26	8.47	25.52	13.15	16.98
85	37.61	69.33	27.59	18.09	48.45
91	26.10	75.34	17.45	5.89	45.95
93	11.51	17.65	4.48	18.90	6.59
99	7.76	51.93	7.48	0.57	22.22
Average, percent	28.93	60.10	20.65	21.43	38.57

by the relative success of the regression equation as a predictive device over simple extrapolation.

The second hypothesis is also confirmed by the data, confirmed so well, in fact, that it almost looks as if the λ_i change sign from one period to the

TABLE 8.5. COMPARISON OF ERRORS OF PREDICTION FOR INDIVIDUAL PREDICTING TECHNIQUES FOR 19 INDUSTRIES

Ad hoc hypothesis	(1) $\lambda_{47} = \lambda_{39}$	(2) $\lambda_{47} = \bar{\lambda}_{39}$	(3) $\lambda_{47} = 0$	(4) $\lambda_{47} = \lambda_{39} + \frac{1}{2}(\lambda - \bar{\lambda})_{39}$
Regression does:				
Better	14	4	9	10
Worse	5	15	10	9
Average error, percent	60	21	21	39

next. Actually, they change sign in 11 out of 19 cases. What is important, however, is the confirmation that the regression relation indicated the change in the value of λ_i by means of the error in the regression. It can be seen by comparing the residuals from the regression with the actual changes in λ_i which occurred in the two periods. This is shown in Table 8.6.

TABLE 8.6

Industry No.	$\lambda_{47} - \lambda_{39}$	$\hat{\lambda} - \lambda_{39}$
3541	$+15.91$	-24.09
42	$+27.77$	$+13.53$
43	$+6.89$	$+20.37$
51	$+340.46$	$+30.45$
52	-19.41	-29.33
53	$+24.80$	$+67.08$
54	$+6.59$	-11.20
55	-82.47	-76.01
59	$+20.10$	$+3.16$
61	-106.01	-46.17
62 + 63	$+86.28$	$+88.16$
66	$+115.59$	$+62.19$
69	-143.66	-105.27
72	$+20.78$	$+19.99$
83	$+7.90$	-25.95
85	$+84.37$	$+38.60$
91	$+78.03$	$+50.99$
93	$+14.15$	$+23.38$
99	-86.83	-73.86

The first column shows the change in λ_i from one period to the next ($\lambda_{47} - \lambda_{39}$). The second column shows the residuals from the 1939–47 regression line. If our hypothesis is valid, we should observe the following: If the original residual from the regression ($\hat{\lambda} - \lambda_{39}$) is positive, the change in λ should be positive. If the initial residual is negative, the change in λ should be negative. In other words, λ_{47} moves away from λ_{39} in the direction of the value predicted by the regression line. An examination of Table 8.6 shows a very strong confirmation of this hypothesis. In 16 out of 19 cases the signs agree, indicating that λ_i does indeed move in the direction predicted by the regression.

The third hypothesis is also borne out by the data. The failure to predict λ_{i47} from the 1939–47 regression line is closely related to the change in the μ_i from one period to the next. Table 8.7 shows the error in predicting λ_{47} from the regression ($\lambda_{47} - \hat{\lambda}$) and the change in

μ_i: $\Delta\mu_i = \mu_{47} - \mu_{39}$. The error from regression is positively related to $\mu_{47} - \mu_{39}$. The correlation between these two terms is $+0.9340$, which indicates quite conclusively that the changes in λ conform to our theory.

TABLE 8.7

Industry No.	$\lambda_{47} - \hat{\lambda}$	$\mu_{47} - \mu_{39}$
3541	$+40.00$	$+101.07$
42	$+14.24$	$+32.68$
43	-13.48	$+4.01$
51	$+310.01$	$+432.54$
52	$+9.92$	$+16.60$
53	-42.28	-6.18
54	$+17.79$	-6.20
55	-6.46	-33.69
59	$+16.94$	$\vert\, 99.06$
61	-59.84	-85.05
62 + 63	-1.88	-59.04
66	$+53.40$	$+43.65$
69	-38.39	-55.74
72	$+0.79$	-69.60
83	$+33.85$	$+32.94$
85	$+45.77$	$+75.51$
91	$+27.04$	$+99.29$
93	-9.23	-45.68
99	-12.97	-82.74

Conclusions

1. The absolute percentage error of predicting the 1954 employment in New England industries from the μ of 1939–47 and the regression based upon the 1939–47 data was 29 per cent. This was lower than every ad hoc method with the exception of methods 2 and 3.

2. In 16 out of 19 cases the λ in 1947–54 moved closer to the value predicted by the regression line.

3. The failure to predict the λ in 1947–54 from the regression line is closely related to the change in μ from one period to the next. Whenever λ_t exceeded that λ predicted on the basis of μ_{t-1}, μ_t exceeded μ_{t-1}. Similarly, whenever λ_t was less than the λ predicted on the basis of μ_{t-1}, μ_t was less than μ_{t-1}.

The analysis of the machinery industry shows that firms can predict the future to some extent. λ_{t-1} was positively and significantly related to μ_{t-1}; that is, the more profitable sectors expanded more rapidly than the less profitable sectors. In so far as expansion tends to reduce the marginal efficiency of investment by raising costs faster than revenues, the economy tends to equalize rates of return among activities. This is precisely what a movement toward intertemporal competitive equilibrium means. We conclude that the U.S. interregional and interindustrial growth pattern seems to be tending towards an intertemporal competitive equilibrium and hence towards intertemporal efficiency.

INTERREGIONAL DIFFERENCES IN GROWTH RATES

Ad hoc hypothesis 2 had a high predictive accuracy. This hypothesis claimed that growth rates in a region are a fixed differential of the U.S. growth rate and that this differential λ is the same for each industry in a region. We now show how hypothesis 2 may be implied by our theory.

Our theory of growth was summarized by Equation (9) in Chapter 4:

$$L_{ij}^* = \left(p^* + \frac{u}{e} k^*\right)_i + v_{ij}^* \qquad (7)$$

where L_{ij}^* is the rate of growth of employment in the ith industry located in the jth region, v_{ij}^* is the rate of growth of the labor-supply function in the ith industry and jth region, and the term in parenthesis is common to all firms in the ith industry regardless of region. The variable λ_{ij} is

$$\lambda_{ij} = L_{ij}^* - \Sigma_j L_{ij}^* b_{ij} \qquad (7.1)$$

where $b_{ij} = L_{ij}/L_i$, the share of employment in the ith industry accounted for by the jth region. Substitute (7) into (7.1) and obtain[22]

$$\lambda_{ij} = v_{ij}^* - \Sigma_j v_{ij}^* b_{ij} \qquad (7.2)$$

Suppose there were no interindustry differences in the growth of the labor-supply curve in a given region, that is, $v_{ij}^* = v_{hj}^*$ for all i and h. Then

$$\lambda_{ij} = v_j^* - \Sigma v_j^* b_{ij}$$

$$\lambda_{hj} = v_j^* - \Sigma v_j^* b_{hj}$$

where $b_{hj} = L_{hj}/L_h$.

If the weights b_{ij} and b_{hj} are not "too dissimilar," i.e., if the geographical distributions of the h and i industries are "sufficiently similar," then $\lambda_{ij} = \lambda_{hj}$, which is hypothesis 2 above. All of region j industries grow faster or more slowly than their national counterparts by a fixed number of percentage points.

Finally, we relate this analysis of interregional differences in growth rates to the analysis described in Figure 8.5. The rate at which the investment demand schedule (mei) shifts is affected by the rate of growth of the cooperating input: labor. In so far as the supply of labor grows more rapidly in region 2 than in region 1, the marginal and average rates of return schedules for region 2 will lie above those of region 1, assuming they were initially identical. If the firms in each region invest at the point where the marginal rate of return is equal to $0r$, the average rate of return (which is our measured rate of return) will be higher in the region with the more rapidly growing supply of labor.

9. GOVERNMENT POLICIES TOWARD GROWING AND DECLINING REGIONS

The economic forces which produce the growth and decline of regions in the United States make themselves felt very slowly over time. For this reason, they are apt to be overshadowed in importance by events with more immediate impact. The attention of economists and public officials is frequently captured by the more dramatic problems of inflation and the business cycle, for these events involve rates of change of economic activity which are far greater than the glacierlike movements of regional economic development. While it is understandable that public attention should be focused on those aspects of our economic life which appear to generate the greatest immediate disturbance, one must never lose sight of the long-run regional growth process and the policy problems it generates, for while the regional growth process may be slow, its movements may for long periods of time be irreversible. The consequence is that the face of the nation is slowly but perceptibly changing in directions which are poorly understood and perhaps improperly controlled.

As a consequence of its partial concealment, regional growth makes its greatest impression on our thinking in the rapidly growing and the declining areas. In the rapidly growing areas of the country, the observer is struck by the immigration of new families, the large volume of new construction, the high incomes of entrepreneurial groups, and the opportunities for employment. In the declining areas, the observer finds low or declining wages, diminishing employment opportunities, and the migration of the most productive sectors of the labor force to other regions. He is struck by the decay of housing and of industrial plants and equipment, by the apathy of entrepreneurship, and by the inexperience of political leaders in the face of new problems.

In the United States, we have never pursued a laissez-faire policy with regard to the allocation of resources among regions. The history of Federal legislation with regard to the tariff, land policy, railways, and agriculture provide examples of the influences that the Federal government has brought to bear on regional development. Today, many

Federal policies have a differential effect on regional growth in the areas of agriculture, natural resources, public power, transportation, and housing, to name a few. These policies have not, however, been formulated in terms of an over-all view of an efficient free-market economy. This may be an understandable consequence of the resolution of political forces in a federated government, but it is deplorable in view of the social burdens which powerful groups are capable of imposing on the economy. We are likely to observe in the future more, not less, government influence on regional development. The passive acceptance of economic change has disappeared from the American political scene. The authors of the Full Employment Act of 1946 responded to concern over unemployment and inadequate aggregate demand. It is a short step from national to regional unemployment as a locus of discontent, and the recent legislation passed by the Congress indicates the growth of Federal government responsibilities.[1] While the two types of unemployment have different causes and call for different remedies, their political consequences are similar.

In this chapter we shall continue the analysis of economic efficiency and apply it to government policy. We shall use the criteria for an efficient growth process to evaluate public policies influencing regional growth. We shall show that certain policies are consistent with the goal of maximizing the national output. Other policies cannot be rationalized in these terms. The latter must be understood in terms of regional political pressures. They represent an attempt to use the taxing power of Federal and local government to insulate individual regions from economic changes. The cost of such protection is a loss of national output.

In a sense, all governmental economic policies have a regional impact. Some laws and regulations are consciously designed to stimulate the growth of one or two regions at the expense of others. Public power projects are an example. Other policies have an implicit regional effect because of the varying geographic location of economic activity. Examples of the latter might be a tight-money policy pursued by the Federal Reserve System or the favorable Federal tax treatment of mineral property depletion. The impact of tight money is likely to be greatest in those regions where a large proportion of resources is devoted to construction. The tax policy will affect the regions where mineral production is located. The identification of regional effects is not made for the purpose of specifying the varying regional political interests in different types of legislation. Our goal rather is to apply standards for an efficient growth process in the nation and indicate the extent to which governmental activities satisfy these goals.

GOVERNMENT POLICY IN GROWING REGIONS

The rapidly growing area is a challenge to anyone concerned with the efficient use of scarce resources. Residential, business, and industrial areas must be laid out with an eye to the avoidance of future slums. Roads, sewers, and schools must be built. New taxes must be raised to provide an appropriate level of public service.

One of the severest problems faced by rapidly growing regions is the assimilation of migrants into the labor and housing markets. On the one hand, these may be regarded as short-run phenomena in the sense that competitive markets are capable of reaching prices which will adjust to and satisfy any changes in either demand or supply conditions. On the other hand, the possible failure of such markets to adjust in the short run, for whatever reason, imposes potentially serious burdens on the affected area. A rapidly growing region like the Los Angeles metropolitan area may receive as many as six thousand net additions to the labor force each month as a result of migration. To these must be added the number generated by reproduction among the local population. If, for some reason, the demand for labor should level off and hence fall short of this increase in supply, a serious short-run unemployment problem can be generated which would call for the use of public relief and unemployment compensation funds.

The same situation is likely to occur in the housing market as a consequence of the migration of new families searching for housing accommodation. Here the increased demand for housing, if not met by new construction, forces doubling up and a reduction in the quality of housing that certain parts of the population may use. This problem becomes unusually severe in wartime, for example, and is evidenced by the shortage faced in the city of Detroit during the early 1940s. The same problem appeared in West Germany in the 1950s with the migration of political refugees from the East. While the problem does not ordinarily appear in such extreme form in peacetime, there are segments of the housing market which may nevertheless approach the conditions of wartime crowding. For example, the restricted supply of housing and public facilities available to Negro families in growing urban areas outside the South poses the same type of problem. With the continued migration of Negroes to these areas, a serious crowding problem arises, and this crowding produces additional drains on public funds for the provision of adequate public services in these areas.

Within rapidly growing regions there are sharp conflicts over the desirability of continued expansion of population. Opponents of further growth may argue that each immigrant family imposes cost burdens on the community which exceed any contribution the immigrant may pay as tax receipts. These burdens arise from the need to provide new arrivals with public services. They also arise from the congestion and decline of privacy accompanying the growth of an area's population. It is frequently argued that the growing area is subsidizing immigration by failing to impose on the migrant the marginal social costs of his decision to move. The actual taxes paid by the immigrant may fall short of the marginal social cost for a number of possible reasons.

First, it is alleged that the marginal social cost of migration exceeds the marginal private cost as a result of the congestion imposed upon the other residents. Even if the migrant were charged, through taxes, the average cost of providing public facilities, the taxes would fail to reflect the higher cost of services resulting from the larger population.

Second, the critic of immigration would contend that the immigrant may make a disproportionate claim on public services if his family includes children requiring public education. Moreover, since public services are not often charged on a use basis, the social cost that the migrant's family imposes upon the community will exceed his tax payments. Hence, the free market is supposed to produce too great a rate of immigration.

Neither argument should be taken seriously as an objection to inter-regional migration. When the migrant moves from region A to region B, additional plant for the provision of public services is demanded in region B to service the larger population. In area A a smaller plant is required to service a smaller population. Hence, in the long run the net marginal social cost of providing public service in the two regions combined is not necessarily positive. Moreover, there will probably be a net marginal social benefit from the migration, since the migrant's income earning prospects are likely to be more promising in area B than in area A.

The additional plant for the provision of public services, such as school facilities and road capacity, may be provided at constant or at rising marginal costs. If marginal costs are constant, then, in the long run, no additional hardships need be imposed upon the original residents, if services were charged on a use basis. If marginal costs are rising, however, the average cost of services would be increased to the original residents. By the same token, the average price received by the suppliers of the plant will be increased. There will merely be a transfer of resources from the purchasers to the suppliers of the public facilities. The marginal social cost of the services consumed by the migrants would be equal to the price paid by them if services were charged on a use basis.

At this point, the second argument supposedly is applicable. The public services are not charged on a use basis, and the migrants may be heavy users of public services but light contributors to tax revenues.

There are several objections to this second argument. We have shown that there is not necessarily any net social cost that migrants impose on the residents of region A or on those of regions A and B combined. That the migrants may not pay their marginal private costs for the use of social services is a fault of the method of pricing used in the region. An indigenous resident with the same attributes as the migrant will also be paying less than the value of the resources he consumes. Why is migration

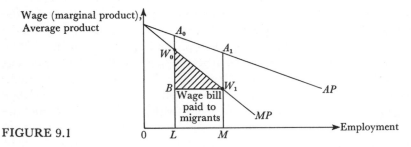

FIGURE 9.1

to be thought of as a source of difficulty, if this situation of "improper" pricing is independent of migration?

Our main theme is that there is a net benefit to the indigenous residents from migration. Suppose that there is an immigration of a certain number of workers per unit of time. The wage of the migrant is equal to his marginal product, but the income gain to the region is equal to the average product of the migrants. The difference is a net gain, which is potentially available to the indigenous residents (Figure 9.1).

Originally $0L$ workers were employed at wage W_0 with an average product A_0. With the inflow of LM workers into the region, the wage will decline from W_0 to W_1. The migrants produce an addition to regional output equal to area LW_0W_1M. Their wages are equal to the area LBW_1M. Hence, the indigenous residents receive a social increment of regional income, equal to the shaded area BW_0W_1, as a result of the migration. There are, of course, indigenous residents who suffer from the immigration. For example, the workers suffer reductions in the wage from W_0 to W_1. There are others, however, who gain from the immigration, for example, the employers of labor, who will now find a larger labor supply available for both the undesirable as well as the desirable jobs. The growth of the supply of labor inhibits the rise in the wage and prevents the rate of return on capital from declining. What Figure 9.1

demonstrates is that, despite the presence of losers and gainers from immigration, there is a net regional increase in real income resulting from the immigration.[2] Consequently, it is theoretically possible to compensate those who have suffered from the immigration and still have additional output for distribution to the rest of the community.

Arguments of a noneconomic nature have also been made against immigration. These arguments relate to the cultural and social characteristics of the migrants and to the possibilities that immigration will produce social conflict and disorganization. Arguments of this type have been raised in the past in connection with the migration of West Indians, Cypriots, and Pakistanis to Great Britain and with the migration of Algerians to Metropolitan France. Similar arguments might be raised with regard to the migration of Negroes from the South to northern, midwestern, and Pacific Coast cities. However, the predominant ethic in the recipient areas of the United States appears sufficiently tolerant to prevent popular support for arguments of this type. In addition, the possibility that recipient cities would resort to legal devices designed to halt the further immigration of Negroes declines as the political strength of their Negro communities grows.[3]

GOVERNMENT POLICY IN DEPRESSED AREAS

The problems of the declining areas are more severe and complex than those raised by the rapidly growing areas. First, there is little agreement over the causes of decline. Second, there are divergent social policies prescribed to deal with economic decline. The process of decline poses the issue of social programs to ameliorate the loss of employment and income-earning opportunities suffered by the residents. In addition, there is a strong possibility that social programs carried out by subnational government units may conflict with the national interest, which may be to maximize the economic choices and income-earning opportunities open to all citizens. That amelioration in some form is desirable in terms of this end is seen by an examination of comparable earnings statistics in declining and rapidly growing areas. Workers in the same industry may be earning as much as $1,200 per annum more in a growing area as compared with a declining area. That this difference is partly due to the number of weeks worked and partly due to differences in wage rates is not germane to the comparison.[4] Moreover, in some declining areas wage comparisons understate the difference in income opportunities because of high levels of unemployment. Income differentials of this order of magnitude have produced considerable migration of the working population out of declining regions. A difference of $1,200 per year over the working life of an entrant to the labor force may mean a rate of return of 30 percent on the cost of moving from one labor market to another. The rate of return is based on the assumption that the worker can enjoy the differential for 40 years and that it costs $4,000 to move. The latter figure might consist, for example, of $1,000 in direct moving expenses and $3,000 in foregone income while searching for a job. Even if the differential is enjoyed for only five years, the rate of return is still greater than 10 percent.

Note, however, that this calculation ignores the possibility that the cost of certain elements of the consumer budget will be higher in high-wage areas. For example, assume that all wages are 25 percent higher in the high-wage areas. Further assume that the wage differential enters the cost of services and that 30 percent of the consumer budget is spent on services. Then the differential of $1,200 per year is reduced to a real differential of $1,110 per year. Another possibility is that housing will be temporarily cheaper in declining regions if rental levels fail to repay construction costs. This situation can last while the stock of housing is declining to a lower level consistent with equilibrium rents. Such an adjustment process may, of course, go on for a considerable period of time.

Many observers of the declining regions have argued that it is the proper goal of government policy to allow the declining regions to be denuded of people and that the maximization of income opportunities is not achieved until the inhabitants of declining regions are given the fullest opportunity (the incentive is already present) to leave. Others have objected to this position on the grounds that economic decline is reversible. As an alternative, it is argued that proper social policy consists of reviving regions which have gone into decline. A policy of renewal is regarded as most realistic in regions which are heavily dependent on manufacturing. The loss of a major export industry may impair the profitability of other investments in the region. More important, it may also impair the confidence and venturesomeness of entrepreneurial groups in the region. It is argued that public policy can revive such an area by stimulating investment in a number of key industrial sectors. This will revive the rate of return on other investments. The term "seed capital" has been used by the more enthusiastic spokesmen for this policy.

The possible scope of such a policy is limited by the economic characteristics of depressed areas in the United States. They fall into two categories. First, there are older industrialized sections of the country where manufacturing firms have gone out of business, leaving behind a group of unemployed workers who must move or adjust as best they can to inferior employment opportunities. This group includes states in the northeastern part of the country. Second, there are older farming and mining areas of the country where, owing to the depletion of natural resources, technological change, and change in demand, employment opportunities have declined. This group includes areas in the Northeast, North Central, and Southern regions of the country.

In both types of areas, industrial and agricultural, the labor force is faced with declining employment opportunities. These reveal themselves in a slower growth of wage and property income, and possibly in lower wages than are paid in comparable occupations elsewhere. The policy choices open to the first type of region are wider than those to the second, for the existence of plant, equipment, and a skilled labor force increases the possibilities of revival in industial regions. The development of industry is likely to be more difficult in the second type of region.

Social investment to induce the revival of a region seeks to raise the productivity of private investment both through large-scale public improvements and through the subsidization of a core group of industries. These eventually are supposed to stand on their own feet and provide the basis of future growth. Private investment in a single plant or firm may not be profitable until the redevelopment of an export base or core industry occurs. This is a variant of the familiar infant-industry argument applied to protective tariffs. There is a question whether it is applicable to declining regions with heavy commitments to manufacturing. It is true that the elements of a revived industrial complex are already present in declining regions in the form of skilled labor living in an urban society,[5] but the infant-industry argument turns on the supposed presence of potential external economies and agglomeration effects which would come into operation at certain minimum levels of industrial activity. The purpose of subsidization is to induce a core industry to expand to a minimum level at which investment in the peripheral industries becomes profitable.

Why should additional external economies and agglomeration effects appear in a depressed area as a result of government-subsidized investment? These effects depend on the existence of indivisible factors of production and minimum utilization rates in certain production processes. As these minima are reached, increasing returns are exploited; and it becomes profitable to invest for the purpose of expanding and duplicating these processes.[6] These effects, however, are typically associated with the development of newer areas which have not yet reached a certain size. They are hardly likely to occur in the well-developed industrial complex of an older depressed area. In order that these effects come into play, there must be a radical transformation of the industrial structure of a depressed area, with the consequence that a new industrial complex is formed and most existing social capital is replaced.

First, what is the agency by which a new complex is formed? It is clear that many depressed areas will be unable to find the new core group of export industries. Some areas are not viable if market rates of return on investment are used as a criteria of choice. Second, even if a new core is found, it may not survive without continued government subsidy. There is no guarantee that the rate of return on investment will rise to or above competitive levels after government subsidy has created the social capital necessary for the new core. If this is the case, the argument for publicly subsidized investment in depressed areas must rest on grounds other than revival.

It is not possible to draw a conclusive judgment on this score by examining the fate of older depressed areas. Their experience has been too mixed. Certain older urban industrial areas, such as the Greater Boston, Springfield, and Hartford areas in New England, have managed to replace a decaying core with one that is presently growing. Other areas have been less fortunate, but one thing is clear. The ability to forecast the development of a new core is an entrepreneurial function which requires a great deal of ability and possibly luck. The success of a "seed capital" policy requires that government administrators possess these virtues.

The dilemma of policy towards depressed areas is frequently stated in the alternatives, "Should government policy move the worker to the job or the job to the worker?" Usually, the question is posed to point up the humanitarian aspects of the latter alternative. Governments in many countries have in the past faced this problem. The Italian Government faces it in Southern Italy and Sicily; the British Government faces it in Wales and Scotland. The idea that the job should be moved to the worker has found expression in a number of "depressed area" bills submitted to the U.S. Congress in the past. One of these was recently enacted into law. The focus of this effort is the revival of the depressed area through the subsidization of a new or redeveloped industrial base. Federal efforts in this direction have been preceded and assisted by locally financed (state and municipal) efforts in the same direction. These programs subsidize the cost of loans (either short or long term) to firms considering the establishment of plants in depressed areas. Some of the local programs have included the development of industrial parks and the building of general purpose plant sites for lease to unspecified users.

The rationale for these programs is that the depressed areas can be revived by the attraction of new sources of employment, which can be accomplished by providing plant sites at less than cost, long-term mortgages and leases, and tax concessions. It is felt that these newer firms, through their own demands for labor, materials, components, and services, will stimulate the revival of older areas. These programs raise three rather interesting issues. First there is the question of whether they can succeed in halting decline and, if so, in what kinds of areas. Second is the question of whether these programs can ever terminate, with the expectation that they have provided enough momentum for the areas to continue to grow. And third is the question of whether these programs are efficient in the sense that they represent a wise use of public funds.

Let us examine the efficiency of alternative government programs. If the job is moved to the worker, it means that private capital, which might be earning a return of 20 percent, would earn, say, 2 percent in the attempt to provide work for an immobile labor force. This return may mean a lower level of real output. The social desirability of the redirection of private capital depends, however, upon a comparison not of 20 percent with 2 percent but of the net marginal productivity of capital in a growing region (20 percent) with the total increment to value added in the declining region. The reason is that the income generated in either region is the sum of the rents *and* wages created minus the opportunity costs of labor. On the assumption that the labor force in a declining region is immobile and would otherwise produce nothing, we use the gross marginal product of capital in the declining region, i.e., the increment of value added. Aid to depressed areas may be economically efficient even if permanent revival is impossible. Nevertheless, a number of alternatives to this use of resources may also be considered.

First, immigration from depressed areas might be subsidized. The government might support the retraining and moving of workers who are displaced from declining industries and cannot find reemployment in their localities. The incentives to make this shift are already present for such workers, particularly the younger ones, although, for a number of reasons relevant to conditions in the United States, it may not be feasible for them to move without government help. Older or unskilled workers frequently find it very difficult to find new jobs. The costs of retraining and moving combined with the uncertainties of finding employment may wipe out the gains, particularly for an older worker whose income-earning span of years is not long. Workers changing jobs and places of employment may find that they must take lower-paying positions than comparable workers are earning in the same area. The fact that average earnings per employee in metal-working are $1,200 per year higher in one area than another does not necessarily mean that a man can achieve this entire differential by moving.

It is worth noting that proposals for migration have not been made by Federal agencies concerned with heavily depressed areas such as the Appalachian region.

A second alternative is to allow the market to determine the regional allocation of investable funds; however, the government would then subsidize the consumption of the unemployed in declining areas. The argument for this policy rests on the belief that the best government policy is one which maximizes the private return to society's resources. If resources can earn 20 percent in growing regions and 2 percent in declining regions, it would, under this argument, be best to allow resources to move to the 20 percent opportunity. A tax and subsidy would then permit income to be transferred to the indigent unemployed of the declining region. Presumably, such a tax would have to fall on the immobile resources of the growing regions to avoid interference with the allocative goal. Proponents of this type of policy would argue that it is preferable to government subsidy of investment in declining regions because this plan yields greater real output than the first. We have already seen that this may not be true. Proponents might also argue that indigent unemployed are better off with a consumption subsidy than being forced to work for a living. This alternative is inefficient for two reasons. First, it fails to obtain the high rate of return derived from investment in the retraining and migration of mobile workers. Second, it fails to utilize the older immobile workers whose employment in the region involves no opportunity cost.

A third alternative is suggested by the original one. It is at least as efficient as the others. Under this policy, the local governments of declining regions would tax immobile resources and use the proceeds to subsidize private employment in the region.[7] The taxes might take the form of taxes on wage income and sales taxes. If the tax were an income tax, it might be avoided by those individuals willing and able to substitute leisure for income and by those who can change legal residence. For this reason, an income tax would be unsuitable, since it might drive away the richer members of society who are for sentimental reasons potential investors in a declining region.

If the tax were on real property, it would discourage investment in the physical plant of business enterprise because a real property tax falls on the profitable and unprofitable with equal severity. Consequently, it changes the probability distribution of rewards in such a way as to discourage the assumption of risk.[8] For this reason, such a tax is an unsuitable source of funds to provide revenue for the purpose of subsidizing investment. This point is worth emphasizing because of the heavy reliance of local government upon revenues from property taxes.

We are left therefore with the wages tax and the sales tax, both of which fall on the low-income household and on the worker. While these taxes would ordinarily be considered inequitable because of their incidence, it is precisely this quality which recommends them as a tool of government policy, for they fall on the immobile resource, namely, the workers who will not migrate to superior job opportunities elsewhere. The proceeds of this tax are then used as a subsidy per employed worker, which is paid to the employer. The formerly unemployed, immobile workers are better off because they are earning a living in the region where they wish to live. The rest of the country is no worse off, since the owners of investment resources have voluntarily chosen to invest in the depressed area in response to the subsidy, and the rate of real output is at least as great as previously.

In examining this proposal, it is pertinent to inquire why wage levels in depressed areas do not adjust by themselves to eliminate unemployment, for the burden of the above proposal is that the real wage must be lowered by the tax and subsidy. Why does not the money wage fall to accomplish this? The answer appears to be that wages, even in unorganized markets, are resistant to downward pressure when there is a decline in the demand for labor. Workers are unwilling to accept reduced earnings for jobs which previously paid more and are frequently unwilling to accept larger work assignments in place of lower earnings. Employers may be unwilling to offend workers by offering substantial wage cuts. In addition, wage cuts may be impossible because of trade union pressure and because of the Federal minimum wage. The virtue of the above proposal is that it provides an immediate cut in the real wage without interfering with wage bargaining or personnel relations between employer and employee. It is a means of artificially producing wage flexibility in depressed regions. In addition, it offers to depressed areas the prospect of continued employment and possibly revival without the need for subsidy from other areas. Finally, it offers mobile workers in depressed areas a choice that they may not have at the moment, namely, a cut in their real wage in return for employment in their native regions. At the moment, their choices may be far more limited, and they may face unemployment if they do not migrate.

The wage subsidy proposal does, however, contain serious limitations. Effectively, it proposes that the cost of labor to the employer be reduced to the existing level of the marginal value productivity of labor. It makes sense to introduce such a scheme in the case of older workers displaced in declining industries. Here the purpose of the subsidy is to keep enough capital in production to maintain these workers in useful employment until they reach retirement age. If such a proposal were carried out, it would have been possible to handle the structural unemployment problem in the New England textile towns. The textile mills would have remained in operation until the labor force retired. The subsidy would eventually end, for the wage level paid in such industries in the North is not sufficiently attractive to induce new entrants into the labor force to take textile mill jobs.

It would be a mistake, however, to regard the subsidy proposal as anything other than a short-run measure. Over the long run, wage subsidies are a form of regional wage cutting that effectively maintain the geographic and industrial immobility of the labor force. Over the long run, labor is mobile, geographically, industrially, and occupationally. Wage subsidies may interfere with the willingness of workers to invest in their own training. It may also interfere with the willingness of public authorities to invest in educational and training facilities. Permanent wage subsidies have been proposed by Moes as a method of developing areas that wish attract new firms. His proposal is directed particularly to small Southern towns which may have a relatively large number of under-employed workers. To Moes the advantage of the subsidy is that it permits workers to find employment without migrating. Presumably, migration is costly and irksome, and many individuals prefer to remain in their native regions. The subsidy can be arranged as a tax on the immobile in the manner described earlier. There are two flaws in the Moes proposal. It may not work, and it may not be desirable if it does work.

Moes does not explain why these towns have failed to develop with their existing levels of low wages. The South as a region has been very successful in attracting manufacturing firms, and it is not clear why these towns have been bypassed. It is not evident that a wage differential between a small Southern town and a larger Southern city will be sufficient to attract employers. Moes cites the existence of Federally determined minimum wages to explain why wages fail to fall below that level. This implies that the private cost of using labor must be pushed below the minimum wage level to induce new firms to enter these areas. It is not clear how much of a subsidy is needed or whether any reasonable subsidy would accomplish the task. Other factors affecting the location of industry may be more important than the wage differential between a developed and an undeveloped Southern town. The same type of argument cannot be levied against the wage subsidy when used in a depressed region, for the plants are already there. There is then no question of using the subsidy as a device to affect the location of new plants.

Second, even if the proposal works, it means that the labor force has paid a tax to attract a low-wage employer, for if the tax falls on wages, the disposable income remaining to the worker is his real marginal product, which, according to the argument, can be lower than the minimum wage. If the scheme can do no more than provide an income below the minimum wage, it may be far less desirable than other proposals which raise the productivity of labor.

This brings us to the question of alternative government policies directed toward raising the productivity of labor. Two types of policy bear examination. One is government subsidy of education, retraining, and migration. The second is government subsidy of natural resource development. The first type of policy is a direct attempt to improve the quality of the worker. The second type of policy attempts to raise the demand for labor.

Government subsidization of education is an area of inquiry which extends far beyond the reaches of regional economic problems. It does, however, contain a regional dimension in the sense that the policies of state and local government may conflict with the well-being of the citizens involved. This is particularly the case in declining regions and low-income regions which are losing population to other parts of the country. In such areas the volume of resources devoted to public education by state and local government may be less than optimal, because education increases mobility. A declining region that invests in education will find that the fruits of such investment are enjoyed in other regions. The college graduate is more likely to migrate than the high school graduate, so that the benefits from education are received in areas where the investment did not occur. For this reason, state and local authorities in declining and low-income regions may refrain from investing in education compared with authorities in growing regions. This is a powerful argument for some type of subsidy by the Federal government in order to maintain opportunities in these depressed areas. The purpose of the subsidy is to insure a sufficiently high level of public investment in education.

These arguments apply with equal force to the problem of vocational training for adult workers and with much greater force to the problem of migration. The need for vocational training for adult workers is greatest in areas where industries have declined. Jobs have been lost with little prospect that the specific industry will revive. A case in point is the decline of coal mining in the Appalachian region. Public investment in such retraining may yield a high rate of return on human capital. Ignorance and the imperfection of the capital market, for investment in human capital, may prevent the optimum rate of investment from being undertaken—in the absence of a government program. State and local authorities in such areas will very likely not be willing to provide sufficient resources. For one thing, the retrained worker may migrate, and thus the returns from the investment are lost to the depressed region.

Perhaps a more immediate consideration in the minds of public authorities is the effect of economic decline on their tax revenues. With declining tax revenues, there would be a disinclination to embark on new education programs. Here again is an area for Federal subsidy of a policy with high returns. In the absence of Federal support, retraining will be inadequately developed.

Finally, migration is the one sensible policy that is likely to receive the least support from state and local governments. We have already seen in Moes' proposal a strong defense of immobility. Moes puts such weight on immobility that he is apparently willing to neglect the increases in income from migration. It is not possible to dismiss out of hand these sentiments as irrational or unworthy, but it is necessary to point out the large potential gains from public investment in migration. These gains may far outweigh any gain from the subsidy proposal. The subsidy proposal promises a low-wage cure for underemployment. Migration and vocational training combined promise a high-wage cure for underemployment. As we have noted, subsidization of migration may be needed to overcome immobility and ignorance. These subsidies must be provided by the Federal government, for state and local governments will be unwilling to use their funds in these directions.

Government subsidization of resource development also has major implications for the development of low-income and depressed areas. Here again is an area where Federal policy is needed to correct possible allocative mistakes by state and local governments. Again there is likely to be too little investment in the development of natural resources by the governmental authorities of such regions. There are two reasons for this. First, these authorities are faced with shrinking tax revenues if there has been a loss of industry. Second, many resource development projects overlap the geographic jurisdiction of several states. Consequently, Federal policy is necessary to provide rational guides to public investment. The first reason explains why public investment may be too small in depressed and declining regions. The second reason is applicable to all regions, growing or declining.

The development of natural resources is not an over-all solution for regional development problems. It may have applicability in particular regions, but it is not likely to apply to all depressed areas. Nevertheless, the income-generating features of such programs are important where there are large groups of unemployed. The effect of resource development is to raise the demand for labor in a given region. The construction of hydroelectric power projects within the framework of a river basin authority is a powerful device for the establishment of a new industrial base.

It is not necessary to repeat the analysis of rational government decision-making as it applies to water resources. This is an area where external effects abound and government investment is necessary.[9] The point of relevance is that government policy in this area will be affected by regional economic conditions, and government investment decisions will influence the region's growth in the future. For example, the presence of unemployed or underemployed labor changes the rational calculation of social rates of return on investment. The social return on investment should properly include any wage income generated over and above the opportunity cost of labor. With unemployed and under-employed labor this opportunity cost may very likely be below the going money wage.

In addition to resource development and education, governments in other countries have attempted to influence the regional demand for labor through large-scale physical planning programs. One example is the development of southern Italy in the Mezzogiorno program. Another is the development of new towns in the United Kingdom. In both cases the program goes beyond the construction of public works, the harnessing of water power, and the establishment of education and training programs. Both programs represent an attempt to produce a gross change in the regional distribution of economic activity. For this reason it will never be possible to assess fairly the return on the social capital so invested. The calculation of rates of return on social investment can be carried out only when the investment occurs in small units. It is then possible to impute a social return by asking how the real income stream would be altered by the absence or presence of the program in question. Note that such a problem does not arise in the same form in the imputation of return to private capital, for under perfect competition, in the absence of externalities, the social and private returns coincide. In the case of public investment, a return is rarely paid to the government, so that imputation requires an indirect procedure.

When the social investment consists of a new town, it is most difficult to measure, even in principle, the return on the investment, for social investment of this type means that the government has anticipated the demand for certain services and has decided to make them available in a specific locality. Whether the private market for land and buildings would have done the same in the same space of time is the unmeasurable problem. As a result, we reach a point where public investment becomes so extensive that it is extremely difficult to evaluate its profitability.

The type of planning mentioned above has not yet emerged in this country, at least on the scale that exists elsewhere. The only equivalent which might be mentioned is still embryonic, namely, the mass rebuilding of urban centers in the United States under the aegis of the Federal government. The areas which have been torn out and rebuilt can be identified mainly by their age. Urban renewal as presently practiced in the United States is not, however, logically connected to the problems of declining and depressed areas, for the urban renewal areas are found all over the country, and the priorities for funds and projects do not appear to be related to the problem of stimulating regional economic growth in depressed areas.

SUMMARY

We should like to summarize our views on appropriate government policies toward depressed and declining areas. The wage-subsidy program is a rational method of solving the unemployment problem in those areas dominated by declining industries. This policy is consistent with economic efficiency, for it is concerned with older immobile workers. It raises the output of the regions affected by a greater amount than any loss of output which might occur as a result in other regions. This conclusion does not seem to apply to the use of the wage subsidy as a means of handling the problem of underemployment in areas which are not presently industrialized. In these areas unemployment is concentrated in people who may be readily employed elsewhere. The wage subsidy, when appropriate, can and should be carried out by state and local governments using their taxing power over immobile resources to provide the revenues for the transfer payment. There is no need for Federal government participation.

The policy of subsidizing investment in depressed areas cannot be rationalized on the same grounds and indeed is less satisfactory than the wage subsidy. For one thing, an investment subsidy induces the use of more capital than is efficient, since, if labor is underemployed, it is not rational to economize on it in production. The efficient capital-labor ratio in a given industry is the one which would be chosen under perfect competition when the private cost of using labor equals the wage which will clear the labor market. This is a lower wage than the one prevailing in depressed areas.

Once the unemployment problem is solved efficiently through a wage subsidy, the rationale for public subsidies to private investment becomes very weak indeed. Its only defense is the desire of local owners of capital and labor to remain employed in their native areas. If they wish to tax themselves to subsidize mobile resources, they should be allowed to do so; but this subsidy is again a function for state and local government. The transfer of tax funds from other regions through the intermediary of the Federal government cannot be defended on efficiency grounds. Federal programs of this sort are serving other ends than the maximization of national income. These ends are the preservation of the identity of local areas.[10]

As we have pointed out, the proper role of Federal government in this area is the subsidization of vocational training, migration, and resource development. Here the Federal government has an important role to play which state and local governments cannot and will not perform. Federal programs of this sort are consistent with economic efficiency and should be developed.

I O. SUMMARY

Chapter 2 presents the regularities which must be explained by a theory of growth and tests the theory developed in Chapter 1 that interstate differences in the rate of growth of per capita income are influenced by the rate at which the intrastate misallocation of resources is being corrected.

Drawing upon earlier studies, it is shown that the convergence of per capita income among states has been associated with the intrastate shifting of labor from the low-wage agricultural sector to the higher-wage nonagricultural sector. There has been some tendency for factor prices to equalize among states, but this tendency has not been very marked for wage payments.

The misallocation of resources *within* a state is a function of (1) the wage differential *between* sectors and (2) the fraction of the labor force employed in the low-wage sector. Assume that the rate at which resource misallocation is being corrected is given. Then we predict that the rate of growth of per capita income is dependent upon variables (1) and (2). This prediction is consistent with the data during the periods 1880–1900, 1900–1920, and 1920–1950. States with the worst allocation of resources at the initial date tended to experience the highest rates of growth of per capita income during the period. This is empirical support for the theory of interstate differences in the rate of growth of per capita income developed in Chapter 1.

As states have become more similar over time in terms of their ratios of agricultural to total employment, the intersectoral wage differential has in fact narrowed. We therefore expect convergence to occur among the rates of growth of per capita income of states.

There is a stable pattern of growth of nonagricultural employment among states. Certain states have experienced rapid rates of growth of nonagricultural (and of manufacturing) employment, relative to the national average; and others have had relatively slow rates of growth.

This phenomenon cannot be attributed to chance. Moreover, there is a positive relation between the growth of employment in manufacturing and the growth of per capita income. This finding is consistent with the theory which we advanced concerning interstate differences in the growth of per capita income.

Economic maturity is defined as the situation where growth has been persistently less than the national average for a long period of time, in terms of significant measures of economic performance. The mature states are then identified. Some characteristics of these states are that (1) there has been net emigration from these states, (2) manufacturing employment has declined in many of these states (between business cycle peaks), and (3) the chronic labor surplus areas are heavily represented in these states.

Economic maturity is not to be explained in terms of the industrial composition of these states. In mature states the component industries tend to grow at slower rates than do their national counterparts. There have been states which experienced declines in manufacturing production-worker employment (between business cycle peaks). These declines were not the result of the industrial composition of the states but rather of the fact that the state industries declined, whereas their national counterparts did not decline. Maturity and decline are long-run phenomena and are not the products of the business cycle. The theories of growth developed here must explain why this occurred.

The explanatory power of a simple and widely used aggregative theory of growth is examined in Chapter 3. This simple theory, usually associated with the names of Hecksher and Ohlin, assumes that those regions with the highest proportion of capital to labor will evidence the highest real wage and the lowest marginal product of capital. In a free market we would observe capital moving from high-wage to low-wage areas, with the consequence that the low-wage areas experience higher rates of growth of capital and of the return to labor. If the regional wage differentials were large enough, we may also observe labor migrating from the low-wage to the high-wage areas. Two testable hypotheses are derived from this theory.

1. Low-wage regions will experience the highest rates of growth of capital and of the ratio of capital to labor.

2. Low-wage regions will experience the highest rates of growth of wages.

Three periods were studied in connection with a test of the simple model: 1919–29, 1929–48, and 1948–53.

The explanatory power of the aggregative model is quite weak. In the first and third periods, capital grew at a greater rate in the high-wage areas than in the low-wage areas.

Moreover, the wage grew faster in the high-wage areas during the same periods. Employment grew perceptibly more rapidly in the high-wage areas only during the middle period. The theory is refuted for the periods 1919–29 and 1948–53 but is compatible with the data during the 1929–48 period.

Several ad hoc explanations are adduced to rationalize these findings. First, there was a greater rate of migration into high-wage areas than into low-wage areas during the 1919–29 and 1948–53 periods. These migrations and population increases induced capital formation in housing and services. Second, during these two periods interstate differences in industrial composition may partly explain interstate differences in growth rates. It could be argued that there was a greater rate of growth of demand for the products of the high-wage areas than of low-wage areas. The weakness of the simple aggregative model stems from its failure to recognize the diversity of economic activities that are conducted in a region. In the long run, there is no significant relationship between the composition of a state's industries and its growth rate, but some weak relationship appears during short periods of time.

A theory of interstate differences in the rate of growth of manufacturing employment is developed in Chapter 4. This theory is designed to avoid the shortcomings of the simple aggregative theory developed in Chapter 3, and it explains the following phenomena. The rate of growth of manufacturing employment in a state, or the probability that manufacturing industry X will grow more rapidly in State A than in the United States as a whole, is (1) negatively related to the ratio of manufacturing employment to total state employment, (2) positively related to the rate of immigration into a state, and (3) not significantly related to the level of the wage prevailing in the state's manufacturing industries.

The theory which explains these phenomena assumes that:

1. The price of a product produced by a given manufacturing industry is the same for each firm, regardless of its regional location.

2. The price of capital goods to each firm in a given manufacturing industry is, on the average, the same for each firm regardless of its regional location.

3. Each firm in a given manufacturing industry has the same production function subject to constant returns to scale, and there is a limit to the size of each firm such that competition prevails.

4. Firms behave competitively.

From these assumptions, the following conclusion is deduced. Interstate differences in the rates of growth of employment in a given manufacturing industry, from one long-run equilibrium to another, arise solely from interstate differences in the rate of growth of the labor-supply function

The determinants of the rate of growth of the labor-supply function are then discussed:

1. The earnings differential in favor of the manufacturing sector, and hence the incentive for labor to migrate from the other sectors of the state's economy, is negatively related to the ratio of manufacturing to total state employment.

2. The natural increase of the population is typically greater in rural than in urban areas. This means that shifts of the labor-supply function from this source are likely to be most pronounced in areas where manufacturing employment is not widely prevalent. Factors (1) and (2) explain why the rate of growth of manufacturing employment is negatively related to the ratio of manufacturing to total state employment.

3. Migration occurs, to a large extent, from low-wage to high-wage states. Hence, the rate of growth of the labor-supply function is affected by interstate wage differentials.

The level of the state wage has two counterbalancing effects upon the rate of growth of employment. On the one hand, the marginal rate of return on capital is higher in low-wage states, in a given industry, than in high-wage states. Capital is therefore attracted to the state. As capital flows in, this generates a demand for labor. Thus, low wages and high growth rates should be positively correlated. On the other hand, emigration of labor occurs in low-wage states, as labor flows from low- to high-wage states. As a result, emigration tends to reduce the rate of growth of the labor supply in low-wage states; and immigration of labor tends to raise the rate of growth of the labor supply in high-wage states. Consequently, we found no significant relation between the level of the wage and the rate of growth of employment in a state.

Further confirmation of the theory of growth developed in Chapter 4 is presented in Chapter 5. It was noted earlier that the industrial composition of a state is a poor predictor of its rate of growth. The actual growth rate in a given state can be viewed as the sum of a hypothetical growth rate and an internal growth rate. The hypothetical growth rate is the rate that would have occurred if each industry in the state grew at the same rate as its national counterpart. The internal growth rate measures the importance of local factors in producing a divergence between the actual state growth and that expected upon the basis of industrial composition. Since we observe no relation between the actual and hypothetical rates, there exists a negative relation between the hypothetical and internal growth rates. This phenomenon is given an economic explanation on the basis of the role of the labor-supply function.

States with high hypothetical growth rates produce products whose demands are growing rapidly in the United States. An expansion of these products requires an increase in the inputs of productive services in these industries. The additional productive services may come either from other industries in the manufacturing sector or from migration into the manufacturing sector of the state. In the first case, the other manufacturing industries in the state must be adversely affected. Their internal growth rates will be reduced, since they are losing resources to the more rapidly growing sectors. In so far as migration occurs into the manufacturing sector, either from other states or from the nonmanufacturing sector of a state, the decline in internal growth rates is mitigated or offset. The same reasoning applies, *mutatis mutandis*, to states with low hypothetical growth rates.

States with positive internal growth rates had more rapidly growing supplies of labor than did states with negative internal rates:

1. Among states with immigration, the rate of immigration was greater where the internal growth rate was positive.

2. Among states with emigration, the rate of emigration was greater where the internal growth rate was positive.

3. Where there was a positive internal growth rate, there was relatively and absolutely more emigration than where there was a negative internal growth rate.

4. States with positive internal growth rates in manufacturing had smaller fractions of the labor force in manufacturing than states with negative internal growth rates, given the hypothetical growth rate and the net migration position of the state. These facts support the view that the growth of the labor-supply function affects the rate of growth.

According to the aggregative model of growth developed in Chapter 3, the growth of the real wage is positively related to the growth of the total ratio of capital to labor in a state. If, however, we disaggregate and consider a region with several industries, then the growth in the real wage does not depend solely upon the growth of the regional capital-labor ratio. This is the theme of Chapter 6.

An increase in the ratio of capital to labor in the region may not lead to a rise in the ratio of capital to labor in each of the component industries.

Instead of a rise in the real wage, a reallocation of the region's output may occur in favor of the commodity produced by the capital-intensive sector. Developing the analysis of Stolper and Samuelson, we conclude that:

1. Accumulation will lead to an increase in the marginal product of labor when it is accompanied by a rise in the ratio of capital to labor in each industry sector.

2. This rise will occur when the price of output of the labor-intensive sector rises relative to the price of output of the capital-intensive sector.

3. If accumulation leads to an increase in the marginal product of labor, it will also result in a decline in the marginal product of capital.

The validity of these conclusions was then tested for the period 1929 to 1953. A positive relationship was found between the growth of the nonagricultural wage payments per worker (Y) and the growth of the total payments to nonagricultural capital per worker (X). This positive relation would reflect the fact that, when the price of the region's output rises, the money wage and rent per unit of capital rise together. If, however, the capital-labor ratio rises in both sectors of the region's economy, when the average price of the region's output increases, then the money wage per worker will receive an additional impetus from the increase in the marginal product of labor, while the total money return to capital will receive a negative impetus from the decline in the marginal product of capital. The theory developed above claims that the marginal product of labor in both sectors will rise when there is a relative expansion of the labor-intensive sector. Can this theory be tested?

We examined the positive and negative residuals from the regression of Y on X (as defined above). The states with positive residuals exhibit a greater growth in wages than that predicted by the growth of the payments to capital when combined with the regression line. Similarly, states with negative residuals show a smaller growth of wages per worker than predicted. We consider the service sector to be labor-intensive and the manufacturing-mining sector to be capital-intensive. We use the relative growth of the service wage to the manufacturing wage as an index of the growth of the price of services to the price of manufactured goods. When this index rises, there is an increase in the demand for the output of the labor-intensive sector. We found that in states with greater than median increases in the ratio of the service wage to the manufacturing wage, there tended to be positive residuals from the regression. That is, the actual wage grew faster than predicted. Similarly, in states with less than median increases in the ratio of the service wage to the manufacturing wage, there tended to be negative residuals; that is, the actual wage grew slower than predicted by the regression. Consequently, we find support for the theory which claims that the marginal physical product of labor will rise when the price of the output of the labor-intensive sector rises relative to the price of the output of the capital-intensive sector.

Chapter 7 provides a picture of an open economy moving along a balanced growth path determined by the rate of growth of the labor supply. We disturb the equilibrium by changing the values of three principal exogenous variables: the rate of growth of the price of exports, the intersectoral wage differential, and the rate of growth of the supply of labor. It is shown how these disturbances alter the allocation of resources, the distribution of factor payments, the rate of growth, and the extent of the capital movements.

Given the rate of return on capital (equal to an exogenously determined interest rate) and the price of imported capital goods, we trace the effects of an autonomous rise in the price of the export good. To keep the rate of return constant, the ratio of capital to labor must rise in the export sector. With given quantities of labor and capital, the price of the domestic good and its rate of output will rise. This rise in price of the domestically produced good will induce a rise in the ratio of capital to labor, to keep the rate of return constant. Moreover, the rise in the relative price of each good compared with the price of the imported capital good will induce capital accumulation. The complete adjustment to the rise of export prices will yield a rise in the output of the export good.

Within the framework of our assumption that domestic goods are relatively labor-intensive, the fraction of the labor force employed in the export sector will rise (when the price of exports autonomously increases) if the elasticity of substitution is less than unity. If the sectoral production functions are of the Cobb-Douglas type (with a unit elasticity of substitution), there is no relative shift of labor between sectors.

The effect on the distribution of income within each sector, consequent to a rise in the price of exports, also depends upon the elasticity of substitution. If the elasticity is less than unity, the distribution will turn in favor of the factor which has decreased in relative quantity, in this case, labor. On the other hand, if the elasticity exceeds unity, the distribution will turn in favor of the factor which has increased in relative quantity, in this case, capital.

We then examine the effects of the narrowing of the intersectoral wage differential. In the final equilibrium, the fraction of the labor force employed in the lower-wage domestic sector will decline so that the rate of output of the export sector will increase. The demand facing the products of the export sector is perfectly elastic at the given price, and the supply price of the capital goods input is given. When capital is sub-stituted for labor in the domestic goods industry, as a result of the rise in the wage relative to that prevailing in the export sector, the liberated labor is available for employment in the export industry. Since the demand for exports is perfectly elastic, its final equilibrium rate of output increases.

Finally, we show that the hypothesized changes in the distribution of factor payments and in the growth rate accord with the empirical evidence cited in Chapter 6.

Chapter 8 is concerned with the question: Is the actual pattern of growth that has occurred in the United States efficient? First, we analyze the concept of an efficient growth pattern. An efficient growth pattern is one that maximizes the amount of good X_i available at period $t = n$, *given* the quantities of the other goods available at period $t = n$ and the quantities of all goods consumed from period $t = 0$ through period $t = n$. It is proved that if firms maximize their profits and invest in such a way as to equalize marginal efficiencies of investment among goods produced, then the growth program will be efficient.

Second, we prove that there can be a competitive equilibrium, and hence an efficient pattern of growth, although there are interregional differences in the rates of growth of employment and capital in a given industry. Balanced growth among regions is not necessary for a com-petitive equilibrium in a nonslave economy.

Third, we inquire whether the most rapidly growing sectors are those which have correctly forecasted the greatest marginal efficiencies of investment. If the answer is "Yes," then we conclude that firms have an ability to forecast the future with some degree of accuracy and that they gear their growth rates to profit opportunities. In this manner the economy tends to equalize marginal efficiencies of investment among activities.

We develop a method of predicting growth rates based upon the assumption that the relative rate of growth of an industry in a region is primarily determined by the relative rate of return that has been earned on investment in this industry in the region. It is shown that:

1. The growth position of an industry is determined by the relative rate of return that has been realized in the prior period. The *predicted relation* between the relative growth rate and the relative rate of return is given by the relation between the relative growth rate and relative rate of return that occurred in the prior period.

2. Where an industry's relative rate of growth was overestimated or underestimated in the prior period, its *subsequent* relative growth rate will conform more closely to the predicted growth rate.

3. If the industry's relative growth rate fails to conform to the predicted growth rate, this failure is due to a change in the realized relative rate of return on investment from the prior to the present period.

We therefore conclude that the U.S. interregional and interindustrial growth pattern seems to be tending towards an intertemporal competitive equilibrium and hence towards intertemporal efficiency.

An analysis of government policies towards growing and declining regions is undertaken in Chapter 9. There are social problems arising from rapid growth and immigration, and there are social problems arising from economic decline. One of the most severe problems faced by rapidly growing regions is the short-run assimilation of migrants into the labor and housing markets. Opponents of further growth have contended that each immigrant family imposes cost burdens on the community which exceed any contribution the immigrant may pay as tax receipts.

We refute the validity of this argument. Moreover, we prove that, despite the presence of losers and gainers from immigration, there is a net regional increase in output resulting from the immigration. Consequently, it is theoretically possible to compensate those who have suffered from the immigration and still have additional output for distribution to the rest of the community.

The problems of the declining areas are more severe and complex than those raised by the rapidly growing areas. We examine the efficiency of alternative government programs. First, immigration from depressed areas might be subsidized. The rate of return involved in the subsidization of migration seems to be quite high. Second, the local governments of the declining regions could tax immobile resources and use the proceeds to subsidize private employment in the region. The taxes might take the form of taxes on wage income. This proposal has merit, as a short-run measure, for the employment of older immobile workers in depressed industrial areas. Over the longer run, labor is mobile geographically, industrially, and occupationally. Wage subsidies may interfere with the willingness of younger workers to invest in their own training. It may also interfere with the willingness of public authorities to invest in educational and training facilities. The wage subsidy proposal is an inefficient long-run proposal.

The most efficient policy is the Federal government subsidy of education, retraining, and migration. This policy is a direct attempt to raise the rate of return on human effort. It must operate on the Federal level because the value of resources devoted to these ends by state and local government is likely to be less than optimal. These suggested policies tend to increase labor mobility. A declining region (especially) which invests in education will find that the fruits of such investment are enjoyed in other regions. Ignorance and the imperfection of the capital market, for investment in human capital, may prevent the optimum rate of investment from being undertaken by private individuals.

NOTES

CHAPTER 1. THE FRAMEWORK FOR AN ANALYSIS OF ECONOMIC GROWTH
AMONG OPEN ECONOMIES

1. Gunnar Myrdal, *Economic Theory and Under-Developed Regions* (London, Gerald Duckworth, 1957), p. 6.

2. *Ibid.*, p. 53.

3. *Ibid.*, p. 28.

4. Simon Kuznets, *Six Lectures on Economic Growth* (New York, Free Press of Glencoe, 1959), Lecture II.

5. *Ibid.*, p. 41.

6. Equation (1) is derived by differentiating the logarithm of $Y = F(K, L)$ with respect to time. The term involving F_K is multiplied by K/K, and the term involving F_L is multiplied by L/L.

7. Since K is the same commodity as Y, M is a percentage per unit of time.

8. This definition is based upon the identity income equals consumption plus savings equal consumption plus investment plus exports minus imports. Government spending can be included in investment, and taxes can be included in savings.

9. $a = \frac{1}{3}, s = \frac{1}{5}$.

10. A productive attempt at quantification is to be found in R. Solow, "Technical Change and the Aggregate Production Function," *Review of Economics and Statistics*, XXXIX (1957), 312–20. See also Edward F. Denison, *The Sources of Economic Growth in the United States* (Committee for Economic Development, Washington, D.C., 1962), and Moses Abramovitz, "Economic Growth in the United States," *American Economic Review*, LII (1962).

11. B. F. Massell, "A Disaggregated View of Technical Change," *Journal of Political Economy*, LXIX (1961), 555.

12. Only if $m_i = m$ and $w_i = w$ for all i will Y be at a maximum. If there is any dispersion of m or w, then the bracketed term in Equation (11.2) will be negative.

13. Kuznets, *Six Lectures*, p. 54.

14. This statement assumes that the prices of the cooperating inputs reflect opportunity costs. If unemployed labor is immobile, there may be a divergence between the private and the social rate of return on capital. (See Chapter 9.)

15. In terms of the first part of this chapter the g of the older regions declines as the rate of growth of the price of its output declines.

CHAPTER 2. EMPIRICAL REGULARITIES IN THE PROCESS OF
GROWTH AND DECLINE

1. We have been influenced by Carl G. Hempel and Paul Oppenheim, "Studies in the Logic of Explanation," *Philosophy of Science*, XV (April, 1948), 135–73.

2. See the valuable study by Harvey S. Perloff, Edgar S. Dunn, Jr., Eric E. Lampard, and Richard F. Muth, *Regions, Resources, and Economic Growth* (Baltimore, Johns Hopkins Press, 1960), Part V in general and Ch. 33 in particular on this point.

3. Easterlin's data do not allow us to determine whether factor returns have been equalized, because he does not identify wage income.

4. Easterlin defines service income as the sum of wages, salaries, and proprietor's income, with the imputed rents of farm dwellings included in the agricultural component. Property income represents the payments of rents, profits, and interest to owners of capital by state. This includes the imputed rents of owner-occupied nonfarm dwellings. Transfer payments and undistributed profits are excluded from these figures. Note that the property income data are on a received basis; that is, Easterlin allocated the payments on the basis of the residence of property owners.

5. For every state, Easterlin computed the percentage deviation of the income measure from the national average, and disregarded sign. He averaged these deviations arithmetically to obtain the unweighted mean deviation for each date. To reduce the effect of states with relatively small populations, he weighted the (absolute value of the) percentage deviation by the state share in total population. Thereby, the weighted mean deviation was derived.

6. These data are taken from G. H. Borts, "The Estimation of Produced Income by State and Region," presented to the Conference on Research in Income and Wealth, April, 1961. The proceedings have been published as Studies in Income and Wealth, No. 27, *The Behavior of Income Shares*.

The data are partially reproduced from Table 4. Note that payments to capital here include proprietor's income and all imputed rents.

7. Richard A. Easterlin, "Regional Growth of Income: Long-Term Tendencies," in Simon Kuznets, Ann Ratner Miller, and Richard A. Easterlin, *Analyses of Economic Change* (Vol. II of *Population Redistribution and Economic Growth, United States, 1870–1950*, Philadelphia, American Philosophical Society, 1960), p. 158.

8. A good description of the use of the F ratio is found in George W. Snedecor, *Statistical Methods* (Ames, Iowa, Iowa State College Press. 1955), Ch. 10. As applied here, the F ratio is simply a test of the homogeneity of four sample means with different sample sizes.

9. Connecticut, Idaho, Wyoming, Washington, Oregon, California, and Wisconsin.

10. Maine, Vermont, and Nevada.

11. This is the form in which Easterlin presents the data.

12. See Everett S. Lee, Ann Ratner Miller, Carol P. Brainerd, and Richard A. Easterlin, *Methodological Considerations and Reference Tables* (Vol. I of *Population Redistribution and Economic Growth, United States, 1870–1950*, Philadelphia, American Philosophical Society, 1957), Table L-4.

13. The data used in this calculation are found in Richard A. Easterlin, "Estimates of Manufacturing Activity," in Lee *et al.*, *ibid.*, p. 684.

14. It can be shown that the above distribution of states is not very likely a phenomenon produced by chance. There were a total of 179 successes out of 360 (= 45 × 8) observations. Let us assume that the event of a success or failure is a Bernoulli trial with a fixed probability of one-half. Then, the distribution of 45 states by successes is given through the term $C_n{}^8(\frac{1}{2})^8$, where *n* equals the number of successes. The expected frequency for each number of successes is 45 times the probability of *n*. The actual and expected frequencies are shown below. The data were subsequently grouped to insure at least five observations per cell.

No. of successes	Actual no. of states	Expected no. of states
0	4 ⎫	
1	3 ⎬ 10	6.5
2	3 ⎭	
3	7	10
4	7	12
5	9	10
6	9 ⎫	
7	2 ⎬ 12	6.5
8	1 ⎭	

A χ^2 test was performed on the actual frequencies to see if they might have been generated by the binomial distribution, where the probability of success is one-half. The value of chi-square is 9.62, with four degrees of freedom. This is statistically significant at the 5 percent level. We may therefore reject the hypothesis that the observed frequencies of success were produced by a binomial distribution with a probability of one-half. Certain states have grown consistently more rapidly than the national average; others have grown consistently less rapidly than the national average.

15. Slowly growing states include New Hampshire, Rhode Island, Vermont, Massachusetts, Pennsylvania, Maine, New York, Connecticut, Maryland, and Delaware. The rapidly growing states include Alabama, Colorado, Georgia, Idaho, Illinois, North Carolina, Ohio, Utah, Oregon, California, Michigan, and Texas.

16. These patterns are significantly nonrandom in the statistical sense. We may form a contingency table showing the possible relation between success and growth in manufacturing employment:

	Rapid growth	Slow growth
Success	17	7
Failure	19	23

We may use a χ^2 distribution to test the hypothesis that the occurrences of success and failure in per capita income growth are independent of the employment growth classification. We obtain a value of $\chi^2 = 4.04$, which is significant at 5 percent. Thus the phenomena are related, for the hypothesis has been rejected.

17. Substantial migration from Rhode Island in the period 1950–60 confirms the validity of our procedure. In effect, it confirms our designation of this area as mature.

18. A complete tabulation on smaller areas is found in the statement by J. M. Robertson, Special Assistant for Labor Surplus Programs, Office of the Assistant Secretary of Defense, *Unemployment Problems*, Part I of Hearings before Committee on Unemployment Problems, U.S. Senate, Eighty-Sixth Congress, First Session, October, 1959, pp. 222ff.

19. The 1948–53 period is an exception to the rule that A and H rates are not correlated.

CHAPTER 3. A CRITIQUE OF A SIMPLE AGGREGATIVE
THEORY OF GROWTH

1. See Milton Friedman, *Essays in Positive Economics* (Chicago, University of Chicago Press, 1953), Ch. I.

2. See George H. Borts, "The Equalization of Returns and Regional Economic Growth," *American Economic Review*, L (1960).

3. This is basically Knight's view on capital. See Frank H. Knight, "Neglected Factors in the Problem of Normal Interest," *Quarterly Journal of Economics*, XXX (1916), 279–310.

4. The Knight measure of capital is in value terms, and it may be expressed as R/r. This is not quite the same as the C in the production function, for C is a physical unit. Nevertheless, the relation between the two concepts is close because of the assumption of a one-commodity world. The capitalization factor r must in equilibrium be identical with the marginal physical product of capital. Hence, the Knight measure of capital is formally equivalent under our assumptions with the physical unit C.

In this aggregative model, increases in the quantity of capital employed would be accompanied by increases in the total return to capital, R, as long as the schedule of the marginal product of capital were elastic in the range in which accumulation were taking place.

5. M. Leven, *Income in the Various States* (New York, National Bureau of Economic Research, 1925).

6. U.S. Department of Commerce, Office of Business Economics, *Personal Income by States since 1929* (Washington, D.C., 1956).

7. The data were derived from Everett S. Lee, "Migration Estimates," in Everett S. Lee, Ann Ratner Miller, Carol P. Brainerd, and Richard A. Easterlin, *Methodological Considerations and Reference Tables* (Vol. I of *Population Redistribution*

and Economic Growth, United States, 1870–1950, Philadelphia, American Philosophical Society, 1957), Table P-1. This table contains estimates of net migration computed by the forward census survival method.

8. χ^2 measures here the interaction between the two classifications w and w^*.

9. This discrepancy between the two coefficients occurs because of the nature of the simple correlations between the variates. The correlation of two ratios, X/Z and Y/Z, will yield the same results as the partial of X on Y given Z when the regressions of X on Z and Y on Z are homogeneous. This condition is not fulfilled in the 1948–53 period. For a proof of the proposition, see Appendix C of J. R. Meyer and E. Kuh, *The Investment Decision* (Cambridge, Mass., Harvard University Press, 1957).

10. The data on service income and migration rates come from Richard A. Easterlin, "Regional Growth of Income: Long-Term Tendencies," in Simon Kuznets, Ann Ratner Miller, and Richard A. Easterlin, *Analyses of Economic Change* (Vol. II of *Population Redistribution and Economic Growth, United States, 1870–1950*, Philadelphia, American Philosophical Society, 1960), p. 171. Service income is not the same as wages, since it includes farm and other proprietors' income. Nevertheless, they are closely related at a point in time.

11. The 20 groups correspond roughly to the following industries from the Standard Industrial Classification used in the Census of Manufactures for 1947:

Durable goods		Nondurable goods	
Group No.	Industry	Group No.	Industry
24	Lumber products	20	Food and kindred products
25	Furniture and fixtures	21	Tobacco manufactures
32	Stone, clay, and glass products	22	Textile mill products
33	Primary metal industries	23	Apparel and related products
34	Fabricated metal products	26	Paper and allied products
35	Machinery (except electrical)	27	Printing and publishing
36	Electrical machinery	28	Chemicals and allied products
37	Transportation equipment	29	Petroleum and coal products
38	Instruments	30	Rubber products
		31	Leather products
		(391, 396)	Jewelry and silverware

12. Let $L_1 = L_{11}/L_{10}$, where L_{11} is the employment in U.S. industry 1 in year 1 and L_{10} is employment in the same industry in the base year 0. Let W_{i0} be the proportion of a state's employment in industry i in year 0. Then the projected employment growth rate is $\sum_i L_i W_{i0}$.

13. See Harvey S. Perloff, Edgar S. Dunn, Jr., Eric E. Lampard, and Richard F. Muth, *Regions, Resources, and Economic Growth* (Baltimore, Johns Hopkins Press, 1960), pp. 541–49; Frank Hanna, *State Income Differentials, 1919–1954* (Durham, N.C., Duke University Press, 1959), Ch. 5 and 6.

14. Price data for the years 1919, 1929, 1948, and 1953 were taken from *Wholesale Prices, 1913–1927*, Bulletin No. 473 (1929); *Wholesale Prices, 1929*, Bulletin No. 521 (1930); *Wholesale Prices, 1947*, Bulletin No. 947 (1949); *Wholesale Prices, 1948*, Bulletin No. 973 (1950); and *Wholesale Prices and Price Indexes, 1954–1956*, Bulletin No. 1214 (1957). Also, data for 1953 were taken from the *Monthly Labor Review* for 1954. All are publications of the U.S. Bureau of Labor Statistics, Washington, D.C. Data on wages and wage growth by industry for the years 1919, 1929, 1948, and 1953 were taken from the relevant Censuses of Manufactures for the years 1919, 1929, and 1947. Also, data for 1948 and 1953 were taken from *Employment, Hours and Earnings*, a publication of the U.S. Bureau of Labor Statistics.

15. The Spearman rank correlation among 34 commodities between the 1929 wage level and the 1929–48 percentage wage growth is −0.36, which is significant in the probability sense at the 5 percent level.

16. The rank correlation among 34 industries between the wage level and relative price growth is +0.49. The rank correlation between the wage level and relative wage growth is +0.71. Both are significant at the 5 percent level.

17. Table 3.5 shows only three observations in one cell, and the expected frequency for that cell equals 8.9. Because of this, the squared difference between actual and expected frequencies contributes 3.88 of 10.35, the total value of χ^2 obtained. While a small number of observations in a cell may bias upward the estimate of χ^2, we feel that the contingency table accurately reflects the population of industrial sectors. There are two reasons for this, one of which is based on additional information.

First, the contribution of this cell to the total χ^2 is not enough to make the difference between significance or its absence. Second, these findings on 69 subindustry groups are confirmed by an analysis of 15 major manufacturing groups. For the group of 15, two statistics were computed: the growth of the ratio (wage bill to value added) between 1919 and 1929 and the 1919 average wage per worker. The rank correlation between the two variates is −0.589, significant at 5 percent. Thus, on this more aggregate level, the high-wage sectors also experienced a drop in the ratio of wage bill to value added.

18. With an elasticity of substitution greater than unity, the share of output paid to capital increases with a rise in the capital-labor ratio.

19. Write the ratio of labor's share to capital's share

$$s = \frac{L f_L}{K f_K}$$

where L and K refer to the input quantities and f_L and f_K refer to the marginal physical productivities of labor and capital, respectively. The value of s fell and L/K fell in high-wage industries. This implies that f_L/f_K failed to rise by a sufficient degree to offset the fall of L/K.

20. Note that these might be constant-cost industries. Only changing factor proportions could then cause a rise of output prices.

CHAPTER 4. INTERSTATE DIFFERENCES IN RATES OF
GROWTH OF MANUFACTURING EMPLOYMENT

1. See Jerome L. Stein, "A Theory of Interstate Differences in Rates of Growth of Manufacturing Employment in a Free Market Area," *International Economic Review*, I, No. 2 (1960).

2. The data underlying the ratio were computed from *Census of Manufactures, 1919*, and *Annual Survey of Manufactures, 1953*. Both are publications of the U.S. Bureau of the Census, Washington, D.C.

3. The data underlying this ratio were taken from *Census of Manufactures, 1939*.

4. Everett S. Lee, "Migration Estimates," in Everett S. Lee, Ann Ratner Miller, Carol P. Brainerd, and Richard A. Easterlin, *Methodological Considerations and Reference Tables* (Vol. I of *Population Redistribution and Economic Growth, United States, 1870–1950* (Philadelphia, American Philosophical Society, 1957), Table P–1.

The numerator of X_2 is the total migration in the three decades. The denominator is the sum of the average population in the three decades. The resulting expression is therefore the weighted average migration rate over the three decades.

5. The industries excluded did not seem to satisfy the assumptions postulated by the theory of growth given in the last part of this chapter.

6. Milton Friedman, *Essays in Positive Economics* (Chicago, University of Chicago Press, 1953), p. 18.

7. Six states were excluded from the analysis because of the small number of two-digit industries in the state reported by the Annual Survey of Manufactures for 1953. We did not use the fuller information contained in the 1954 Census of Manufactures because of the disturbing influence of the recession of that year on regional growth patterns.

8. In the regression reported earlier for the 1919–53 period, the correlation between X_1, the manufacturing employment ratio, and X_2, the rate of migration, was $+0.25$. This correlation was not significant at the 5 percent probability level.

9. Frank A. Hanna, "Analysis of Interstate Differentials: Theory and Practice," in National Bureau of Economic Research, *Regional Income* (Vol. XXI of *Studies in Income and Wealth*, Princeton, N.J., Princeton University Press, 1957), Table 1.

10. The following contingency table was used:

	Success	Failure	Total	Frequency of success
High wage	59	101	160	0.3688
Low wage	71	50	121	0.4868
Total	130	151	281	0.4626

11. A test was carried out on the 48 states using the data for M, L, and ΔM which had been employed in the multiple regression shown earlier in this chapter.

The null hypothesis and the actually observed events are summarized in the figure. The null hypothesis, which the data rejected, are described by the line

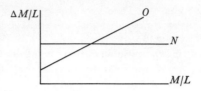

labeled N. The observed events are consistent with the line labeled O; namely, the positive relation between $\Delta M/L$ and M/L and the negative relation between $\Delta M/M$ and M/L.

12. The following contingency table is obtained, yielding a value of $\chi^2 = 8.32$ significant at 1 percent:

		Above *median*	*Below* *median*
	M/L		
$\Delta M/L$	Above median	17	7
	Below median	7	17

13. R. G. D. Allen, *Mathematical Analysis for Economists* (London, Macmillan, 1949), pp. 80–82.

14. One may consider the price Z as the rental per unit of time. Under competition the rental will equal the interest rate plus depreciation on the unit of equipment.

15. According to our model, $w = pF(q)$. Since p, F, and q are the same for firms in each state, long-run equilibrium implies wage equalization. Since $F' > 0$, given q and p, a unique w results.

16. Let w_0 be the initial equilibrium wage and w_0' be the new equilibrium wage, in both states. State 1 is the low-wage state where w_1 was initially below w_0', but state 2 initially paid the equilibrium wage. Suppose that capital flows into both states and wage rates rise to w_0'.

In state 1 wages will rise by $(w_0' - w_1)/w_1$ and in state 2 wages will rise by $(w_0' - w_0)/w_0$:

$$\frac{w_0' - w_1}{w_1} = \frac{(w_0' - w_0) + (w_0 - w_1)}{w_1}$$

Let

$$\frac{w_0' - w_0}{w_0} = y \quad \text{and} \quad \frac{w_0 - w_1}{w_1} = d$$

Then

$$\frac{w_0' - w_1}{w_1} = d(1 + y) + y$$

17. Assume that $s_1 = s_2$.

18. See the analysis in Harvey S. Perloff, Edgar S. Dunn, Jr., Eric Lampard, and Richard F. Muth, *Regions, Resources, and Economic Growth* (Baltimore, Johns Hopkins Press, 1960), Ch. 33.

CHAPTER 5. INTERINDUSTRY REPERCUSSIONS OF GROWTH
AND DECLINE

1. Let L_0 be a vector of employment in the industries in a state at the initial period and L_1 be the vector at the final period. Let g be the vector of growth rates in each of these industries, in the state, and let 1 be the unit vector. Then $L_0 \cdot g = L_1 \cdot 1$, where $(\cdot)$ denotes the inner product operation. The actual growth rate A is

$$A = \frac{L_0 \cdot g}{L_0 \cdot 1}$$

Let h be the vector of U.S. growth rates in each industry. Then the hypothetical growth rate H is

$$H = \frac{L_0 \cdot h}{L_0 \cdot 1}$$

The internal growth rate I is defined as $A - H$:

$$I = A - H = \frac{L_0 \cdot g - L_0 \cdot h}{L_0 \cdot 1} = \frac{L_0 \cdot (g - h)}{L_0 \cdot 1}$$

We seek to discover the relative importance of H and I in determining A among states.

2. The theory presented above is not the only possible rationalization for the negative relation between hypothetical and internal growth rates, or (to say the same thing) the independence of actual and hypothetical growth rates. One could maintain that demand is a regional rather than a national phenomenon. If, for example, employment in the automobile industry is growing rapidly nationally, it does not mean that the demand for automobiles is growing rapidly everywhere in the United States or that employment in this industry is growing rapidly everywhere. The same would be true for the other products of manufacturing industries. Hence, there might be no relation between actual and hypothetical growth rates, because there are profound interstate differences in the growth of demand. This theory does not explain why demand grows at different rates in different regions, nor does it tell us why we should expect each state to produce its own automobiles.

We maintain that our theory is to be preferred to the "regional demand theory" for several reasons. First, our theory explains interstate differences in internal growth rates, whereas the "regional demand theory" cannot. Second, with one theory we can explain both the negative relation between hypothetical and internal growth rates as well as the interstate differences in internal growth rates. Third, the theory is very similar to the one advanced and tested in Chapter 4. It is compatible with all the data we have examined. Fourth, our theory is simpler and more fruitful than the regional demand theory. It is simpler because less initial knowledge is needed to make a prediction. It is more fruitful because the resulting prediction is more precise. It yields predictions within a wider area and suggests additional lines for further research.

CHAPTER 6. MODELS OF GROWTH AND ALLOCATION

1. Using the numbers provided in the hypothetical production functions and given the stock of resources, we have $Xa = Ya = 9.09$.

2. The original development of this framework is to be found in W. F. Stolper and P. A. Samuelson, "Protection and Real Wages," *Review of Economic Studies,* IX (November, 1941), 58–73.

On the question of uniqueness, see Harry G. Johnson, *International Trade and Economic Growth* (Cambridge, Mass., Harvard University Press, 1958), pp. 19–24.

3. See F. M. Bator, "The Simple Analytics of Welfare Maximization," *American Economic Review,* XLVII (March, 1957), 22–59; G. D. N. Worswick, "The Convexity of the Production Possibility Function," *Economic Journal,* LXVII (December, 1957), 748–51; H. A. J. Green, "Mr. Worswick on the Production Possibility Function," *Economic Journal,* LXIX (March, 1959), 177–80.

4. For discussion of these relations, see G. H. Borts, "Professor Meade on Economic Growth," *Economica,* XIX (February, 1962), 72–86.

5. A complete demonstration is to be found in T. M. Rybczynski, "Factor Endowment and Relative Commodity Prices," *Economica,* XXII (November, 1955), 336–44. Also comment by E. J. Mishan, *Economica,* XXIII (November, 1956), 357–59.

6. It should be noted that points on the contract curve are consistent with long-run equilibrium in each industry. Short-run equilibrium positions which are not long-run equilibrium positions represent movements off the contract curve.

7. The payments to capital are on a where-produced basis, as discussed in Chapter 2.

8. There are errors of measurement in the X variable, since the growth in proprietary income is not identical with the growth of capital. Hence, the regression coefficient of X is biased downward, and the intercept is biased upward, This bias does not affect the subsequent argument.

9. The value of X' is found by setting Y equal to X in the regression equation and solving for X. The value of X' obtained is 1,351, larger than any X observed in the sample.

10. The states are as follows: Y deviation positive, X deviation negative in Kansas, California, North Carolina, and South Carolina; Y deviation negative, X deviation positive in West Virginia, Kentucky, Wyoming, Ohio, Indiana, and Wisconsin.

11. Using the χ^2 distribution to test the independence of the classification, we obtain with two degrees of freedom a value of χ^2 of 7.32, which is significant at the 5 percent level.

12. The growth of capital relative to employment is the variable X in the previous regression. It was formed by subtracting the percentage growth of employment from the percentage growth of capital.

CHAPTER 7. ECONOMIC GROWTH, DISTRIBUTION OF
INCOME, AND MOVEMENT OF CAPITAL

1. Similar two-sector models for closed economies may be found in J. E. Meade, *A Neo-Classical Theory of Economic Growth* (London, George Allen and Unwin, 1961).

2. If foreign borrowing had occurred in the past, then some of the social product would be devoted to paying interest to foreign capitalists. We might introduce a variable T to represent such payment. Equation (16) would then include T on the right-hand side as an additional method of disposing of produced income. The present level of T is exogenous, in the sense that it is determined by past borrowing. Changes in T are endogenous, however, because they are determined by future borrowing. The effects of changes in T could be analyzed by introducing another variable, $Z_R = Z - T$, where Z_R is received regional income. We would then convert Equations (17) to (19) into functions of Z_R. Note that the above suggestions constitute only one of a number of possible ways to introduce T into the analysis.

3. See G. H. Borts, "The Estimation of Produced Income by State and Region," presented to the Conference on Research in Income and Wealth, April, 1961. The proceedings will be published as Studies in Income and Wealth, No. 27, *The Behavior of Income Shares*.

4. The fitted regression line has the following values. Written under the coefficients are the estimates of their standard errors.

$$A = 0.530E + 0.631$$
$$(0.099) \quad (0.652)$$

5. As an example, suppose an additional disturbance had been present, namely $P_k{}^* > 0$. This is a rise in the price of capital goods. Then Equation (33) would have the following form:

$$\frac{W^* - R^*}{w_x{}^* - P_k{}^*} = 1 - \sigma$$

If $P_k{}^*$ had different values in different states, this would yield an error in the estimate of σ.

6. The fitted regression line had the following values (standard errors in parentheses):

$$A = 1.104E + 0.129$$
$$(0.293) \quad (0.726)$$

7. Investment is properly measured in money units, so that $I_0 = P_k K_0 L^*$. We have, however, deleted P_k from the analysis, since it is assumed unchanged.

8. J. Thomas Romans, *Capital Exports and Growth among U.S. Regions*, unpublished doctoral dissertation, Brown University, 1963, mimeo.

CHAPTER 8. INTERTEMPORAL EFFICIENCY AND ACTUAL
GROWTH PATTERNS

1. We are indebted to Martin J. Beckmann for comments on several sections of this chapter.

2. The phrases "growth program" and "growth pattern" are used synonymously. No control planning is implied by the word "program."

3. The concept of intertemporal efficiency was developed in Robert Dorfman, Paul A. Samuelson, and Robert M. Solow, *Linear Programming and Economic Analysis* (New York, McGraw-Hill, 1958), Ch. 12; Paul A. Samuelson, "Efficient Paths of Capital Accumulation in Terms of the Calculus of Variations," in Kenneth J. Arrow, Samuel Karlin, and Patrick Suppes, *Mathematical Methods in the Social Sciences* (Stanford, Calif., Stanford University Press, 1960), pp. 77–88.

4. By a vector of consumption at time t, we mean the set of real consumption enjoyed by the economy during a given period. For example, the vector may consist of X_1 pair of shoes, X_2 loaves of bread, X_3 movies, etc.

5. If the vector of consumption of goods A and B in periods $t = 0$ and $t = 1$ is a_0, b_0, a_1, $b_1 = C$, then the movement along the efficient path gives vector C and final stocks A_1, B_1. Along the inefficient path the economy consumes vector C but has stocks A_1', $B_1' < A_1$, B_1. The ratio of B to A is given by the ray from the origin.

6. In effect we are holding all stocks but one constant, and we seek to maximize the quantity of the remaining stock.

7. The ratios in parentheses are slopes of functions.

8. $p_i(t)$ is the price of the ith good at period t.

9. This equation can be put in terms of own rates of return and price appreciation: $\Delta B_1/\Delta B_0 = 1 + b$, where b is the own rate of return, $p_B(1)/p_B(0) = 1 + q$, where q is the rate of price appreciation; hence, $(1 + b)(1 + q) = 1 + i$. This equation is approximately equal to $e^{b+q} = e^i$, as can be seen by expanding $e^b e^q$ and e^i as a Taylor series and eliminating all terms above the first degree. Thus, we obtain the equation $b + q = i$. The interest rate (i) must equal the sum of the own rate (b) and the price appreciation (q).

10. D. Gale, *The Theory of Linear Economic Models* (New York, McGraw-Hill, 1960), pp. 310–18.

11. R. Radner, "Paths of Economic Growth That Are Optimal with Regard Only to Final States," *Review of Economic Studies*, XXVIII, No. 2 (1960–61), 98–104.

12. The theory developed here is based on Chapters 4 and 5 and Jerome L. Stein, "A Theory of Interstate Differences in the Rates of Growth of Manufacturing Employment in a Free Market Area," *International Economic Review*, I, No. 2 (May, 1960). The evidence supporting this hypothesis need not be repeated here.

13. J. M. Keynes, *The General Theory of Employment, Interest and Money* (New York, Harcourt, Brace, 1936), p. 148.

14. This is the mean value theorem for integrals.

15. This section has benefited from the perceptive comments of Daniel Creamer.

16. And if I_1/P_1 is approximately equal to I_2/P_2, where the subscripts refer to regions.

17. Jerome L. Stein, *Economic Factors in the Location of Industry: Part One, The Chemical Industries* (1957); George H. Borts, *Economic Factors in the Location of Industry: Part Two, The Metal Working Industries* (Brown University, College-Community Research Program, 1959).

In these studies we constructed estimates of depreciation on a regional and industrial basis. We used the ratio of gross investment to value added as a rough measure of the rate of net investment for an industry group in a region. Write this as

$$a_{ij} = \frac{\text{gross investment, } ij}{\text{value added, } ij}$$

where i stands for four-digit industry group and j stands for the region. We then say that if

$$m_{ij} > m_i \text{ (US)} \qquad \text{(marginal rate of return on gross investment)}$$
$$a_{ij} \geq a_i \text{ (US)} \qquad \text{(ratio of gross investment to value added)}$$

then the industry i has a higher rate of return on net investment in the jth region than it has in the United States as a whole.

The use of the ratio a embodies the assumption that the ratio of depreciation to value added is roughly the same for all geographic sectors of a four-digit industry. When this assumption is satisfied, a expresses regional differences in the ratio of net investment to value added. This assumption leaves much to be desired, for the higher the rate of expansion of reproducible capital, the lower is the ratio of depreciation to gross investment. Since no data on depreciation are available, we are forced to use gross investment as our denominator.

18. This section has benefited greatly from the comments made by Richard Muth.

19. In a number of cases it was necessary to reconstruct the composition of the four-digit group in New England for 1939. The reason is that data on gross investment, wages and salaries, and value added are not available on a region basis for 1939. Further, gross investment was not available on region or state basis in 1939.

Estimates of wages and salaries and value added for four-digit industries in New England were derived as follows:

(1) In a given four-digit industry we know from the Census the production worker employment in 1939 for New England.

(2) We also know for each New England state the number of production workers, the wage bill, and the value added in the industry. The information given for the states will fall short of the New England total because the disclosure rule will eliminate some of the state information.

(3) Estimates of the wage bill and value added for New England were made by using the ratio of total production workers in New England to the production workers reported by state. This involves using the assumption that the wage

bill per production worker and value added per production worker are the same in the known and unknown sectors of the industry. For the 19 industries data available for 1939 included on the average 75 percent of the total production-worker employment in each of the categories.

Estimates of gross investment for 1939 for New England four-digit industries were derived as follows: for each industry in New England the ratio of gross investment to value added was formed for 1947. This ratio was then applied to the 1939 value added for each industry. This estimate assumes that the ratio remains the same over time, but, of course, differs by industry and region.

20. We are indebted to Richard Muth for this observation.

21. Let the straight line in the figure connecting the dots be the true regression equation. As a result of normally distributed errors in the measurement of μ, our observations are the x's. The dispersion of the x's raises the *measured* variance of

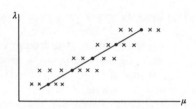

the μ's, but it does not affect the covariance $\Sigma(\lambda - \bar{\lambda})(\mu - \bar{\mu})$, because for a given λ, the $\Sigma(\mu - \bar{\mu}) = 0$. Since the regression coefficient is cov $(\lambda, \mu)/\text{var } \mu$, the measured regression coefficient is less than the slope of the true line. A similar argument explains the lower correlation coefficient.

Moreover, the existence of a positive intercept can be explained in the same manner. The intercept is

$$\bar{\lambda} - \frac{\text{cov }(\lambda, \mu)}{\text{var } \mu}\, \bar{\mu}$$

Since var μ is exaggerated, so is the intercept.

22. This occurs because $p^* + (u/e)k^*$ is the same for all regions in this industry.

CHAPTER 9.   GOVERNMENT POLICIES TOWARD GROWING
AND DECLINING REGIONS

1. Area Redevelopment Act of 1961, Public Law 87–27 of the Eighty-Seventh Congress, First Session, May 1, 1961, an act to establish an effective program to alleviate conditions of unemployment and underemployment in certain economically distressed areas.

2. Let $y = f(L, K)$ be the production function in the region, given capital K. Let employment rise by ΔL as a result of migration. Initially, the real wage was $f'(L_0)$ and then falls to $f'(L_1)$. The increase in output is $dy = f'(L^*)\Delta L$, where

$f'(L^*)$ is a marginal product between $f'(L_0)$ and $f'(L_1)$. The wage bill paid to the migrants is $f'(L_1)\Delta L$. The difference between $f'(L^*)\Delta L$ and $f'(L_1)\Delta L = [f'(L^*) - f'(L_1)]\Delta L$ is nonnegative. It represents the net gain potentially available to the indigenous residents from the migration of ΔL workers.

3. Legally, immigration cannot be restricted. Nevertheless, changes in the rules regarding social welfare payments to immigrants can affect the rate of immigration. For example, a change in the social welfare rules that would require a person to be a resident for at least one year before he is eligible for social welfare benefits would decrease the rate of immigration.

4. G. H. Borts, *Economic Factors in the Location of Industry: Part Two, The Metal Working Industries* (Brown University, College-Community Research Program, 1959), p. 19, contains a comparison of average annual earnings per employee in the metal-working industries in Rhode Island, New England, and the United States. There are a number of metal working industry groups where wages in the United States are $1,200 per annum in excess of those paid in Rhode Island.

5. The declining regions possess the "external economies" described by Alfred Marshall in his *Principles of Economics* (8th ed., London, Macmillan, 1920).

6. G. Stigler, "The Division of Labor Is Limited by the Extent of the Market," *Journal of Political Economy*, LIX (June, 1951), 185–93.

7. See a stimulating article by J. M. Buchanan and J. E. Moes, "A Regional Countermeasure to National Wage Standardization," *American Economic Review*, L (June, 1960), 434–38. Also see the book by J. E. Moes, *Local Subsidies for Industry* (Chapel Hill, N.C., University of North Carolina Press, 1962).

8. See M. P. Stoltz, Chairman, *Report of the Mayor's Committee on Municipal Finance* (City of Providence, R.I., 1959).

9. See John V. Krutilla and Otto Eckstein, *Multiple Purpose River Development* (Baltimore, Johns Hopkins Press, 1958), Ch. 2.

10. See the following analysis of a depressed area, in which the author adopts this view: A. K. Cairncross, *Economic Development and the Atlantic Provinces* (Atlantic Provinces Research Board, Fredericton, New Brunswick, 1961).

INDEX

Abramovitz, Moses, 8
Age of manufacturing industry, see Maturity, economic
Agglomeration effects, 14–15
Allocation of resources, 87, 102, 104, 106, 112; effect on wages and productivity of capital, 101–05, 117, 119, 137; effect on factor proportions, 105–08
Area Redevelopment Act, 189, 196; see also Depressed areas; Government policy

Bator, F. M., 103
Borts, G. H., 24, 48, 105, 138, 176, 193
Box diagram, 103–04, 106–07, 128–29, 132, 135
Buchanan, J. M., 198

Cairncross, A. K., 205
Capital, 49; movements, 3–7, 12, 42, 50, 102, 124, 141–46; productivity, 5, 49–51, 58, 79, 81, 101–02, 105–08, 117, 132, 175; returns to, 23–25; elasticity of marginal product, 80, 133; productivity influenced by intersectoral allocation, 101–40; see also Capital accumulation; Capital growth
Capital accumulation: and real wage 105–08; effect on factor proportions, 105–08; and inefficiency, 108–11; efficient program, 162–87
Capital growth, 5, 6, 50, 125–32, 141–50; in nonagricultural industries, 19, 138; and wage level, 50–51, 53–55, 57–64; measured, 51–52; and population, 55–56; and labor migration, 55–56, 97–100; and industrial composition, 57–64; and ratio of manufacturing to state employment, 97–100; affected by export prices, 133, 153–61; unequal among regions, 168–69

Capital-intensive sector, 52, 108, 111–23, 131
Capital-labor ratio, 105–08; see also Capital, productivity
Chronic labor surplus areas, see Depressed areas
Competition, 49, 168–87
Contract curve, 103–04, 107, 119, 128–29

Denison, Edward F., 8
Depressed areas, 19, 42, 44–47, 196; government policy in, 193–99; retraining program, 197, 201; wage flexibility in, 199; subsidy in, 199, 201 204–05; planning in, 204
Domestic sector, 131–33
Dorfman, Robert, 162
Dunn, Edgar S., Jr., 21, 59, 84

Easterlin, R. A., 20, 22, 24, 28, 35, 37, 56
Eckstein, Otto, 203
Economic efficiency, 8–13, 25, 29–33, 36–37, 112, 162; effect on growth of income, 25–37; and elimination of misallocation, 100–12; intertemporal, 162–87; and government policy, 189
Elasticity of substitution, 134–46
Emigration, see Migration
Employment growth, 19, 52, 83, 113–15, 117; convergence of ratio of nonagricultural to total, 23, 28–37; manufacturing, 38–42, 47, 88–91; actual, hypothetical, and internal rates, 46–47, 58–59, 79, 88–98, 168–69, 186–87; and wage level, 29–33, 65–86; and elasticity of labor supply, 66; ratio of manufacturing to total, 67–76, 85; and migration, 67–76, 85, 93–98; and industrial

Employment growth (Continued)
    composition, 69–76; equilibrium rate,
    125–32, 141–50; prediction of, 169–87
Entrepreneurship, 13–14
Expectations, 171
Exports: response to demand, 121, 135–46,
    153–61; base, 195
Export prices, 124, 132–34, 140–41; effect
    on allocation of labor, 134; effect on
    distribution of income, 134–35
External economies, 14–15, 193–99

Factor price equalization, 21–25, 53–55
Factor proportions, *see* Allocation of
    resources

Gale, D., 167
Government policy: toward growing and
    declining regions, 188–205; in growing
    regions, 190–93; in depressed areas,
    193–99
Green, H. A. J., 103

Hanna, Frank, 59, 74

Immigration, *see* Migration
Income: per capita, growth, 3, 5, 7, 29–37,
    40–44, 83; per capita, convergence, 4, 7,
    19–46; equilibrium growth, 5; service,
    per worker, convergence, 21–37; pro-
    duced vs. received, 24–25; intersectoral
    differential, 29–33, 37; service, per
    worker, agricultural vs. nonagricultural,
    29–37; per capita, and growth of
    employment in manufacturing, 41–42;
    per capita, retardation in growth, *see*
    Maturity, economic
Income distribution, and allocation of
    resources, 132–40, 150
Increasing returns, 64
Industrial parks, 196
Inefficiency, *see* Economic efficiency
Infant industry, 195
Interest rate, 5, 6, 168
Interindustry allocation of labor, *see*
    Allocation of resources
Investment, 5, 6, 141–44, 176; marginal
    efficiency, 57, 58, 167, 169–76; deter-
    mined by profit maximization, 171–87;
    marginal efficiency in machinery in-
    dustry, 177–78; subsidy in depressed
    areas, 204; *see also* Capital
Isoquants, production, 104

Johnson, Harry G., 103

Keynes, J. M., 172
Knight, Frank H., 51
Krutilla, John V., 203
Kuznets, Simon, 3, 10, 13

Labor: returns to, 23–25 (*see also* Income;
    Wages); marginal product, 49–51, 58,
    79, 167 (*see also* Wages); elasticity of
    marginal product, 80; intrastate, inter-
    industry allocation, 88–100, 111–23
Labor supply: function, 16–17, 51, 65–66,
    79–85, 141; interstate differences in
    growth of manufacturing employment,
    67–86; influence upon internal growth
    rate, 96–97
Labor surplus areas, *see* Depressed areas
Lampard, Eric E., 21, 59, 84
Lee, Everett S., 53, 68
Leven, M., 52

Machinery industry, case study, 176–87
Manufacturing-mining sector, 52, 108,
    111–23, 131
Massell, B. F., 9
Maturity, economic, 13–17, 42–47, 195;
    and convergence of per capita incomes,
    37–44; resulting from elimination of
    resource misallocation, 16; and indus-
    trial composition, 44–47
Meade, J. E., 125
Migration, 50, 71, 73, 84, 87–90, 93–94,
    102, 169, 190–93; national barriers to,
    17; and growth of manufacturing
    employment, 77; social costs, 190–93;
    benefits to indigenous residents, 192;
    non-economic effects, 193; from de-
    pressed areas, 193–99, 202
Miller, Ann Ratner, 36
Mishan, E. J., 106
Misallocation, 100–12
Moes, J. E., 198, 200
Muth, Richard F., 21, 59, 84
Myrdal, Gunnar, 3–4

Output: growth of per capita, 6, 141;
    composition of, *see* Allocation of Re-
    sources; *see also* Income

Perloff, Harvey S., 21, 59, 84
Production function, 49–51, 102–03, 126
Production possibility curve, 101–04, 131,
    162–67
Population growth, 84, 90
Product, *see* Income

Radner, R., 167
Retardation, *see* Maturity, economic
Romans, J. T., 145
Rybczynski, T. M., 106

Samuelson, Paul A., 103, 105, 162
Savings, 5–6, 141–44
Schupack, M. B., 178
Services sector, 52, 108, 111–23
Solow, R. M., 8, 162
Stein, Jerome L., 65, 167, 176, 178
Stigler, G., 195
Stolper, W. F., 103, 105
Stoltz, M. P., 199

Technological change, 5, 7–10, 17, 64
Transformation function, 101–04, 131, 162–67

Unions, trade, 15–16, 199

Wage differentials: among sectors, 29–33, 108–11, 114–24, 126, 129–32, 135, 138–41; among regions, 66, 111–15, 193; and allocation of resources, 101–05, 117, 119, 139
Wage growth: and wage level, 51, 53–55, 60–62; and industrial composition, 57–64; and migration, 98–100; in depressed areas, 199
Wages, 101–02, 106, 108, 117–19, 168; and employment growth, 29–33; and growth of capital-labor ratio, 55, 61–63; convergence and divergence, 59–64; long-run equilibrium, 79; and allocation of labor, 101–40; and profitability of investment, 121; and migration, 121, 194; minimum, 200
Welfare, social, 162
Worswick, G. D. N., 103